D1290069

# CyberRegs

## Addison-Wesley Information Technology Series

*Capers Jones and David S. Linthicum, Consulting Editors*

The information technology (IT) industry is in the public eye now more than ever before because of a number of major issues in which software technology and national policies are closely related. As the use of software expands, there is a continuing need for business and software professionals to stay current with the state of the art in software methodologies and technologies. The goal of the Addison-Wesley Information Technology Series is to cover any and all topics that affect the IT community: These books illustrate and explore how information technology can be aligned with business practices to achieve business goals and support business imperatives. Addison-Wesley has created this innovative series to empower you with the benefits of the industry experts' experience.

For more information point your browser to http://www.awl.com/cseng/series/it/

Sid Adelman, Larissa Terpeluk Moss, *Data Warehouse Project Management.* ISBN: 0-201-61635-1

Wayne Applehans, Alden Globe, and Greg Laugero, *Managing Knowledge: A Practical Web-Based Approach.* ISBN: 0-201-43315-X

Michael H. Brackett, *Data Resource Quality: Turning Bad Habits into Good Practices.* ISBN: 0-201-71306-3

Frank Coyle, *Wireless Web: A Manager's Guide.* ISBN: 0-201-72217-8

James Craig and Dawn Jutla, *e-Business Readiness: A Customer-Focused Framework.* ISBN: 0-201-71006-4

Gregory C. Dennis and James R. Rubin, *Mission-Critical Java™ Project Management: Business Strategies, Applications, and Development.* ISBN: 0-201-32573-X

Kevin Dick, *XML: A Manager's Guide.* ISBN: 0-201-43335-4

Jill Dyché, *e-Data: Turning Data into Information with Data Warehousing.* ISBN: 0-201-65780-5

Jill Dyché, *The CRM Handbook: A Business Guide to Customer Relationship Management.* ISBN: 0-201-73062-6

Dr. Nick V. Flor, *Web Business Engineering: Using Offline Activites to Drive Internet Strategies.* ISBN: 0-201-60468-X

David Garmus and David Herron, *Function Point Analysis: Measurement Practices for Successful Software Projects.* ISBN: 0-201-69944-3

Capers Jones, *Software Assessments, Benchmarks, and Best Practices.* ISBN: 0-201-48542-7

Capers Jones, *The Year 2000 Software Problem: Quantifying the Costs and Assessing the Consequences.* ISBN: 0-201-30964-5

Ravi Kalakota and Marcia Robinson, *e-Business 2.0: Roadmap for Success.* ISBN: 0-201-72165-1

David S. Linthicum, *B2B Application Integration: e-Business-Enable Your Enterprise.* ISBN: 0-201-70936-8

Sergio Lozinsky, *Enterprise-Wide Software Solutions: Integration Strategies and Practices.* ISBN: 0-201-30971-8

Joanne Neidorf and Robin Neidorf, *e-Merchant: Retail Strategies for e-Commerce.* ISBN: 0-201-72169-4

Patrick O'Beirne, *Managing the Euro in Information Systems: Strategies for Successful Changeover.* ISBN: 0-201-60482-5

Mai-lan Tomsen, *Killer Content: Strategies for Web Content and E-Commerce.* ISBN: 0-201-65786-4

Bill Wiley, *Essential System Requirements: A Practical Guide to Event-Driven Methods.* ISBN: 0-201-61606-8

Ralph R. Young, *Effective Requirements Practices.* ISBN: 0-201-70912-0

Bill Zoellick, *CyberRegs: A Business Guide to Web Property, Privacy, and Patents.* ISBN: 0-201-72230-5

Bill Zoellick, *Web Engagement: Connecting to Customers in e-Business.* ISBN: 0-201-65766-X

# CyberRegs

## A Business Guide to Web Property, Privacy, and Patents

Bill Zoellick

ADDISON-WESLEY

Boston • San Francisco • New York • Toronto • Montreal
London • Munich • Paris • Madrid
Capetown • Sydney • Tokyo • Singapore • Mexico City

Many of the designations used by manufacturers and sellers to distinguish their products are claimed as trademarks. Where those designations appear in this book, and Addison-Wesley, Inc. was aware of a trademark claim, the designations have been printed with initial capital letters or in all capitals.

The author and publisher have taken care in the preparation of this book, but they make no expressed or implied warranty of any kind and assume no responsibility for errors or omissions. No liability is assumed for incidental or consequential damages in connection with or arising out of the use of the information or programs contained herein.

The publisher offers discounts on this book when ordered in quantity for special sales. For more information, please contact:

Pearson Education Corporate Sales Division
One Lake Street
Upper Saddle River, NJ 07458
(800) 382-3419
corpsales@pearsontechgroup.com

Visit AW on the Web: www.awl.com/cseng/

*Library of Congress Cataloging-in-Publication Data*

Zoellick, Bill.
CyberRegs : a business guide to Web property, privacy, and patents / Bill Zoellick.
p. cm.
Includes bibliographical references and index.
ISBN 0-201-72230-5 (hc)
1. Electronic commerce—Law and legislation—United States. 2. Copyright and electronic data processing—United States. 3. Patent laws and legislation—United States. 4. Intellectual property—United States. 5. Privacy, Right of—United States. 6. Internet—Law and legislation—United States. I. Title.

KF889.3 .Z6114 2001
343.7309'944—dc21

2001026677

Copyright © 2002 by Addison-Wesley

All rights reserved. No part of this publication may be reproduced, stored in a retrieval system, or transmitted, in any form, or by any means, electronic, mechanical, photocopying, recording, or otherwise, without the prior consent of the publisher. Printed in the United States of America. Published simultaneously in Canada.

ISBN 0-201-72230-5
Text printed on recycled paper
1 2 3 4 5 6 7 8 9 10—MA—0504030201
First printing, August 2001

*To my business partners,*
*Mary Laplante and Lee Fife*

# Contents

# Acknowledgments

A number of people made important contributions that resulted in a book that is more accurate, more complete, and easier to read than it would have been without them. In particular I would like to acknowledge the contributions from Randolph A. Kahn in sharpening the arguments regarding electronic signatures; Sarah V. Greenberg for clarifying a number of legal points and, in particular, for helping me sort out a number of FTC actions; Sol Bermann for his review of the privacy section; Seth Finkelstein for his careful reading and critique of the sections on copyright and patents; Dan Carroll for his help in sharpening the focus for senior management; Jon M. Garon for his careful overall review of the book both in terms of law and in terms of audience; Scott Allison for providing early help in understanding patent law and for helping set up my interview with Jay Walker; David Weinberger for his willingness to help me think about the book's audience; and Adina Levin for demanding that my arguments be clearer and more forceful. I also acknowledge a debt to Lawrence Lessig for making the fundamental problem that this book addresses visible enough for me to tackle. Needless to say, perhaps, any mistakes or misunderstandings of law or technology that remain, despite this help from others, are my own.

I also owe thanks to the team at Fastwater LLP, the consulting firm in which I am a partner, for keeping the business running while I was tied up with the research and writing that went into this book. In particular, I owe thanks to my two partners, Lee Fife and Mary Laplante.

I owe a special debt to my wife, Pauline Angione. When I write, the days are long and, though I am physically present, I am mentally and emotionally in another place. Her consistent support throughout the process is essential and much appreciated.

Finally, I want to thank my editor at Addison-Wesley, Mary T. O'Brien, for her very early, strong, and substantial support of a book that was, at the outset, not much more than a concept—and a different concept, at that. This is the second book that we have worked on together that took on a life of its own, turning out to be something different than what I had planned; I appreciate her patience and confidence.

# Introduction

THERE is no "innate nature" of the Web. This was one of the key insights that Lawrence Lessig expressed in his important book, Code.[1] The coast of Maine has an innate nature. The Great Plains have an innate nature, as do the slickrock canyons of Utah. In each of these places, someone starting a business must contend with truly immutable dimensions of climate and geography. The fundamental character of such a place does not change except in geologic time; it exists apart from the people who live and work there.

The Web is not like that. It is made up of computer code, which is made by people. If people don't like the effects of the computer code, they can change it, quickly. The typical way to change a complex application that is in daily use, like the World Wide Web, is to add layers. The layers can consist of new computer code that changes the way people and companies access and use the Web. The layers can also consist of legal code, often coupled with encryption and other technical constraints, that has the same effect.

The fact that the face of the Web can be changed relatively quickly, over a matter of a year or two, means that talking about the "nature of the Web" is risky, if not out and out misguided. This has not stopped people from writing thousands of books and articles that do just that. The formula for such "Web nature" books is simple and, by now, familiar. They start by asserting that the Web changes everything and that old strategies cannot work in the new Internet era. Then, building on some set of assumptions about the supposed nature of the Web, the books reason forward to projections about what to do and what will succeed in the new Internet era of business.

Starting a business built on assumptions about the nature of the Web is even riskier than writing books about it. For example, it was supposed to be in the nature of the Web to do away with the middleman ("disintermediation"), creating a new world in which digital content moved freely and without control. But the Digital Millennium Copyright Act and the rest of copyright law has intervened to change all of that. People involved in creating technologies to enable free exchange of DVD movies are now involved in lawsuits that could ultimately lead to jail terms. Napster, the free music-exchange Web site, is, as I write this, facing possible shutdown by the major music labels.

Here is another example: it was supposed to be in the nature of the Web to enable new, personalized, one-to-one shopping, thus creating enormous new retail opportunities. Many things have gone wrong with this idea over the past three years, transforming it from an article of faith to something that is now viewed with deep suspicion. One critical thing that got in the way is that consumers became uneasy about the collection and use of personal information on the Web. This consumer malaise has a good chance of transforming itself into federal privacy legislation. The new legislation, if enacted, will create a new Web nature.

The nature of the Web was also supposed to usher in a new era of business innovation. But it turns out that evolving patent law makes it possible for companies to own monopoly rights to such innovation for a period of 20 years. Sperry and Hutchinson, the S&H Green Stamps company that pioneered buyer incentive programs for retail stores, now licenses patented technology owned by Netcentives in order to offer incentive promotions on the Web. Once again, the intersection of law and the Web has transformed Web nature into something very different than people first expected.

## The Web Grows Up

Not long ago people believed that the Web, by the force of its innate nature, would radically change business, opening enormous new opportunities. It was a great time to be in the stock market. It was a great time to be starting companies. There was the expectation of new beginnings.

Many things came together to change such expectations. The change came, in part, because many Web businesses were built on naive, though hopeful, ideas. Another problem was that investment extended itself too far, indulging in "irrational exuberance," to use Alan Greenspan's memorable phrase. Part of the problem was simple miscalculation and poor execution.

Web companies also lost sight of the fact that they work in a firmly established context of existing property rights, power structures, and laws. Like an exuberant, self-confident kid, Web business has discovered that it needs to learn some lessons about how the world really works.

This metaphor of "growing up" is useful because it captures both what is necessary and what is dangerous as we come to terms with the Web. The necessary part is the recognition that the Web exists in a powerful context of constraints. The once-popular notion that the Web's freedom-loving, anarchistic "nature" will sweep away existing rules, business arrangements, and even governments is, of course, romantic and a poor foundation for planning, policy, or new business strategy.

The dangerous aspect of the current transition is that vision and excitement about the future could be replaced with cynicism and control. The other side of the belief that the Web is an inevitable, irresistible force of positive change and growth is the belief that it is a force of chaos and destruction that must be controlled. For every John Perry Barlow who proclaims to the governments of the world that Cyberspace has no elected government and that governments are not welcome,[2] there is a Jack Valenti who sees "brazen disdain for laws and rules."[3] Neither approach is good for Web business.

## Business and Policy

I wrote this book because it is clear that government regulation and new legislation, coupled with technology, have the potential to dramatically change the nature of the Web. Lawrence Lessig is right: the intersection of new Web architectures, new laws, and commercial business interests will create a new kind of Web business reality. The new Web business has the potential to be so radically different from the Web of the late 1990s as to be nearly unrecognizable to a denizen from the old world of "Net 95."

Here's the critical thing: you can change the outcome of this story. The shape of Web business—its nature, if you like—is in flux. Most legislation regarding key Web business issues is still tentative and uncertain. The arguments for and against different kinds of regulation or new government action are still taking shape.

What this means is that there are two really good reasons for you to pay more attention to the way that laws, business interests, and Web architecture are intersecting to change Web business. The first is, of course, that it is in your own business interest to understand the changes and to be able to anticipate the next stage of developments. The second and even more interesting reason is that you can work to ensure that the new developments make sense for you and your business.

I have found that most business managers are ill prepared to capitalize on either of these potential benefits. It is clear that they need to

- Come up to speed quickly on the last decade of developments in patent policy, copyright policy, and privacy policy so that they can be conversant about current issues
- See the bigger picture about how these legal and policy developments could affect business activity on the Web
- Begin to articulate a coherent viewpoint that expresses their particular interests with regard to these areas of policy

This book strives to respond to these needs.

## An Emerging Viewpoint

This book is not a tract. The business community is always characterized by a broad diversity of viewpoints. Businesspeople from all points of view are well served by a careful review of recent developments and by an attempt to sort through the issues and set them out fairly. I have tried to produce such a review and attempt at explication.

But it is inevitable that, in spending so much time working with policy issues and talking with experts, a point of view emerges. What emerged was not what I expected when I started out gathering material for this book. At the outset, I saw that the issues that this book examines—copyright, patent law, privacy, and electronic identity—would have big impacts on the nature of the Web and on the shape of Web business. Naively, I hoped to uncover policy programs and proposals that were as large and striking as the issues themselves.

What emerged instead was a strong sense that we should be cautious and parsimonious in proposing regulations and legislation. In some cases we already have new legislation that is potentially dangerous, changing the Web and the fundamental relationship between producer and user in ways that seem to me to be too rapid and far reaching, given our current level of understanding. In other cases we seem too anxious to patch problems and to use bailing wire to effect quick solutions before we understand the bigger picture of what is going on. So, the result of all this research, for me, was increased respect for the argument that we should proceed with restraint, understanding that the full development of the Web will take decades. Far from being a "do-nothing" point of view, this emergent viewpoint argues strongly for forceful, articulate intervention against some of the current proposals being put forth by different interest groups that want rapid development of new policies to "fix" the Web.

Whether you agree with my arguments for this emergent viewpoint or not, I hope you find the background perspective and the arguments that I present useful in establishing your own point of view. Debate is a good thing; we need more of it, and more effort to inform and support it.

## Taking Responsibility for the Web

This is a difficult time. We are about five years into what was supposed to be a revolution in the way we use information and collaborate with others. As with any difficult revolution, not everything has worked as planned. Reactionary forces have mobilized and have, in some cases, aligned with government forces in order to use the original momentum and strength of the revolution as a way to consolidate power and position. At times like this what is needed is not renewed revolutionary zeal but careful, clear thinking about outcomes, about the mechanisms of change, and about the arrangements of property and power.

This sounds like radical stuff. It's not. The business community as a whole has a vested interest in continued growth, change, and innovation. The Web has been a prime generator of these benefits for the last five years. We now know that there is nothing inevitable about continued growth, change, and innovation. We have learned that the Web will only reflect the "nature" that we create for it. It is time to stop acting on the basis of an innocent hope in the power of the Web as something that is real in itself, apart from the businesses and people that use it and shape it. It is time to start accepting responsibility for creating the policies that will make the Web the kind of place that we want it to be.

It is my hope that this book contributes to your participation in that process.

## Notes

1. Lawrence Lessig, *Code* (New York: Basic Books, 1999). See Chapter 5 for more about his book.
2. John Perry Barlow, "A Declaration of the Independence of Cyberspace," February 8, 1996. Available in May 2001 on the Web at http://www.theconnection.org/archive/category/technology/barlow.shtml.
3. Jack Valenti, President and CEO of the Motion Picture Association of America, testifying before the House Commerce Committee's Subcommittee on Telecommunications, Trade and Consumer Protection on February 16, 2000 (106th Congress, Second Session, "Video on the Internet: iCraveTV.com and Other Recent Developments in Webcasting").

# Part One
# Copyright

COPYRIGHT is where the intersection of law, technology, and new business models is striking visible sparks. It is where the collision of old distribution mechanisms and the new capabilities of the Web are most obviously forcing new terrain to the surface.

One of the most visible, notorious collisions between old and new took the form of the lawsuit between Napster, a music-sharing service that gives people access to free music, and the major record labels. The participation of rock stars in the debate guaranteed that it would receive media attention. But beneath the surfaces and the posturing in the Napster suit lie serious questions about copyright policy and how it is applied in a digital world, where the notion of a "copy" does not have the same meaning that it does when a copy is a physical thing. The Napster case provides an excellent introduction to the problems, costs, and complexities of applying copyright in a digital era. Consequently, it is where we begin.

In attempting to understand how new laws fundamentally change the nature of the Web, copyright makes an excellent starting point for reasons that go beyond notoriety: it is one of the areas where Congress has been most active in creating new legislation. Copyright laws actually give us a chance to see the effects of new policies.

Finally, copyright provides an excellent introduction to a phenomenon that recurs frequently in matters of Web policy: the Web changes the underlying context of legal and business arrangements and thus opens up a broad array of other questions, opportunities, and problems. In the case of copyright, the big shift is that new copyright laws, coupled with new approaches to contracting and licensing and then married with encryption, change the balance of power between information users and information producers. In so doing, copyright policy combined with the Web will ultimately impact hundreds of billions of dollars of business. As you will see, it is not necessarily the users who win.

In short, if you are trying to understand how laws can change the nature of the Web, the place to start is by looking at copyright and Napster.

CHAPTER 1

# Creating and Resisting Change

*This case is not about any diminution in the value of Plaintiffs' copyrights; none has occurred or is reasonably foreseeable as the result of Napster. This case is about whether Plaintiffs can use their control over music copyrights to achieve control over Napster's decentralized technology and prevent it from transforming the Internet in ways that might undermine their present chokehold on music promotion and distribution.*

**—from Napster's reply to the District Court ruling, presented to the Ninth Circuit Court of Appeals[1]**

*. . . lack of harm to an established market cannot deprive the copyright holder of the right to develop alternative markets for the works. . . .*

**—from the Ninth Circuit Court of Appeals ruling, substantially upholding the District Court ruling against Napster[2]**

PERHAPS it would have been better if the first tests of copyright on the Internet had centered around, say, medical journals. Maybe then we would have had a more reasoned consideration of the trade-offs between owning information and using it. But it would have also resulted in a big yawn.

Copyright and the Internet got on the evening news because of music, and the centerpiece was Napster, the company that made its name by creating a system that gave people access to copyrighted music for free. The lawsuit that resulted from the giveaway was a battle between the powerful recording industry and an in-your-face start-up company that claimed 40 million people using its service. Recording stars, star lawyers, and star politicians lined up on both sides of the controversy.

The lawsuit and media coverage created a strange but very visible forum for the debate over copyright and its application to digital media. Looked at more closely, the Napster controversy is also an excellent illustration of how the Internet collides with existing physical distribution systems for information and entertainment content. There are important insights in the Napster story for any business that has an investment in intellectual property that can be distributed digitally.

## Brief Background

Napster is a software utility and a service that allows people to exchange files with others on the Internet. The sending and receiving is direct; in computer-speak, it is a *peer-to-peer exchange.* If you have a music file on your computer that you are willing to share, and if I want that file, our machines interact directly over the Internet. The Napster software allows each of our machines to act as Web servers in order to complete the file exchange. It is important to the Napster copyright dispute that Napster's servers are not in the middle of the actual exchange.

The Napster client software also provides access to the Napster real-time directory service, which is how I find out who has the songs I want. When someone logs on to Napster using the Napster software, the program adds to the global directory the list of digitally compressed MP3 music files that the person is willing to share. (MP3 is a standard compression scheme used so that the files can be sent over the Internet more quickly.)

The upshot is that people searching for music on Napster have access to a live, continually updated directory of all the music that is available from other users who happen to be online at that time. This directory is where the Napster servers *are* involved. Napster provides both a meeting place for people who want to exchange music files and a mechanism for completing the exchange.

Even when viewed strictly as software, apart from its application to music, Napster is important and interesting. It provides a very scalable, flexible mechanism for bringing together a community with shared interests and with information to exchange. It does not require uploading and maintenance of some massive central repository. Instead, the collection is fully distributed, living on the machines owned by the community's members. The collection can grow and change as quickly as the needs and interests of the community change. The core Napster technology could provide a powerful infrastructure for any community with voluminous information that members would like to share. It happens to work very well among the community of people interested in exchanging digital music files. The problem for Napster is that most music is protected by copyright.

## Copyright and Policy

Copyright has always been a political construct, and it's no different now. The shape of copyright has changed over time to reflect the struggle between different interest groups over who gets to benefit from the publication of ideas, stories, music, and other works valued by the public. The current controversy over digital music and, more generally, over how to handle digital publishing and the Internet is just the next step in a long history of adjustments to copyright policy to align it with new technologies and with the concerns of new interest groups.[3]

This is an important perspective for managers in charge of content distributed over the Internet. It is easy to be fooled into thinking that digital publishing is the first significant challenge to a set of ancient and long-accepted principles about authorial rights. In fact, we are participating in a new chapter of a debate with a long history. As has always been the case, the outcome will reflect the changes in power among the competing interest groups as well as policy considerations about what is "right" and what is most likely to stimulate continued progress and economic health.

As an example of the extent to which copyright is a constructed and flexible notion, rather than something engraved on a stone tablet and passed down through the ages, consider that in England copyright began as a censorship tool used by the Crown to control what was printed. Copyright grew from laws passed in the early 1500s that required any printed work to be licensed by the Stationer's Company, which was controlled by the Crown. Later, copyright evolved into a tool that, combined with apprenticeship requirements and other constraints imposed by the printers' guilds, created a printing and publishing monopoly for London booksellers. Authors sold their works to printers for a flat fee, giving up all rights in the work. The copyright was the right enjoyed by a bookseller to print copies of particular works, including works by authors who had been dead for hundreds of years. As property, copyrights were bought and sold by the booksellers.

The booksellers' cozy arrangement was threatened by external factors, much like the high prices for CD music currently enjoyed by music publishers are threatened today by the external factors of Napster and the Internet. In the case of the London bookselling cartel, the unification of England and Scotland in 1707 represented a grave threat because Scottish booksellers were reprinting copyrighted books and undercutting the prices charged by the London cartel. At the same time, the Crown was interested in placing some limits on the perpetual property rights enjoyed by the bookselling cartel. The Statute of Anne, otherwise known as the Copyright Act of 1709, sought compromise between the conflicting political interests by granting an exclusive monopoly to publishers for a limited period of time.

The Statute of Anne was historically important because it formed part of the background for U.S. copyright law, which appropriated the idea of monopoly rights granted for limited times. The Statute of Anne also was important because it was followed by a long period of debate over just how the law would be interpreted by the English courts. It was during this period that the new idea of the author as someone with rights to the work began to emerge. Foreshadowing today's assertions by the record companies, it was the booksellers who argued that copyright was important in protecting the author from villains who would otherwise appropriate his work (in the eighteenth century the assumption was that authors were male), ruining his life and destroying his family. The booksellers, of course, were just the right group to protect the poor author from villainous pirates by assuming and defending the copyright. In the eighteenth century, as is true today, it was much more politically effective for publishers to argue on behalf of the authors than on behalf of their own interests in monopoly rights.

Although U.S. copyright law was derived primarily from British law, the United States differed from Britain and the rest of Europe by making it clear at the outset that copyright was not in any sense a moral or natural right enjoyed by authors, apart from action by Congress. The United States, starting with the language of the Constitution and with the Federal Copyright Act of 1790 and continuing up to recent times,[4] has viewed copyright as a utilitarian construct and as a *privilege*—not a *right*—granted by Congress in order to meet Congress's policy objectives.

As an example of this utilitarian view of copyright, consider the fact that until 1891 the United States did not recognize foreign copyrights. This meant that until 1891 it was legal in the United States to publish work by any foreign author without returning any royalties to the author. Using today's terminology, the United States in the nineteenth century was the leading "pirate" nation with regard to intellectual property. But to fully grasp the utilitarian, changeable, and expeditious view of copyright that has shaped policy in this country, it is important to realize that, to nineteenth-century Americans, this aggressive policy was not seen as piracy. It was understood as doing what was necessary for a nation that was, at that time, still a net importer of ideas and technology. The appropriation of works from authors outside the United States just made good business sense. To the extent that there was concern about protection of authors, that concern was also utilitarian and focused solely on U.S. authors.

Today, copyright provides authors of original works with the exclusive right to reproduce, display, make copies of, perform publicly, and create derivative works of the original work. The copyright owner can transfer these rights to others. The right extends for the duration of the author's life plus 70 years. In the case of a work made for hire, the right extends for 95 years from the date of publication or 120 years from the date of creation, whichever is shorter. Copyrights apply to unpublished works as well as to published works. The copyright is granted to the author automatically; the author is not required to register the copyright in order to have copyright protection.[5]

Copyright applies to a broad range of creative activity. The key thing is that the work must be available in a fixed, tangible form of expression, since that fixed expression is what the copyright protects. That means that copyright can be applied to literary works, music, paintings and drawings, sculptures, sound recordings, motion pictures, computer programs, and other tangible creations of a fixed nature. It cannot be applied to ideas, methods, processes, concepts, or devices. (Some of these things can be protected by patents, however.) And copyright cannot be applied to works that consist entirely of common property and that contain no original authorship, such as tables of weights and measures or information taken from public sources.

The granting of copyright grows from the U.S. Constitution's empowerment of Congress in Article I, Section 8: "To promote the progress of science and useful arts, by securing for limited times to authors and inventors the exclusive right to their respective writings and discoveries." As Supreme Court Justice John Paul Stevens wrote in *Sony* v. *Universal Studios*:

> The monopoly privileges that Congress may authorize are neither unlimited nor primarily designed to provide a special private benefit. Rather, the limited grant is a means by which an important public purpose may be achieved. It is intended to motivate the creative activity of authors and inventors by the provision of a special reward, and to allow the public access to the products of their genius after the limited period of exclusive control has expired.

The goal of obtaining public benefit is balanced against the monopoly privileges by imposing limitations on the copyright holder's exclusive control. The most well known of these limitations is the "fair use" restriction, which says that copying "for purposes such as criticism, comment, news reporting, teaching (including multiple copies for classroom use), scholarship, or research" is not necessarily an infringement on the owner's rights.[6]

A survey of the other limitations on exclusive control, beyond fair use, reflects both the utilitarian nature of copyright law and its history of dealing with particular problems and special cases. There are limitations on rights that allow libraries to make copies of works, that allow users of computer programs to make backup copies of the programs, that protect secondary satellite transmissions by TV superstations and by PBS from infringement claims, that deal with retransmission among repeater stations in a radio network, that deal with playing songs on jukeboxes, and so on. Each limitation on rights is driven by the needs of some business or interest group.

Viewed in the aggregate, copyright law looks a lot like a computer program that has been patched and patched again until the overall design is nearly obscured. The one thing that is clear is that copyright is a vehicle for balancing the complex, conflicting interests revolving around the tangible expressions of creative work. At the very highest level copyright is driven by the utilitarian notion of promoting progress. In practice, since copyright is fundamentally all about property, the question of just how to best promote progress is answered in terms of the propertied interests that are politically dominant at any given time. Copyright is a work in progress. It is also a mirror reflecting the struggle between established interests and the challenges to those interests. The conflicts between new Internet-based businesses and established ways of publishing and distributing information are just the next chapter in this struggle.

One quick disclaimer is in order before we return to consideration of Napster and its impact on copyright law and on your business: Copyright law is complex, and any questions about a particular work or instance of potential infringement should, of course, be discussed with an attorney. My focus here is on providing you with a context for thinking about copyright policy, rather than with advice that you can apply directly to your particular legal needs.

## Setting the Stage for Napster

By the time that the Napster dispute finally ends, it is likely that it, in combination with similar cases, will have stimulated yet another adjustment in the way that copyright law balances the interests among authors, publishers, distribution channels, and the consuming public. A recent report by the National Research Council referred to the dispute over copyright and music as "Intellectual Property's Canary in the Digital Coal Mine," stressing the general importance of these early decisions over music copyrights.[7] The decisions made here will propel and constrain the decisions that are ultimately made about other media and the other challenges to established business models arising from the Web. In short, whether you are involved in music publishing or not, you want to pay attention to the legal activity surrounding Napster and other companies that are challenging the existing structure of music distribution. So, some background and some elaboration on the main points in the lawsuit are in order.

The charge that the record companies leveled against Napster is that it is *contributing* to copyright infringement. This is different than charging that Napster itself is infringing on copyrights. The difference is part of what makes the Napster case so important. Like the Internet as a whole, Napster is providing the *means* to do something. If laws are being broken because copyrights are being infringed, it is Napster's users who are doing the breaking and infringing. But Napster provides the means, and so Napster is the record industry's target. If the record industry can shut down Napster and any similar services, so the theory goes, then they can put an end to the infringing.[8]

This is not the first time that a company providing new technology has been accused of contributory infringement. In 1976 a group of motion picture and television studios sued Sony over what was at that time the new technology of the video cassette recorder (VCR), embodied in the Sony Betamax. The studios claimed that, by offering the Betamax for sale, Sony was guilty of contributory copyright infringement because people used the machines to make copies of television programs and movies for which the studios owned copyrights.

The Sony case was in the courts for eight years, finally reaching the Supreme Court in 1982. The Court issued its decision, ruling in favor of Sony and continued sales of VCRs, in 1984.[9] Its decision turned on three points, all of which are relevant to the Napster case:

1. Only Congress can expand the scope of copyright privileges. As new technologies emerge, the courts must guard against expansion of copyright protection without a clear expression of intent from Congress. As Justice Stevens wrote in his opinion, writing for the majority of the Court, "Sound policy, as well as history, supports our consistent deference to Congress when major technological innovations alter the market for copyrighted materials."
2. The assertion that merely supplying the means for copyright infringement can be the basis for a claim of liability for infringement must be evaluated with great care. Blanket acceptance of such claims would, for example, lead to a ban on photocopying machinery. The key question is whether there are substantial noninfringing uses of the technology. This matter is so important that it is sufficient to be able to simply identify *potential* noninfringing uses.
3. "Time shifting," which consists of recording a program for viewing at a later time, is an example of a substantial noninfringing use.

The use of the Internet and peer-to-peer file exchange to enable free exchange of music files, as implemented in Napster and similar services, raises many of the same issues that were present in the Sony case. Once again, we have a major technological innovation that has altered the market. So, one key question is whether, in addition to infringing uses, there is the potential for substantial noninfringing use. Answering this question requires that one looks first at what Napster's users are doing.

## Infringement by Users?

If Napster's users are not infringing on copyrights, then there is certainly no case to be made for contributory infringement. If they *are* infringing, then the question is more complicated, requiring a look at both infringing and noninfringing uses.

If you put a CD audio disc into the CD drive of your computer, you can play it, but you cannot copy it unless you have some special software. What you need is a "ripper"—a device that allows you to capture a track from the CD so that you can store it on your computer's magnetic disk in MP3 format, the compression format used for digital audio files on Napster and other Internet music exchanges. Once you have "ripped" a track and have turned it into an MP3 file, then you are ready to participate in copyright infringement—or not.

The infringement question is not straightforward. If you rip a track from a CD that you already own and then store it on your notebook computer for listening on planes, are you infringing on copyright? Napster argues that this is merely "space shifting"—analogous to the time shifting that you might do with a VCR. Aren't you just transforming something that you already own into a different format so that you can use it elsewhere? Isn't that fair use?

What if you combine a number of your favorite tracks—again, taken from discs that you own—and then write them to a new CD, compiling a collection of personal "greatest hits" that you can then listen to in your car? Now you have created your own CD. That seems more like infringement, but, in other ways, it just seems like more space shifting.

Now let's bring Napster into the picture more directly. Suppose that, rather than ripping a file from your own CD, you download a file from Napster—once again, a song that is on a CD that you own—so that you can assemble your own CD of favorite songs. Is that copyright infringement or just, once again, space shifting? Surely it cannot matter whether you use a ripper or use Napster.

What if you make a copy of your personal "greatest hits" CD and then give it to a friend? What if you use Napster to sample songs from a CD before you buy it? What if you don't buy the CD? What if you actually use Napster as your music source instead of going to the store?

If we constructed a list of questions like this, arranging them from more innocuous uses to more aggressive ones, we would find that, for most people, there is some point where they cross over to deciding that a use is, in fact, an instance of infringement. If we asked a lot of people to respond to such a list, we would find that the crossover point occurred in different places for different individuals. Most important, we would find that we could construct similar lists for intellectual property other than music, extending the process to digital copies of books, to research reports, to copies of magazine articles, and so on. In other words, the questions of infringement that are being addressed in the Napster case are questions that are important for digital publishing in general, and they are not easy ones. The fact that the Napster debate may be addressing them in a haphazard, limited way without considering the full range of potential uses does not decrease the potential impact of the case; it only increases the cause for concern.

## Contributory Infringement?

Napster does not deny that some of its users are breaking copyright laws. In fact, Napster has barred some users from its site because of copyright violations. But the company does claim that there are also substantial noninfringing uses of the Napster service. And, it argues, that is what should matter. In the Sony Betamax case the Supreme Court wrote:

> The sale of copying equipment, like the sale of other articles of commerce, does not constitute contributory infringement if the product is widely used for legitimate, unobjectionable purposes, or, indeed, is merely capable of substantial noninfringing uses.[10]

Using an analogy that states the matter in an obvious way, the fact that Ford knows that its vehicles are used in bank robberies does not make Ford liable for the robberies through some kind of theory of contributory responsibility.

Clearly, making a judgment in the case of Napster is harder than it is for Fords. Fords are a "staple article of commerce." Most uses of Fords are legitimate; the fact that some uses are illegal is no concern of Ford's. For Napster, the proportion of illegitimate uses is much higher. On the other hand, Napster is still young and unformed. In the first years of the Web a very large proportion of Web business was pornography. But that did not mean that the Web could be used only for pornography; it was clearly capable of more legitimate uses. These uses simply needed time to develop. Couldn't it turn out to be the same for Napster? Isn't Napster—just like the Betamax once was—a new technology that is just beginning to develop important, legitimate uses?

Judge Marilyn Patel, the District Court judge who first ruled on the recording industry's request for an injunction against Napster, didn't think so. Judge Patel's ruling is long and detailed, but it can be boiled down to the following points (quotations are from the ruling)[11]:

1. Napster users are definitely infringing on copyrights: "Virtually all Napster users engage in the unauthorized downloading or uploading of copyrighted music."
2. Noninfringing uses of Napster are minimal: "The substantial or commercially significant use of the service was, and continues to be, the unauthorized downloading and uploading of popular music, most of which is copyrighted."
3. What Napster users are doing is not "fair use." Judge Patel points out that an argument in favor of fair use is undercut by the fact that users copy the works in their entirety. "Even after Sony, wholesale copying for private home use tips the fair use analysis in plaintiffs' favor if such copying is likely to adversely affect the market for the copyrighted material."
4. Napster, in reducing the cost of copyrighted music to zero, is likely to adversely impact the market for copyrighted music.
5. Napster is aware that its users are infringing on copyrights and plays an active role in facilitating this infringement.

Taking all of this into account, Judge Patel concluded that there is a reasonable likelihood that a contributory infringement claim against Napster could be successful. Given that likelihood, and given her assessment of the likelihood that the plaintiffs are suffering grave harm, Judge Patel enjoined Napster from assisting users in any further unauthorized copying of copyrighted material. Writing in her conclusion that Napster had "contributed to illegal copying on a scale that is without precedent," she ordered what would have been, for all practical purposes, a shutdown of Napster's operations.

Two days after Judge Patel's ruling, the Ninth Circuit Court of Appeals issued a stay to her injunction, citing concerns about "both the merits and form of the injunction."[12] Although the two-judge panel issuing the stay did not provide a detailed analysis of the ruling (that would have been premature at that point) two things were clear. The first was that, without a stay, further inquiry into the matter was probably moot, since Napster would almost certainly cease to exist.

The second point—and the more important one for people trying to understand the collision between copyright and new technologies—was that Judge Patel's ruling tended to look only at the present and past operations of Napster. For example, the judge's language used to evaluate Napster's claim that it has significant noninfringing uses was,

"The substantial or commercially significant use of the service was, and continues to be . . . " This focus on past and present was consistent throughout her decision. She either feels that future uses are not important to the question before her or believes that past use is a good predictor of a new technology's future use and benefit to society. Apart from the legal merits of such reluctance to include broader consideration of future uses, it is important to note that the judge's viewpoint is very different from that of someone trying to think strategically about building a future market position. Investors and entrepreneurs base their livelihood on creating futures that break from the past.

There have been some other interesting developments subsequent to Judge Patel's initial ruling. But, before I move on to describe the next, surprising chapter in the Napster story, it is necessary to get above the legal details to have a look at the conflict between Napster and the recording companies in a market context.

## Taking Care of Business in the Courts

Speaking before the House Judiciary Committee, Jack Valenti, president of the Motion Picture Association of America, warned that "the growing and dangerous intrusion of this new technology" threatens an entire industry's "economic vitality and future security." Driving his point home with a most striking analogy, he told Congress that the new technology "is to the American film producer and the American public as the Boston Strangler is to the woman alone."[13]

Mr. Valenti was not talking about Napster or the Internet. This particular example of Mr. Valenti's rhetorical style dates back to 1982, and the presumed victim was the movie industry at the hands of the VCR. We now know that, rather than turning out to be the Boston Strangler, the VCR was more like a character in a Jane Austen novel, marrying the lonely woman and bringing a fresh new fortune to her impoverished family. Videotape transformed the distribution mechanism and economics of the movie industry. Virtually all parties—the industry, film producers, and film viewers—benefited from the change. The Supreme Court was wise in proceeding cautiously, leaving it to market forces and to Congress to sort out how the new videotape technology should intersect with the interests of content providers. It is this caution that is missing in Judge Patel's decision.

But, apart from playing armchair judge and second-guessing the courts, what might the future alignment of peer-to-peer file exchange and the music industry look like? Does the technology behind Napster and similar music-swapping services have the same potential for transformation that video recorders had twenty years ago? Are we once again looking at the first instances of a change that is likely to meet an unfilled customer need, opening up new opportunities for growth?

Napster's peer-to-peer file exchange is demonstrably filling some kind of important market need. Use of the service has grown rapidly, at times supporting up to 10,000 exchanges per second according to testimony that Napster presented in response to the lawsuit. Nearly 40 million people have downloaded the Napster software and registered to use the service. That makes the Napster "customer" base larger than AOL's.

The quick and superficial conclusion to draw about such rapid growth is, "Well, yeah, Napster is giving music away for free. It is responding to the 'unfilled customer need' to get something for nothing. It offers nothing to the record industry and can only hurt it."

Such simple analysis overlooks the fact that other industries, such as magazines and newspapers, have been able to build business models that successfully take advantage of free Web distribution. As one friend of the court briefing points out, these other owners of copyrighted works have not seen "a stampede of angry users away from their product to obtain it on the Internet. The public has demonstrated that it is willing to pay a fair and competitive price for a product even though it may be available for less through an unauthorized market."[14]

What's different about music? It is true, of course, that the fact that Internet distribution can supplement physical distribution for magazines and newspapers does not necessarily mean that such combinations will work for music. But the observation does raise the question of why the music distribution business, unlike other content distributors, has been so slow in developing Internet channels. And why, when Napster did provide an Internet alternative, was there actually a stampede of angry users that suddenly abandoned traditional distribution channels? What is different about the music business?

These questions are important because it was the inaction by the established players in the industry that opened up the opportunity for Napster in the first place. Why didn't music publishers jump on the Internet opportunity and foreclose Napster's options before it ever got started? Viewed in terms of market dynamics rather than in terms of points of copyright law, the face-off between the recording industry and Napster is intriguing and even surprising. How could it have ever happened? Was the music industry sleeping? Is it a really tough business and logistics problem?

### Controlling the Market

One plausible explanation for the recording industry's reluctance to open up and change its distribution network is that it had been successful in controlling the existing network as it was. The Federal Trade Commission (FTC) investigated the music distribution industry in the late 1990s. It found that record companies began exercising illegal control over distribution in response to a loss of control in the early 1990s, when new music retailers entered the market and began to cut the prices on CD recordings in a bid to gain market share. Other retailers began to pressure the distributors for a cut in wholesale prices so that they could maintain workable margins while still competing with the newcomers.

According to the FTC complaint, rather than reducing prices, the record distribution companies instituted penalties for retailers who advertised prices lower than a "Minimum Advertised Price" (MAP) set by the distributor. The penalties consisted of a suspension of cooperative advertising funding for the retailer. Since these penalties applied even if an "advertised price" consisted merely of a sign used only inside a store, the MAP program effectively penalized a retailer for any sales at prices below the price set by the distributor.

These efforts not only put an end to the price wars but also restored such effective control over the distribution channel that distributors were actually able to *raise* wholesale prices for CDs in the years that followed. The FTC estimates that this price-fixing activity cost U.S. consumers nearly half a billion dollars over the last three years. In May 2000 the FTC entered into agreements with all five major music distributors that force them to end price fixing.[15] It is clear that the recording industry will go to substantial lengths to control distribution in its market. Market control and innovation are often opposed to each other.

## An Alternative and a Threat to Control

*NAPSTER has turned music into baseball cards and the consumer base of kids are leading the pack, ENTHUSIASTIC ABOUT MUSIC.*
**—Chuck D.[16]**

Chuck D. is speaking to the potential for innovation through Napster. He is the lead vocalist for the rap group Public Enemy, which uses the Internet and music downloads to promote its music and message while also maintaining a very successful business in selling CDs. His analogy between the collection and trading of music tracks and the collection and trading of baseball cards points to a problem and a potential solution. The problem is that the current approach to "packaging" a new hit song consists of an expensive program that combines music videos, staged appearances, and extensive advertising. Chuck D. sees the consequences for the artist as follows:

> Long ago the majors upped the ante on what it took to promote and market a song, thus totally squeezing the small, independent entrepreneur out of the distribution game. With

> radio choosing the more traditional popular favorites, the skyrocketed video costs, and even college jocks on the take, getting a record to the fans was becoming impossible.[17]

So, there were fewer opportunities for new artists. The focus on lavish promotion also created a kind of vicious circle. The result of loading such a large cost structure on top of the sales and distribution of new music is that the distributors are under pressure to sell as many full-length albums as they can at $16.99 a pop. The increased pressure to create big hits increases the focus on promotion. The spiral continues upward, and new artists and artists with smaller audiences continue to get squeezed.

Napster puts this whole edifice at risk. As the recording artist Prince explains it:

> All [the music industry] cares about is that kids on the Internet are downloading MP3s of the one hit song on the latest crappy release they put out with a huge promotional campaign, hoping to sell 2 million copies of the album when there is actually only one decent song on it. They don't care about copyright infringement. They only care about lost sales.[18]

The innovative opportunity that Chuck D. sees in Napster is that it provides an alternate channel for promotion that gets around the big expenses. Reducing the cost of promotion could shift control back to the artist and away from the record companies. He sees Napster as a "new radio"—as an alternative to old radio, which is dominated by the record distribution industry. When fans collect songs and swap songs, like baseball cards, Napster provides new artists with an economical way to build a following and sell music. Chuck D. envisions a distribution environment in which an artist gives two or three songs away in order to sell three or four more and where CD recordings are shorter and much less expensive. He thinks that the "new radio" channel will enable more new artists to come to market on their own, without backing from a major distributor. He sees a return to an emphasis on music rather than on packaging.

### Does Anyone Have the Time?

We don't need to decide whether Chuck D.'s argument is right or not and whether his "new radio" and the swapping of tunes will work out as he predicts. It is sufficient to note that the current industry structure has concentrated a great deal of control in the hands of a small number of companies and that distribution models such as the ones that Chuck D. is contemplating provide plausible alternatives.

There is, of course, no question that new distribution models with reduced transaction costs will threaten existing models. But why is it in the public interest—or even in the interest of the larger business community—to protect the existing distribution scheme? Why should we want to use the legal system to retard and possibly even prevent the development of new, more efficient ways to move music from artists to their audiences? Arguably, the best path forward to promoting "the progress of science and useful arts" is to find a way to enable Napster and other Internet-based music distribution schemes to break new ground.

Moving beyond the specifics of the music business, the general problem that business people face in figuring out how to create value using the tools provided by the Internet and the Web is that we need time to try things out and we need time for new markets to develop. New business development is always a huge chicken-and-egg problem. We typically proceed by starting both with a few chickens and with a few eggs.

For example, in the 1970s there was no ready market for prerecorded videotapes because there were very few VCRs. So, the people who bought VCRs used them to record copyrighted material. They did this to time shift, to get something for nothing, to infringe on copyrights, or to simply use their new toys. As there were more VCRs, there was more incentive to create tapes for sale. This became the incentive for more people to buy machines. More volume, in turn, brought the price of machines down. Then even more people could buy them. And, over a period of years, a new market for prerecorded tapes—a market that was not even dimly glimpsed in the Betamax ruling—emerged.

Most businesses in emerging markets need to be able to proceed in the same way, with a few chickens, a few eggs, and a rough start. In other words, businesses need time because new market development takes time. Rigid application of copyright without consideration of future benefits, as Judge Patel very nearly demonstrated, can run out the clock. The game is over, established investments are protected, but innovation loses.

## Business Takes Care of Business

On October 31, 2000, the Napster saga took a very different turn when Napster surprised nearly everyone with an announcement that it had reached an agreement with Bertelsmann, the giant German media company that owns BMG, one of the major recording companies participating in the Napster lawsuit. The exact financial terms of the deal were not announced, but the general structure is that Bertelsmann provided Napster with a loan, estimated to be more than $50 million, to enable Napster to create the technology required to track what is being exchanged between Napster's users. If Napster could somehow keep track of the songs that users are sending back and forth, then it would be possible to pay royalties to BMG and the other record companies.

Bertelsmann promised that once the tracking capability was in place, BMG would withdraw from the lawsuit. The deal also guaranteed Bertelsmann the option of taking an equity stake in Napster. The arrangement was not exclusive, and Bertelsmann encouraged other plaintiffs in the suit to work out similar arrangements.

What this deal did was buy time. It resolved none of the substantive issues. The lawsuit was still in place, and BMG was still participating in it. But it avoided a rush to a judgment that would either disregard the record companies' copyright claims or, on the other hand, shut down Napster. It bought the time and provided Napster with the funds to explore the potential to turn Napster's peer-to-peer technology and its user base into a new kind of music market, delivering music in new ways. As Thomas Middelhoff, Bertelsmann's CEO, said in speaking of Napster's 38 million registered users, "They can't all be criminals."[19] Put another way, where some saw criminals, Middelhoff saw a new market.

It is actually the fact that this agreement *does not* attempt to resolve any of the substantive issues that makes it such an inspired piece of deal making. Bertelsmann looked at the bigger picture and saw that peer-to-peer file sharing is an issue that goes beyond a simple copyright dispute. It looked at Napster's user base and saw that some kind of need, beyond getting free music, was being met. Bertelsmann saw that, given its financial resources and those of the other record companies, and given Napster's dwindling resources, it could probably crush Napster in court, but it also recognized that doing that wouldn't address the real market issues.

Bertelsmann also knew that there were substantial technical and business problems that needed to be solved before it could develop a new business around file sharing. No one knew if there really would be an effective way to monitor file exchanges on a peer-to-peer network. It was not clear whether it would be necessary to encrypt each music file in some way, tying it to a user's machine, to prevent people from running around the Napster system. It was even less clear how to provide enough new value to Napster's customers to induce them to start paying for something that used to be free. But Bertelsmann recognized that Napster was now in a position where it was highly motivated to try to solve these problems. So Bertelsmann came up with some money to let Napster do just that, and it put itself in a position to enjoy some of the benefits if Napster succeeds.

## Postscript

There has been a great deal of activity surrounding the Napster lawsuit in the three months that elapsed between the completion of this chapter and taking the book to press.[20] I still have time to sneak in a last-minute update. Briefly summarized, the key developments of early 2001 are outlined below.

January 25 Good news for Napster—TVT Records, one of the largest independent labels in the United States, agreed to drop its $1.5 billion lawsuit against Napster. Terms of the deal were not disclosed, but TVT said it will provide Napster with access to TVT's recording masters for use in Napster's file-sharing service. TVT said that Napster's agreement with Bertelsmann was a factor in deciding to reach its own agreement with Napster.

January 29 Bertelsmann announced that it expected to relaunch Napster as a for-fee service as early as summer 2001. Bertelsmann's surveys of Napster users indicate that 70 percent are willing to pay a fee for guaranteed good downloads of new music. Details of planned fee structures were not announced; analysts speculated that the fees will probably run in the range of $10 to $15 per month. Bertelsmann expressed confidence that other major music companies will quickly come on board and back the new Napster service.

February 12 The Ninth Circuit Court of Appeals issued its ruling in response to Napster's appeal of Judge Patel's decision from the previous summer. The Appeals Court ruling substantially affirmed Judge Patel's decision. One small point of departure dealt with the issue of looking at current versus future uses of technology:

> We depart from the reasoning of the district court that Napster failed to demonstrate that its system is capable of commercially significant noninfringing uses. . . . The district court improperly confined the use analysis to current uses, ignoring the system's capabilities. . . . Consequently, the district court placed undue weight on the proportion of current infringing use as compared to current and future noninfringing use.[21]

Although this is an important legal point because it preserves the precedent set in the Sony Betamax case, in the end it makes no difference to Napster. The Appeals Court, like the District Court, decided that Napster's users are not engaged in fair use and are therefore breaking the law. Therefore, if the recording companies provide Napster with a list of the works that are being pirated, Napster is under an absolute obligation to prevent such piracy. The Appeals Court also tipped its hat to the future, noting that Napster is potentially interfering with the opportunity for copyright holders to develop their own digital distribution mechanisms.

The Ninth Circuit Court sent the matter back to Judge Patel so that she can issue a modified injunction that is consistent with the Appeals Court ruling. Napster once again faced imminent shutdown unless it could block the exchange of copyrighted music. An estimated 250 million songs were downloaded by Napster users during the weekend preceding the ruling.

February 20 Napster revealed its plan to begin charging users between $3 and $5 per month for "basic service" and between $6 and $10 per month for "premium service," with the intent of providing the major record producers with $150 million per year in additional revenues. Over a period of five years Napster projected the ability to provide $1 billion in new revenues for the industry as a whole.

March 2 In anticipation of Judge Patel's new injunction, Napster announced that it was prepared to start blocking user access to copyrighted music. This was the first time that Napster agreed that such control is possible. Commentators speculated that Napster was hoping to convince Judge Patel that they could police their own site. During the weekend following the announcement Napster's users, estimated to number 65 million, poured onto the site, and Napster confessed to having significant difficulty putting its filters in place due to the complexity of handling all the different names that might be used to identify a song.

March 6 Judge Patel gave Napster three days to remove all pirated music from its site, starting from the time that Napster received a list of the pirated titles from the copyright owners. Napster admitted that it has received no favorable response from the recording industry to its plan to produce $1 billion in additional revenues. Bertelsmann said that even if the site were shut down for a short while, it would be back up and running as a legal site by July.

March 14 Napster announced that it had managed to avoid the threat of closure by meeting the court deadline to remove titles of copyrighted music from its site. It said that it had successfully removed two-thirds of the titles from a list of 135,000 offending tracks provided by the record companies. The remaining one-third could not be removed immediately because the record companies had provided insufficient or incorrect data.

March 22 Major record labels announced that they were planning new legal action against Napster in the following week because Napster had not been able to comply with demands to remove 500,000 music tracks from its service. Napster's efforts to remove the listed tracks were being made more difficult by misspellings. Further, other sites began offering software that systematically garbles the spelling of tracks so that they will slip past Napster's filters. Record industry spokespersons said that they expect all copyrighted tracks to be removed: the fact that users misspell names or intentionally garble them is Napster's concern, not the concern of the companies that own the copyrights to the music. A new ruling could impose stricter sanctions on Napster or could shut down the service completely, by court order.

If I waited another month to go to press with this book, this list would be longer. It seems at this point (April 2001) that Bertelsmann will be unsuccessful in bringing the other major recording companies on board in its effort to turn Napster into a legitimate service operating for the broader benefit of the industry. There are probably a number of reasons for this. One might be that some companies see important symbolic, political value in getting rid of Napster. Another is that companies might prefer to start up their own digital distribution services to compete with Bertelsmann and Napster. In February, for example, Vivendi Universal and Sony announced that they would start up their own music service, named Duet, to compete with Napster, saying "Napster cannot be alone in this market. We are setting up our own platform, which will be open to others to join and which will offer the maximum amount of legitimate music over the maximum number of platforms."[22]

However the Napster story eventually turns out, many of the important lessons that it offers are already clear and independent of the final shape of the arrangements.

## Lessons from Napster

The Napster story, viewed within the broader context of the history of copyright in the United States, provides useful insights into the actual, practical role of copyright law during times of technological innovation.

- **Political basis**: Copyright today, as in the 1500s, is shaped by the political and economic climate of the times.
- **Utilitarian basis**: Copyright provides important protections for business. These protections are supposed to be consistent with the broader aim of protecting the interests of society as a whole. Despite rhetoric about the rights of authors, the protections are fundamentally utilitarian. Copyright is built around the *quid pro*

*quo* principle that providing publishers and authors with the potential to profit from their work will lead to more creative work and more general benefit. In the past, the focus on utilitarian benefit has consistently trumped claims to authorial or property rights.

- **Conservative stance regarding innovation**: Copyright protections tend to be conservative with regard to technical innovation. Consequently, since innovation is important and since copyright must, over the long run, meet tests of utility rather than some external, objective notion of protecting "rights," copyright law changes with time.
- **Competing notions of utility**: There are, of course, many kinds of business interests looking in many different directions. Some business interests are well served by copyright's conservative tendency. However, in general, businesses interested in developing new capabilities on the Web need more room for innovation than strict application of copyright can provide.
- **Value chain**: In trying to understand the balance between different interests and benefits, it is important to look at the roles of the different actors in the value chain stretching from the initial creator of the work to the ultimate user. In particular, although publishers and distributors argue that they represent the interests of the authors and artists, this claim should be examined closely: in times when distribution mechanisms are changing, both the artist/author and the public as a whole might benefit if market activity can force distributors to adapt to the changes. This can create a conflict between the broader aim of achieving public benefit and the particular aims of protecting copyrights, since the distributor often holds the copyright.
- **Court limitations regarding change**: The courts are not well positioned to deal affirmatively with this tension between the need to enable innovation and the need to protect established interests, particularly in times when the structure of markets and the concept of public benefit are shifting. Some farseeing courts have been sensitive to these limits and to the potential for important new developments, even when the potential benefits were more projected than real. Less visionary courts have simply come down on the side of the status quo, strengthening copyright's conservative tendencies. Even the most visionary courts are limited to acting by forbearing from action.
- **Enlightened management's view beyond the horizon**: It is important for businesses to rise above the details of copyright law to look at the bigger picture of technological and market change. Copyright is not a moral issue; it is a prac-

tical one. In times when technology is changing distribution options, it is in the interest of the business community as a whole to consider embracing new opportunities as well as protecting established investments.

Perhaps the most powerful and important lesson that can be drawn from the Napster story is that active, enlightened business leadership can initiate solutions to the copyright versus innovation dilemma that are simply beyond the reach of the courts. No jurist, no matter how visionary in temperament and ability, could effect the kind of shift of the debate to the higher, more forward-looking plateau that Bertelsmann attempted to reach. Along with the alleged infringement, Bertelsmann was able to see that Napster had created something new that was worth exploring and developing. Part of what Bertelsmann brought to this situation was the financial wherewithal to provide support for that exploration and development. The other quality that Bertelsmann brought was the ability to see the forest as well as the trees.

The Napster case is complex. Digital distribution of music is inevitable. It is also difficult to figure out how to do it and make money, so the music industry initially moved forward slowly. That opened an opportunity for Napster. In its creation of such a large, vigorous music exchange, Napster has forced the music industry to move more quickly in coming to terms with digital distribution. Napster may be out of business next year, but it has served the important purpose of shaping the industry's focus and direction. Copyright, up to this point, has served the important purpose of giving the industry a way to put the brakes on the changes and reassert some control over copyrighted content. The industry gets another shot at creating a digital distribution scheme that works for it. But the bigger story is still a long way from ending.

Once established ways of doing business are upended there are usually a number of different directions that future development can take. One direction might involve the kind of loss of control that Napster embodies (and now has to struggle with, itself). Another direction might involve the use of a combination of law and technology to establish more control than ever before. To do that, Congress would need to change the copyright laws. The next chapter looks at what is happening in that direction.

## Notes

1. From Napster's Reply Brief to the RIAA Appellee's Responding Brief filed with the U.S. Court of Appeals, Ninth Circuit, pursuant to Appeal Nos. 00-16401 and 00-16403 on September 12, 2000. Accessed on the Web at http://www.law.washington.edu/lct/files/Napster/Napster/9th_reply_brief.pdf in May 2001.

2. From *A&M Records* v. *Napster,* No. 00-16401, U.S. Court of Appeals for the Ninth Circuit. Accessed on the Web at http://www.ce9.uscourts.gov/ in May 2001. Search for the opinion by the date of February 12, 2001.
3. The history of copyright is complex and circuitous and is, itself, subject to political interpretation. Reading through the history is an excellent way to get a strong sense of how much copyright is a pragmatic notion that has evolved in response to changing political philosophy and to lobbying by interest groups rather than any kind of long-established "natural" right. Deborah Halbert, in her book *Intellectual Property in the Information Age: The Politics of Expanding Ownership Rights* (Westport, CT: Quorum Books, 1999), provides an excellent survey of this history. The very brief account of copyright history that I include here reflects her research and thinking. For anyone interested in a deeper look at the topic, I recommend her very readable book, which synthesizes a great deal of conflicting research and different viewpoints on the history.
4. The most recent strong expression of the United States' rejection of any claim of moral rights for authors is the fact that, although it agreed to the primary rules set down in the Berne Convention for the Protection of Literary and Artistic Works in 1989, it rejected moral rights claims asserted by European nations.
5. The Library of Congress, which is the branch of government that administers the United States Copyright Office, provides an excellent, thorough introduction to copyright basics on its Web site at http://www.loc.gov/copyright/.
6. From 17 *U.S. Code* §107, "Limitations on Exclusive Rights: Fair Use."
7. See *The Digital Dilemma: Intellectual Property in the Information Age*, Computer Science and Telecommunications Board, National Research Council (Washington, DC: National Academy Press, 2000).
8. There is reason to question whether the record industry can put the genie back in the bottle by going after Napster and other centralized exchange services. There are other peer-to-peer mechanisms, such as Gnutella, that allow users to exchange files without any need for a central organization like Napster. Some analysts argue that the existence of such software tools makes the record industry's attempts to protect its interest by going after Napster moot. The counterargument is that turning music exchange into a business requires some kind of centralization, and only a business can pose a serious threat to the record industry. This argument is, essentially, that shareware like Gnutella is a sideshow.
9. *Sony Corporation of America* v. *Universal City Studios*, 464 U.S. 417 (1984).

10. Ibid.
11. *Napster* v. *A&M Records et al.*, C 99-5183 MHP, and *Napster* v. *Jerry Lieber*, C 00-0074 MHP, U.S. District Court Northern District of California, Judge Marilyn Hall Patel. Available in May 2001 on the Web at http://www.canada.cnet.com/News/Pages/Special/Napster/napster_patel.html and other places.
12. Stay of District Court ruling by Ninth Circuit Court of Appeals on July 28, 2000, Appeal Nos. 00-16401 and 00-16403. Available in May 2001 on the Web at http://www.law.washington.edu/lct/files/Napster/9th_stay.pdf.
13. As quoted by Adam Liptak in "Is Litigation the Best Way to Tame New Technology?" *The New York Times on the Web* (http://www.nytimes.com), accessed on September 2, 2000.
14. Association of American Physicians and Surgeons, Inc. and Eagle Forum Education and Legal Defense Fund, Brief for Amici Curiae Filed in Support of Appellant Napster, Inc. Supporting Reversal, Karen B. Tripp, 1100 Louisiana St., Suite 2690, Houston, TX 77002.
15. Information about the FTC investigation, the complaint, and the record industry's settlement is available in a press release from the FTC titled "Record Companies Settle FTC Charges of Restraining Competition in CD Music Market" and in a document titled "Analysis to Aid Public Comment on the Proposed Consent Order." As of May 2001, the press release and analysis were available at http://www.ftc.gov/opa/2000/05/cdpres.htm and http://www.ftc.gov/os/2000/05/mapanalysis.htm, respectively.
16. From Chuck D.'s "Terrordome" column for May 1, 2000, on the Public Enemy Web site, http://www.publicenemy.com/terrordome/, accessed in May 2001.
17. Ibid.
18. As quoted by the Associated Press in "Napster's Effect on Sales Unclear," *The New York Times on the Web* (http://www.nytimes.com). Accessed on August 18, 2000.
19. As reported by Matt Richtel and David D. Kirkpatrick in "Napster to Charge Fee for Music Rights," *The New York Times*, November 1, 2000.
20. *Financial Times* has been maintaining a timeline of key events in the Napster story, dating back to Shawn Fanning's creation of the original Napster service in January 1999. The timeline was available in May 2001 on the Web at http://www.ft.com/napster/.

21. From *A&M Records* v. *Napster,* No. 00-16401, U.S. Court of Appeals for the Ninth Circuit. Available in May 2001 on the Web at http://www.ce9.uscourts.gov/. Search for the opinion by the date of February 12, 2001.
22. As quoted by Jo Johnson and James Harding in "Vivendi and Sony Tighten the Screws on Napster," *Financial Times*, February 22, 2001. Accessed in March 2001 at http://www.ft.com/napster.

CHAPTER 2

# Congress Asserts Control

JON JOHANSEN is a bright Norwegian teenager who, like many other young computer programmers, thinks that Linux is one of the greatest things to happen to computing.[1] His involvement with Linux and his desire to use it to watch DVD movies on his computer led to a conflict that helps illustrate the scope of Congress's recent changes to copyright law.

Linux got started in 1991 as a hobbyist's operating system. It was initially created by a Finnish computer science student, Linus Torvalds, who wanted a true multitasking operating system that he could run on his PC. Torvalds couldn't afford to buy a commercial version of such a system and, besides, he wanted a system where the source code was available so that he could play with it and modify it. Realizing that creating an operating system was more than he could do by himself, he sent out a call to the Internet community asking for help in creating the system. He made copies of Linux freely available to anyone who wanted to contribute to its development or simply use it on their own equipment. The surprising result was that Linux quickly attracted interest from the commercial community as well as the hobbyist community. It turned out that having so many different people working on a system, critiquing it, and finding errors and weaknesses produced a system that can be very robust and secure. Linux became a powerful operating system that someone like Johansen can not only use but can also help build.[2] Jon Johansen is a Linux disciple.

Jon had a problem, and within the problem was an opportunity. He found that when he purchased or rented movies on DVD discs he couldn't watch them on his Linux-based computer. The computer had a DVD drive, and if Jon had been running

Microsoft Windows he could have used that DVD drive because Windows includes software that can decode the Contents Scramble System (CSS) encryption used to protect DVD movies from copying. But the Linux system did not yet have a CSS descrambler. So, Jon took on the project of figuring out how to write one.

Jon got together with two other Linux hobbyists, one in Germany who had managed to decrypt the CSS code and another in the Netherlands. Working together, the three friends wrote the Linux software required to create DeCSS, their DVD code descrambler.

Consistent with common practice among Linux programmers, Jon and his friends shared their work with the worldwide membership of the Linux community so that all Linux users could review the DeCSS code, use it, critique it, and improve on it. In the United States, a magazine called *2600: The Hacker's Quarterly* emerged as one of the more visible publishing vehicles for distributing DeCSS in print and on its Web site.

That's where the trouble began.

## The Digital Millennium Copyright Act

Eight of the major motion picture studios sued Eric Corley, editor and publisher of *2600: The Hacker's Quarterly,* for publishing DeCSS. (Jon Johansen, though not involved directly in this U.S. suit except for a brief appearance as a witness, is also under investigation by Norwegian authorities for posting and advertising DeCSS.) The problem with DeCSS, from the studios' point of view, is that it serves the same function for DVD movies that "rippers" serve for CD audio discs: DeCSS allows people to make a digital copy of a movie that can be compressed and stored on a computer disk. Once you have a computer file, rather than a DVD disc, it is possible to start sending movies around on the Internet. Pretty soon the studios could find themselves dealing with the same difficulties that record companies now have with Napster.

The interesting thing about this action is that it doesn't look like a typical copyright infringement case. Nobody is accusing Corley or Johansen of making illegal copies of copyrighted movie files. Instead the crime is "circumvention." The accusation is that Johansen helped create and Corley published software that circumvents encryption code used to protect DVD movies.

The idea that it is a criminal act to create and distribute a software product that unlocks encrypted, copyrighted material is not just some claim being asserted by the movie studios. It is, instead, a direct expression of Congress's intent in the Digital Millennium Copyright Act (DMCA), passed by Congress in 1998 and now included as one of latest in the long series of patches to the copyright law. The DMCA says that it is illegal to

> manufacture, import, offer to the public, provide, or otherwise traffic in any technology, product, service, device, component, or part thereof, that is primarily designed or produced for the purpose of circumventing a technological measure that effectively controls access to a work protected under this title.[3]

Prohibiting circumvention devices is a new step in copyright law. It is a big change. It used to be perfectly legal to create products that, for example, defeated the copy protection system on floppy disks used to distribute software. The software to circumvent copy protection was understood to serve a substantial legitimate purpose in that it allowed software users to make backup copies of their disks.[4] Making copies of copyrighted software to use on other machines or to distribute to others was illegal, to be sure, but the copyright owner had to go after the copyright violator, not after the company that created the software to defeat the protection scheme.

To decide otherwise is a little like saying that, in the case of a murder with a handgun, one could convict the handgun manufacturer as well as the person who pulled the trigger. Even more pointedly, it is like saying that because a handgun *could* be used in a murder, whether or not an actual murder was committed, the handgun manufacturer has broken the law. Depending on your feelings about handguns you might think that this is a great idea or a bad one, but there is little doubt that it would represent an expansion of the reach of the law. Johansen helped create DeCSS and Corley provided access to it. Consequently, in the eyes of the major movie studios, they are both trafficking in circumvention technology and therefore breaking the new law.

*Universal* v. *Corley* is similar to *Napster* v. *A&M Records* in important ways. In both cases the plaintiffs are not going after the people who are infringing on the copyrights but are instead suing organizations that are viewed as enabling the infringement. In both cases the resolution turns on the question of whether the product or service in question, Napster or DeCSS, has significant uses other than the illegal ones. In both cases the consequences will reach well beyond the plaintiffs and defendants.

The important difference is that in the Napster case, the question of "contributory infringement"—the question of Napster's culpability for infringement by its users—leaves room for judicial discretion regarding future beneficial uses that are not yet realized. *Universal* v. *Corley* shows us that the DMCA provides courts with much less discretion when it comes to circumvention.

## The DMCA in Action

*Universal* v. *Corley* is one of the first lawsuits to make use of the DMCA's anticircumvention provisions. That's why it is an important case to look at closely. By making the effects of the law concrete, *Universal* v. *Corley* makes it easier to see how the DMCA changes the impact of copyright law. There are two aspects of the DMCA that *Universal* v. *Corley* brings into focus:

1. *Universal* v. *Corley* shows the scope of the DMCA in determining what is a legal decryption device and what is considered to be circumvention.
2. The case shows how the DMCA constrains a user's *access* to material as well as outlawing circumvention.

### Scope: The Question of Commercially Significant Purpose

A software debugger, in the hands of a skilled programmer, could be used to circumvent a copy protection scheme. The DMCA does not intend to outlaw debuggers. So, the DMCA confines the scope of its prohibition to devices with "only limited commercially significant purpose or use other than to circumvent a technological measure that effectively controls" protected works.

The defendants in the case argue that enabling Linux users to view DVD movies is a commercially significant use; indeed, it is the use that motivated the creation of DeCSS. But the representatives for the motion picture industry argue for a much narrower reading of the DMCA, saying that whether DeCSS is used to watch movies on Linux is beside the point. They argue that even when used to view a DVD movie owned by the viewer, DeCSS is clearly circumventing CSS protection, which is precisely what the law forbids.

The motion picture studios contend that Corley and his *2600* magazine compounded Johansen's mistake of writing DeCSS by then distributing the DeCSS code. The defendants reply that their publishing of source code written as part of an open-source operating system is simply in keeping with the long-established and respected practice within the open-source community, which routinely publishes, critiques, and improves upon the engineering work performed by other members of the community. They claim a First Amendment right to publish the code.

The District Court judge, Lewis Kaplan, described the facts of the case as "simply put" in the opinion that he wrote. The concluding statement in his opinion characterizes the defendants as "adherents of a movement that believes that information should be available without charge to anyone clever enough to break into the computer systems or data storage media in which it is located." In short, Judge Kaplan found in favor of the movie studios and a reading of the DMCA that gives broad scope to its anticircumvention provisions. The case has been appealed.

### Restriction of Access

One of the most important aspects of the DMCA is that by making circumvention devices illegal it constrains the choices available to the *user* of the copyrighted material. This is a very important insight, but it is not one that is immediately obvious; it is worth spending some time to understand how this works.

The key to understanding how the DMCA shifts control from users to publishers starts with the recognition that unlike information on paper, you cannot use digital information without the aid of some kind of computer program. If the information comes to you as a Web page, e-mail, or in some other form that can be interpreted by commonly available readers, then there are not many constraints on your use of the content. But if the information is encrypted so that it can be accessed only with the help of a specialized reader, the situation is suddenly very different. Under the DMCA, only the copyright owner can legally supply the decryption mechanism. This gives the copyright owner monopoly control over the reading devices as well.

To make this concrete, consider the difference between Linux DeCSS and the "official," sanctioned DVD playback software included with Microsoft Windows and with Macintosh computers. The official version of the software only transmits the DVD content to the computer screen. DeCSS, on the other hand, allows a user to actually create a file that contains the content. This means that DeCSS enables a user to grab brief excerpts—essentially, "quotations" from the copyrighted work—that could be used in teaching, criticism, and scholarship. Similarly, the decrypted files could be used in archival storage by libraries. All such uses have been traditionally treated as "fair use" of a copyrighted work, essentially an exception to the control granted to the copyright owners to ensure that the public derives benefit in return for its grant of copyright protection. In designing the sanctioned readers, the copyright owners have chosen to do away with such fair use—a choice that they can effect simply by building viewers that don't permit such activities. Ordinarily, that might create an opportunity for some other company that creates a more flexible, highly functional DVD player. But the DMCA completes and secures the elimination of fair-use activities by making it illegal for others to construct alternative, unlicensed players.

Stated more generally, by giving copyright owners complete control over the decision of what is an "approved" reading or decoding device—and outlawing all other devices that would circumvent the protection scheme—the DMCA is allowing the copyright owners to dictate how copyrighted material will be used. This new power could extend beyond simple elimination of fair use. An authorized player could, for example, implement a pay-per-view billing scheme. Alternatively, it could be constructed to play a particular disk only a limited number of times and then require the user to pay a license renewal fee. It could be constructed to keep track of viewing habits and send this information back to the copyright owner. A user wanting access to the copyrighted content has no choice but to accept the structure and the constraints of the player authorized by the copyright owners. There is no legal alternative source of decryption capability and therefore of readers, players, and viewers.[5]

In the past, copyright has not been used to grant the copyright holder exclusive control over ordinary, private use. The copyright owner controlled the process of *producing and delivering* the content, but the user controlled the process of *reading, listening, or viewing*. By giving the copyright owner the power to prosecute anyone who provides alternatives to the owner's authorized playback device, the DMCA changes this balance. It expands the power and value of copyright protection at the expense of the readers, viewers, and listeners who purchase and use such materials.[6]

## Consequences and Causes

Looking at the DMCA and at its concrete application in *Universal* v. *Corley* raises two questions: "Is this a good thing?" and "How did this happen?"

In the short run, owning a lock on how content is used in addition to how content is distributed looks like a good thing for the handful of companies that own the rights to most entertainment content.

For most other companies, however, changing the balance between information users and information producers looks like a bad thing. Most companies acquire and use much more information than they produce. Call it information entropy, information refinement, or what you will, but the simple fact is that you take in more than you put out. Shifting the control over *use* of information to the *producer* is not only unprecedented, it will also get in the way of information use for most of us. The information producer cannot anticipate how I will—from my standpoint—most profitably make use of particular information. A law that shifts control over my use of information to someone else is almost certainly a bad law.

How did we get such a law? Three factors appear to be at work:

1. A belief that copyright is a moral issue rather than a pragmatic one, and the consequent conclusion that the issues are simple
2. Lack of engagement in the issue by the broader business community
3. The unavoidable difficulty in anticipating consequences when technologies are changing rapidly

## Making Problems Simple

We face a tough challenge. We need to be able to make room for the development of new, as yet poorly understood business models. We also need to protect the interests of those who have already made investments in the businesses on which we depend today.

It is almost certainly true that companies with valuable content are reluctant to put that content on the Web for fear that it will be pirated. This is how inability to provide strong protection for content can diminish the value and quantity of what is available to the public on the Internet. More simply, it chills the development of Web-based businesses. From this viewpoint, strong copyright protection looks like the surest way to ensure more online access to content and more business vitality.

At the same time, as the exploration of the issues in *Universal* v. *Corley* shows, the new combinations of technology and law can have the opposite effect, radically shifting the balance between the interests of the copyright holders and the interests of the reading, viewing, and listening public. So, in addition to strong protection, we need the right kind of protection. But it is, of course, hard to create the right solutions all at once.

To the extent that businesspeople or members of Congress respond in a simple, single-minded way to one side or another in this controversy, we decrease our chances of creating policy that might achieve the objectives of balanced benefit and continued innovation and growth. The issues raised here are difficult ones; we are not well served by people who want to announce that "it's simple."

Unfortunately, there is apparently a strong impulse to do just that. For instance, in September 2000 Janet Reno, Attorney General at that time, made reference to cases such as the one we have just examined during a speech she gave on protecting intellectual property in the digital age:

> I have been quite concerned reading accounts of individuals who have been charged with committing computer-related crimes—especially statements by young people in the

> U.S. and other countries—who brag about their technological accomplishments. Some young people talk about these activities as if they were harmless hobbies or, at best, intriguing challenges. We need to change the cultural acceptance of theft of intellectual property, whether the theft is committed by stealing from a retail store or stealing using a computer. Either way, we are talking about theft, pure and simple.[7]

Former Attorney General Reno was the nation's chief law enforcement officer, and so perhaps her desire to have things simple is understandable. Given the apparent disregard for copyright shown by the general public in its broad exchange of copyrighted material using Napster, the Attorney General was probably wanting to deliver a moral lesson along with her analysis of the situation. But her reading of the issues in a case such as *Universal* v. *Corley* as theft, pure and simple, should be a real cause for concern among businesspeople. Such a view leads to a focus on protecting property above all else, even if the result is less ability to make legitimate use of information. The DMCA is a work in progress and cases such as *Universal* v. *Corley* help us see what work is left to be done. We won't get good, workable policy by reducing the problem to a game of cops and robbers.

## Engagement and Time to Learn

Our current tendency to see copyright issues in high-contrast black and white is not wholly the government's fault. The government is responding to what it hears. For example, Jack Valenti, president of the Motion Picture Association of America (yes, the same Jack Valenti who compared videotape to the Boston Strangler) described the situation to the House Commerce Committee's Subcommittee on Telecommunications as follows:

> As legitimate businesses emerge on the Internet, illegitimate intruders find the Internet a haven. These invaders steal copyrighted works, assault legal business sites and otherwise disrupt the normalities of Internet conduct. Piracy comes in all sizes, ingenuity and motivation. Which is why at this moment we confront attacks by those who profess to defend technological advancement but in truth who treat Copyright with a brazen disdain for laws and rules which guide and govern the daily labors of Americans.[8]

During the debate on the DMCA the presentation from the business community primarily reflected the point of view of the entertainment industry articulated here by Mr. Valenti. Record companies, motion picture studios, and publishers comprise a relatively small number of companies that have concentrated ownership over the full range of entertainment and information media. These companies exercise enormous political power. Their assertion is that business is under assault by immoral invaders who are out to undermine the American Way. The message, in short, is one of alarm and calling for strong action, quickly, to build a legally fortified wall around copyrighted content. It is this line of reasoning that is reflected in Ms. Reno's remarks. It was successful in persuading Congress to pass the DMCA.

During the debate on the DMCA the primary opposition to the assertions from the entertainment industry came from legal scholars, other academic groups, professional organizations such as the American Library Association and the Association for Computing Machinery, and citizen organizations such as the Electronic Frontier Foundation. These groups are just as concerned as Jack Valenti about the preservation of the American Way, but they see the DMCA as an instrument in its destruction. Here, for example, is an excerpt from the American Library Association's press release in response to the final issue of rules regarding the DMCA's anticircumvention provisions in October 2000:

> This ruling is not some narrow legalism. It has real consequences for the American people, because it is a direct threat to public access to information. It appears to give in to the demands of the proprietary community, which seems determined to lock up information—requiring citizens to pay for glancing at any kind of information in the digital age.[9]

Notable in its absence in this debate, to date, is the business community beyond the boundaries of the entertainment and publishing industries. Copyright, as always, reflects competing interests and Congress's perception of the alignment of power and benefits as the legislation is passed. What is currently missing from Congress's view is the understanding that the peculiar, narrow, short-term interests of the entertainment industry do not necessarily reflect the broader concerns of the business community in general, which needs access to and use of information for its long-term health.

Another thing that is missing is the broader business perspective that Bertelsmann was able to bring to the Napster dispute. Someone needs to step up to the task of dealing with the bigger picture of how digital information and distribution changes the operation of the information marketplace. The business community seems to have, for the moment, bought into the view that this is a face-off between the entertainment industry and would-be pirates and is otherwise of little interest.

That view is wrong. The question of how to provide reasonable protection for information while still ensuring broad access will require the same time and investment that the information distribution questions require in the Napster case. In fact, ultimately the Napster questions and the DMCA questions become the same question: In a world of digital distribution, how should we balance the trade-off between protecting information and ensuring that it gets used? The DMCA is almost certainly not the answer.

The next chapter looks at questions of control and access in more detail and offers pragmatic suggestions for finding the right blend for your company. Understanding the protection and use options open to companies that want to derive value from content is a prerequisite to beginning to think about solutions.

## Keeping Up with Developments

Like the Napster suit, the activity surrounding DeCSS, *2600: The Hacker's Quarterly*, and the DMCA is ongoing. The Berkman Center for Internet and Society at the Harvard Law School maintains an open forum that is a good source of news, opinion, and new developments related to DeCSS and the DMCA. Interested readers can access the site at http://eon.law.harvard.edu/openlaw/DVD/.[10]

## Notes

1. The facts in these presentations about Jon Johansen are drawn from Carl S. Kaplan's story titled "Norwegian Teenager Appears at Hacker Trial He Sparked," which appeared in *The New York Times on the Web* on July 21, 2000. It was available in May 2001 at http://www.nytimes.com/library/tech/00/07/cyber/cyberlaw/21law.html.
2. A readable, concise history of Linux is available on the IBM Developers site: Thomas Schenk, "Linux: Its History and Current Distributions." Accessed in September 2000 at http://www.developer.ibm.com/library/articles/schenk1.html.
3. 17 *U.S. Code* §1201(a)(2), "Violations Regarding Circumvention of Technological Measures."
4. See, for example, *Vault Corporation* v. *Quaid Software Limited*, United States Court of Appeals for the Fifth Circuit 847 F.2d 255, 7 U.S.P.Q.2D (BNA) 1281, decided on June 20, 1988.
5. Lawrence Lessig, in his book *Code* (see Chapter 5) presents a careful and valuable analysis of how computer code, such as the authorized viewing devices provided by copyright owners, provides more powerful constraints on user activity than legal code could ever hope to provide. He also focuses on how computer code and legal code can be used together, as in the instance of the DMCA, to perfect the control by outlawing alternative versions of computer code.

6. Actually, the DMCA contains prohibitions on circumvention that affect users even more directly than do the prohibitions on manufacturing and distributing circumvention devices. Section 1201(a)(1) of the DMCA reads, "No person shall circumvent a technological measure that effectively controls access to a work protected under this title," thus addressing the end user in person. The relationship between the language in this section and fair use is murky at best. But the general tendency to constrain the end user and to provide more power to the copyright owner is certainly consistent with the analysis of *Universal* v. *Corley* that I present here.
7. U.S. Department of Justice, "Statement by the Attorney General. Symposium of the Americas: Protecting Intellectual Property in the Digital Age. September 12, 2000." Accessed in September 2000; available as of May 2001 at http://www.usdoj.gov/archive/ag/speeches/2000/91200agintellectualprop.htm.
8. Jack Valenti, President and CEO of the Motion Picture Association of America, testifying before the House Commerce Committee's Subcommittee on Telecommunications, Trade and Consumer Protection on February 16, 2000 (106th Congress, Second Session, "Video on the Internet: iCraveTV.com and Other Recent Developments in Webcasting").
9. American Library Association news release, "New Digital Copyright Rules Seen As a Defeat for Library Users and the American Public," October 26, 2000. Accessed in December 2000 at http://www.ala.org/washoff/copyright1000.html.
10. A resource for more technical and historical information on the DeCSS case, including useful links to sites with technical and legal documents related to DeCSS, its use, and its licensing, was available in May 2001 at http://www.lemuria.org/DeCSS/decss.html.

# Control Put into Practice

CONTROL over the distribution of content is critical for any business that hopes to derive revenues from publication of content. Moving from paper to electronic distribution threatens that control. However, it also can provide a publisher with a degree of control that is unimaginable with paper media.

In the mid-1990s, as publishing on the Internet first emerged, I was in a business where I suddenly had to publish on the Web. It was clear that the change to electronic distribution could break us, and it also looked like it could lead us to new growth. My own experiences in dealing with the problem of controlling access to content can serve as the jumping-off point for a broader look at the issues surrounding control of electronic content.

## Electronic Distribution as Threat and Opportunity

I was running a market analysis service that followed a number of software and early e-commerce markets. My job was to ensure that my division of the company grew and made money. Our business model was the traditional one for industry and market analysts at the time: we counted things, did surveys, made market projections, and published what we discovered in a series of substantial reports or as loose-leaf updates to a three-ring binder. Clients bought the reports by subscribing to our information service. A subscription cost around $20,000 a year.

A big report containing survey results and analysis might be hundreds of pages long. When we printed such reports we often printed only a hundred or so copies. Because we didn't "unbundle" the service, selling the reports apart from the service package, the effective cost to you if you wanted a particular report was $20,000. You had to buy a year of the service to get any part of it. Given that kind of pricing scheme, we were of course concerned about the possibility that people would make copies of the reports and distribute them to associates. There were often just a few reports—usually the ones with market projections and competitive analysis—that provided much of the motivation for buying our service. A little unauthorized copying and distribution could go a long way toward reducing our potential market and revenues.

We were wary about electronic distribution of our reports, despite (or, perhaps, because of) the fact that we were covering markets such as "Internet Publishing," "Content Management," and "Electronic Document Distribution." Our concern was that if we provided clients with digital versions of the documents, we would soon be selling only one copy to an entire company, and perhaps even only one to a company and its close partners. The nice thing about paper documents was that they didn't circulate much—if someone else had your copy of the report then you didn't have it. They were also difficult and time consuming to copy, particularly if we bound them with a glued spine. Besides, since we printed "Do Not Photocopy" on each page and included a strong prohibition against photocopying in the contract agreement for the service, we found that most of our customers respected those rules. Our concern was that if we provided the document in electronic form, all of this would change. It would be just too easy to send an electronic copy to a business partner or to stick the report on a server someplace and give everyone access to it.

Around 1996, however, our clients began to demand electronic copies of our research. They were demanding them for precisely the reasons that we feared: they wanted to be able to share the information more broadly among different departments and information users within their companies. Since we were a relatively small research firm competing against some much bigger players, we decided to try to turn electronic distribution into a competitive advantage. If we could use electronic distribution to enable a client to get more use out of our service, perhaps we could find new ways to sell against our bigger rivals who were still distributing reports on paper. In short, we saw that in the long run we really didn't have a choice with regard to electronic distribution, and so we decided to see whether, by accepting fate quickly and gracefully, we could gain some advantage.

## Four Strategies

We used a combination of four different approaches to protect our research as we began distributing it electronically. The four approaches consisted of:

1. Technical protection services (TPSs)
2. Contracts and licensing agreements
3. Changes to our publishing and distribution model
4. Changes to our business model

In varying degrees these same four approaches are useful for almost any company trying to come to terms with digital content distribution and protection. Note that "aggressive pursuit of copyright violators" is not on this list. We needed to be willing to do that after some point, of course, if we wanted to put any bite behind our bark. But, as a practical matter, pursuing copyright violators in the courts was too expensive for us to use as anything other than a last resort. Our approaches were more pragmatic.

## Technical Protection Services

We used relatively simple forms of technical protection. We assigned a separate password and login to each client, which allowed us to monitor downloads and access. We were interested in behaviors that were unusual in either direction. If we saw that a client was not accessing the site to use the materials, this was a cause for concern, since lack of use could mean that we were somehow not meeting the client's needs. The key to running a successful market research service is to keep renewal rates high, and clients who don't use the service don't renew. So, minimal use of the site meant that it was time to give the client a call. On the other hand, if we saw an unusually large amount of use, it was also time to make a call. Perhaps the client was having trouble using the system, perhaps the staff was working on a project where some consulting help was in order, and perhaps it meant that we needed to look at renegotiating the license agreement.

There are many other TPSs that we could have used to provide us with additional and different kinds of protection. We could have encrypted each document and required a password in order to open it. When using Adobe's PDF format or other file formats that can be made secure, we could have restricted use of the document to prevent changing it or to prevent selection of text. Because we were not publishing a large number of copies, it would have been simple to personalize each document with the client's name to discourage unauthorized circulation. We could have disabled printing of the documents, an important (but, from the user's point of view, irritating) precaution that protects against printing the document to a file in order to defeat document protection schemes.

There are now even more TPSs than were readily available in the mid-1990s. For example, it is now a simple matter to encrypt publications and to then tie the decryption to specific information about a customer's computing environment such as the computer's internal system identification or serial numbers on storage devices (even cheap, removable storage devices such as Clic disks have serial numbers).[1] This restricts use of a publication to some particular set of computers or media, greatly reducing the risk of unauthorized sharing or copying of information.

In general, the basic approach behind all TPS-based content protection schemes is to lock the document up, usually through encryption, and to then restrict access through passwords, decryption keys, and special readers. The use of special readers is essential if you want to impose special constraints (for example, no printing). Special readers provide a powerful way to extend control over documents. A publisher could, for example, check on date information and require the payment of a renewal fee after some period of time if the user wants to enjoy continued access to the content. Such an approach would have provided my company with substantial leverage when it was time to negotiate service renewals with clients but certainly would have also produced vocal objections from clients. We could have used the combination of encrypted content and specialized readers in order to gather information about what our clients were doing with the data, using the readers not only as a way to control access but also as a way to track client activity.

## Contracts and Licensing Agreements

Copyright, as its name implies, deals with the making and sale of physical copies of a work. A book is manufactured and sold. Atoms change hands. A license, on the other hand, does not necessarily involve a transfer of ownership and atoms. A license is a limited transfer of *rights* to use information under particular terms and conditions.

Contracts and licenses provide important mechanisms for extending, modifying, or limiting the rights of copyright holders and users that are granted under copyright law. In our efforts to find innovative ways to distribute our market research in electronic form, my company certainly made use of contracts and licenses. Viewed from the standpoint of our business objectives, perhaps the most important reason to negotiate contracts and license agreements with our clients was to enable us to offer a service rather than just content. We coupled the delivery of the content with telephone and face-to-face consultation that assisted clients in understanding and using the content. Just as important, we delivered content over a period of time. It was the combination of service and serial publishing that enabled us to structure an offer that supported a continuing business based on annual contract and license renewals, rather that just on one-time sales of content. As we focused more on electronic delivery, the license agreements also provided rights and value to clients that would not be available under a simple sale and copyright arrangement. For example, site licenses gave a client the right to provide employees with simultaneous access to multiple electronic copies of a report within a department or project team, sometimes even within an entire enterprise.

It is important to note that the contracts and license agreements we negotiated with our clients were agreements between sophisticated parties. We each not only read the terms of the agreement but also often modified the agreements to meet needs, preferences, or policies that were unique to a particular deal. We were, after all, doing deals that were worth tens of thousands of dollars apiece. All of this changes when a publishing operation focuses on selling to a broader market where the business consists of many smaller transactions. Rather than an individually negotiated agreement you may, instead, have a standard license. In place of sophisticated buyers you may have someone who does not bother to read the agreement. Rather than written signatures and a handshake, assent to the agreement might involve nothing more than the click of a mouse. The use of license agreements in place of traditional copyright law for mass distribution of content has enormous implications for the balance of rights and control between publishers and users.

### Licenses as a Way to Constrain a User's Rights

If you write a book and then copyright, publish, and sell it, your copyright protection preserves certain rights for you after the sale. The buyer cannot make copies, for example, and he or she cannot create "derivative works," such as a translation or condensed version of your original. But your sale of a copy of your book also exhausts certain rights that you had in that particular copy of the book before its sale. For instance, the buyer can choose to give the legally purchased copy of the book away as a gift or can rent it, resell it, or in other ways treat the book as something that he or she owns. This limitation of the copyright holder's rights over the distribution of a copy of a work after its sale, known as the *first-sale rule*, is an important mechanism for insuring that there is broad access to copyrighted work.

First sale is not the only limitation on copyright holder rights. There are also the important limitations imposed by fair-use requirements, which keep a copyright holder from interfering with excerpts and other uses of the work for purposes of criticism, commentary, news reporting, teaching (including making multiple copies for classroom use), scholarship, and research.

Taken all together, these limits on the copyright holder's control of a work create important avenues for learning about and benefiting from the content of a book without actually having to purchase it. They are avenues that most of us use. They include reading book reviews, borrowing copies from friends, checking books out from libraries, reading magazine stories about a new book, and learning about the content in educational settings. When an important new business book or policy book hits the market it usually sells a great many copies, but much of the general impact of the book comes from the excerpts and commentary that are delivered through all of these secondary sources. This additional use and extraction of value that is not directly related to a purchase happens by design: it is part of the trade-off in copyright law between advantage to the publisher through limited monopoly rights and advantage to society in return for granting those rights.

The powerful thing about licensing content, as opposed to selling a copy of it, is that it provides a publisher with a way to shift this balance of benefits in the publisher's favor. Licensing provides publishers with a mechanism for controlling reuse that can take away most of the user's customary rights to fair use and to ownership of a copy of the work. For example, a license can be written to prohibit use of multiple copies in a classroom without the payment of an additional fee. A license can also replace first-sale rights—since no copy is being "sold"—imposing tight restrictions on the sharing of a work, prohibiting resale of the license, and prohibiting use of the work by anyone other than the licensee. Sometimes publishers even include license terms that prohibit the licensee from writing about the licensed product, describing the product to others, and criticizing it.

Licenses can combine with electronic access to provide publishers with a particularly powerful model for control when the use of content is through online access rather than through electronic delivery. Providing users with access to a large data repository that is simply used as needed can offer advantages to users in terms of currency of the information and ease of access, but it also gives publishers the ability to simply turn off access if a license is not renewed.

### Digital Distribution and New Laws Make Use of Licensing Easier

The problem with licenses is that they require an agreement between the information provider and the information user, rather than just the simple sale of a published product. In the past, securing such an agreement increased the cost of the sale. This was not a problem for us, since we were making $20,000 deals, but it was much more of an issue for someone selling a $15 report or a $2.50 copy of a newspaper article.

The barriers to broad use of licensing in place of the sale of copies are falling, however. The key to this shift is the increased use of "click-wrap" agreements, which allow a user to indicate agreement to the terms of a license through some simple electronic mechanism such as, for example, clicking on an "I Agree" button displayed on a computer screen. Recent court decisions have ruled in favor of enforcement of such agreements.[2] Perhaps even more important, the Uniform Computer Information Transactions Act (UCITA), a model state law for dealing with online transactions that was developed by the National Conference of Commissioners on Uniform State Laws (NCCUSL), contains specific language that makes shrink-wrap and click-wrap agreements enforceable as contracts. UCITA has been adopted in Maryland and Virginia and is under consideration in a number of other states. If adopted generally, UCITA will potentially enable publishers to selectively prohibit many of the familiar ways of sharing and using information that we have come to take for granted under copyright law.[3]

## Changing the Publishing and Distribution Model

The use of TPSs and licensing agreements were important tools in my company's attempt to survive and, if possible, profit from the transition to electronic publishing of our content. But, as tools, they were only a means to an end. Our principal focus was on rethinking our model for publishing and distributing our market research. In a superficial sense this was inevitable: we were moving from paper to electronic delivery. But the changes quickly cut below the surface and began to touch on matters such as how frequently we published and what we published.

One of our most important insights was that the reduction in our ability to protect individual publications (we did not use strong TPS technologies) could be offset by publishing more frequently and by changing the content of the publications to focus more on opinions and analysis and less exclusively on static data. In a sense, we made each individual publication less valuable but made the entire corpus of publications more valuable. Our goal was to deliver value in a way that caused our clients to want to "tune in" each week, week after week, rather than just waiting for an occasional big report.

In practice this meant that, when we completed a significant piece of research, rather than making clients wait for months as we prepared an extensive report containing all the data and analysis, we delivered the analysis week by week, as we did it. The publications took the form of a weekly e-mail message that typically dealt with some particular finding or issue that was especially interesting. Judging from the favorable client response, this format turned out to be much more useful for our clients: it delivered the results and analysis more quickly and, just as important, it delivered the analysis in bite-sized chunks that made it easy to absorb the findings and think about business implications. We did always, eventually, deliver a report that summarized the findings in one place, but these summary reports seemed almost anticlimactic after the clients had received weeks and weeks of data and analysis via e-mail.

## From Specific to General

There are a couple of aspects of this story about how we addressed our particular problems that make it more generally interesting. Like many firms, we were confronted with a need to take our paper reports and distribute them electronically. Our experience was also typical in that we found that the simplest thing to do was to publish the reports in Adobe Acrobat PDF format and place them on our Web site. We recognized that simply placing PDF files in password-protected areas did not provide us with much protection against illegal copying. But, rather than cranking up the level of encryption and using more sophisticated TPSs to place more secure locks on our data, we changed our publishing and distribution model to make locks unnecessary. We decided that our best security lay in the direction of making ourselves even more valuable to our clients, and valuable in a way that would make them want to build a continuing relationship with us, rather than just filching an occasional report.

This change in focus transformed our starting question from "How can we protect our content on the Web?" to "How can we use electronic delivery to do a better job of meeting client needs that we could not easily meet with paper?" It is interesting that the answer to this second question led us in the somewhat surprising and initially uncomfortable direction of not encrypting or otherwise securing our weekly reports at all. Keeping the customers happy meant minimizing use of new technologies that they had to learn to use. But by changing the distribution model to one that focused on regular, serial installments of information, we effectively reduced the value inherent in copying any one issue of our publication and increased the value in paying for a continuing relationship.

The details of such an approach will vary from business to business, of course, but the general principle is clear: electronic delivery opens an opportunity to rethink your publishing and distribution model from one of periodic purchases to one of an ongoing relationship. One approach to the risks inherent in electronic distribution is to stick to your old publishing and distribution model and to make aggressive use of TPSs and litigation to try to protect your content. This is what the movie industry is attempting to do with regard to DVD distribution. An alternative approach is to see whether electronic distribution offers interesting new ways to build an ongoing relationship with customers. It may be that the new approach still requires technical protection and litigation, but it may also be that switching to a new publishing model can permit you to set some of the protection and litigation aside. This is the insight that was behind Bertelsmann's offer of a substantial loan to Napster in exchange for warrants. Bertelsmann recognized that Napster is, in fact, experimenting with new publishing and distribution models. Even more exciting, Napster might be able to move from a model depending on sales of individual discs to a subscription model. Bertelsmann recognized that, over the long run, reconsidering the publishing and distribution model would be an easier and more successful strategy than would be building a fort.

## Changing the Business Model

When a company that makes money from content begins looking at the publishing and distribution model, consideration of the broader business model can't be far behind. In the case of the market research business that I directed, our changes to our distribution model eventually led to a restructuring of our pricing scheme and an ability to address a broader market. Over time, the weekly publication became so valuable in the eyes of our clients that we were able to offer it as the core of the service, actually unbundling the individual summary reports. Our primary customer base wanted both the weekly analysis and the summary reports and so continued to subscribe to a full-service offer that included everything we published. But we were also able to address a larger market of more peripheral clients who would never have paid for the full-service offer but who would gladly pay a few thousand dollars for an individual report. The shift in publishing medium led to a shift in our publishing model, which in turn changed our business model and, ultimately, our notion of what we did.

Once again, a comparison with Bertelsmann and Napster suggests that the business principles that worked for my small customer base and high-value content might be useful, as well, at the other end of the spectrum. If Bertelsmann, working through Napster, can move from sales of individual CDs to a subscription model, that will open up new business opportunities as it did for my company. Could Bertelsmann/Napster become the complete music source for customers? If so, what add-on sales opportunities, surrounding, say, concert ticket sales, might become part of the business? Questions like these arise only when a company begins to look beyond mere technical protection to the broader issues of publishing, distribution, and business models. The real potential of doing business on the Web emerges only when your questions about how to protect and profit from your copyrighted content begin to elicit answers that are broader than "lock it up."

## Convergence: Complete Control

The Napster case and other high-profile news reports about the difficulties that publishers have experienced in protecting their copyrighted materials have contributed to a general sense that the Internet has put publishers and their property at risk. The perception is that the combination of the Internet and its associated technologies has shifted the balance of benefits between publisher and user dramatically in favor of the user. We are back to Jack Valenti's image of the publisher as unaccompanied woman walking dark streets prowled by the Boston Strangler.

It is critically and even urgently important for businesspeople, who are always users of information and only sometimes publishers, to realize that it is equally likely that the balance is shifting the other way. The combination of TPSs, licensing, and new copyright laws provides the publisher with nearly complete control of content, to the great disadvantage of people who need to use such content. In order to help you see that this assertion is more a certainty than a supposition, let's assemble the pieces of the puzzle presented over this chapter and the last one into a single picture.

### Technical Restriction

The critical fact that makes TPS protection of content possible is that electronic information needs a computer program to be usable. Unaided, I can read a paper document. With a magnifier I can even read film. But there is nothing at all that I can do with a CD-ROM or a magnetic disk unless I have a computer or some other kind of electronic reader. If you can control the device that makes bits intelligible, you have complete control over access to the information.

A TPS is really nothing more than a set of constraints placed on the reading device. (I will use the term *reader* to refer to the broad class of hardware and software devices that turn bits into usable information, whether the information is intended to be read, viewed, heard, felt, or smelled.) If a document is made up of bits representing ASCII characters and organized as HTML, there are a great many available readers that a user could deploy to extract value from those bits. If you encrypt the information in the bits, the value is available only to users with an appropriate reader *and* the right encryption key. This gives you a way to control *who* accesses the information. You can extend control even more completely if you represent the information in a nonstandard way so that it requires a proprietary reader to be rendered intelligibly. By owning the design of the reader as well as the information content, you can impose control not only on *who* accesses the information, but also on *how* they access it and what they can do with it.

Control over both "who" and "how" is at the heart of the motion picture industry's lawsuit over the production of a Linux DVD viewer. If the motion picture industry can constrain the market so that consumers can use only approved, licensed viewers, the industry can control use so that it does not include making excerpts or making copies for use on other devices that a licensed user might happen to own. Never, in the era of paper distribution, could the publisher control the "who" and "how" of access; electronic distribution coupled with TPSs and special readers opens the door to taking such control.

### Licensing: The Second Side of the Triangle

Licensing is a key element in the use of technical protection to extend control and constrain user rights. Without licensing the publisher is stuck with the balancing of user and publisher interests expressed in copyright law, including fair use, multiple copies for classroom use, and so on. The use of licenses makes it possible for the publisher to get the user's agreement to give up such rights. The new UCITA model legislation, described above in the discussion of licensing, makes the resignation of rights as easy as a mouse click and asserts that the resulting agreement should be recognized as a binding contract by the courts.

### Closing the Triangle: The DMCA

Given the conjunction of technical protection and proprietary readers on the one hand and on the other the realignment of rights through licensing, now made cost effective and legally binding in UCITA, we have most of the components in place to radically shift the old division of rights and values between publishers and users.

The only remaining risk, from the publisher's point of view, would be that such a strong shift in value from user to publisher would create a market demand among users for new products that would restore the old balance or perhaps even tilt it in the reader's favor. This is precisely why publishers advocated and received strong legal measures within the DMCA.

The DMCA closes the third side of the triangle that began taking shape with TPSs and licensing. Now publishers can use special reading devices to rearrange the distribution of rights between themselves and the users, they can economically make this rearrangement legal and binding through the use of licensing, and they can eliminate the user community's ability to restore the old balance through market demand for alternative readers. Far from diminishing a publisher's control over content, the movement from paper to electronic distribution now opens the possibility of perfecting control in ways that were not even conceivable ten years ago.

## A Complex Message for a Complex Problem

There are several messages here.

1. **More than just TPSs**: If you are a publisher or you manage a company that, in some other way, depends on extracting value from the delivery of content, you should look beyond simply using technical protection and litigation to preserve the value of your product and assets. The use of licensing agreements in place of the sale of copies, reconsideration of your publishing and distribution model, and examination of new business models, taken all together, will provide you with much better protection and opportunities for growth.
2. **New technologies and laws favor the publisher**: The fact that there can be no unmediated use of digital information confers enormous power on the group that can control the design and operation of information readers. The combination of technical protection, mass market licensing, and the use of the law to destroy the market's ability to restore balance places control over access in the hands of the publisher.
3. **Momentum builds**: Most publishers have not yet learned to use such control, and consequently they persist in fears of the Internet marketplace and continue to ask for new laws and support from Congress and elsewhere.
4. **We may have overshot the mark**: Such powerful disruption of the balance between publisher and user should be, at the very least, a cause for caution and concern.

We all consume and process more information than we produce. The book that you are holding in your hands is an example of that fact. It is a unique and, I hope, useful integration and analysis of a great deal of information that I have assembled from other sources. I certainly hope to preserve the rights that my publisher and I share in this work so that we can profit from it directly. But the work would not be here in the first place if I had not had broad access to enormous amounts of other information at reasonable cost. It would not be available if I had been constrained in citing, critiquing, and in other ways building upon the work of others.

The same is true for most of the work that we do. The framers of the Constitution did not put it this way, but they were concerned with the same basic truth: increasing the velocity of information exchange and reuse benefits business and society as a whole. We need to make sure that, in our zeal to protect information, we do not diminish its broader utility.

## Notes

1. See, for example, Adobe's PDF Merchant technology. Adobe describes this product in white papers that were available in May 2001 on the Adobe Web site, http://www.adobe.com.
2. For an excellent discussion of these court precedents and of the licensing agreement in general, see Pamela Samuelson's "Does Information Really Have to Be Licensed?," reprinted in *Intellectual Property in the Age of Universal Access* (Association for Computing Machinery [ACM], 2000; order number 300991). For a more technical but still very useful discussion of these issues, see Samuelson's "Intellectual Property and Contract Law for the Information Age: Foreword to a Symposium," *California Law Review*, 87(1), January 1999, which was accessible in May 2001 at http://www.sims.berkeley.edu/~pam/papers/CLR-2B.pdf.
3. UCITA is a surprisingly radical attempt to create a body of new legislation to deal with electronic transactions. It changes many of the traditional models for doing business. For example, it provides online vendors with broad capabilities to modify the terms of an agreement after the customer has agreed to pay. UCITA enjoys the strong backing of the Software Publisher's Association and software publishers such as Microsoft but is opposed by many other computer and information industry groups such as the ACM, the IEEE, the Newspaper Association of America, the Motion Picture Association of America, and 26 state attorneys general. Jean

Braucher has summarized the principal objections to UCITA in an article titled "Proposed Uniform Computer Information Transactions Act (UCITA): Objections from the Consumer Perspective." The article was accessed in October 2000 from the Computer Professionals for Social Responsibility Web site at http://www.cpsr.org/program/UCITA/braucher.html.

CHAPTER 4

# Copyright Policy and Progress

COPYRIGHT has the difficult task of reconciling two objectives that are not always well aligned. On the one hand it must ensure that the people who create, publish, and distribute information have the chance to profit from their activity. On the other hand, copyright, as a privilege granted by the government, must serve the broader interests of our society. When the balance is just right, copyright encourages the creation of more published work while at the same time ensuring that the society as a whole gets access to this productive output. The history of copyright is a history of adjustments to maintain and restore this balance in the face of changes in technology and in the nature of the nation's needs (for example, the decision to begin protecting the works of foreign authors at the end of the nineteenth century when the United States began to see benefit in demanding reciprocal copyright agreements).

The digitization of information challenges the structure of copyright in fundamental ways, upsetting the balance once again. Making sense of this challenge in terms of either policy or business practice requires at least a brief consideration of these fundamental shifts.

## The Perspective from Mars

Imagine that we convened a panel of visionaries whose thinking is not tainted by familiarity with the past few hundred years of copyright law and practice—perhaps a panel of reasonable, fair-minded Martians. Suppose we asked them to make recommendations about how (quoting from the U.S. Constitution) "to promote the progress of science and useful arts, by securing for limited times to authors and inventors the exclusive right to their respective writings and discoveries" in a world where all work is in digital form.

One of the important things about digital information, unlike information on paper, microfilm, or some other physical format, is that it is cheap and easy to make a perfect copy. For example, if you want a copy of an article published on the Web, a couple clicks of the mouse will get you one. Your copy is indistinguishable from the original. You can make millions of them if you want. Times have changed: making a copy used to require making a photocopy, with its obvious degradation and difficulty, particularly for longer works. The changes are even greater if you look back, say, about fifty years, when the only efficient way to make copies was to print more of them.

However, as the cost of making perfect copies has gone down, so has the *value* of doing so. Broadly distributed and easily accessible digital networks tend to make "making a copy" unnecessary. Suppose that you know that a particular article on the Web is always available there and that the publisher is committed to maintaining that availability. In that case, the value of making a copy at all goes down. Simply saving the URL is just as good as saving a copy. If you want to share a copy with colleagues, you can just point them toward the URL rather than bothering with making and transmitting new copies. As bandwidth increases and as mobile connectivity becomes less expensive, this shift from sharing copies to sharing *references* to copies will accelerate.

So, making digital copies involves only microscopic costs and, if the original is known to be available on the Web, provides little in the way of benefit. Given these facts, it seems extremely unlikely that our panel of Martian experts would consider counting and controlling of copies as a credible solution, much less the best approach, to our goal of promoting the progress of science and useful arts by providing authors with limited exclusive rights.

However, as its name suggests, copyright law is centered around the notion of a physical copy of a work. Copyright attempts to control distribution of copies. It is an awkward approach to controlling digital information.

## Licensing

The structure and impact of the DMCA, illuminated by the DeCSS case, are evidence that Congress is making heroic efforts to shore up the concept of protecting copies. The response to the realization that digital copies are easily and perfectly shared is to reverse those facts, making them difficult and illegal to share. Not surprisingly, these extreme exertions to focus on *copies* and *copying* in the face of the unfavorable economics of digital copies are having side effects. Most notably, the new law is changing fundamental notions of ownership and use of intellectual property.

But the reason for putting Martians on the panel is that they might have a broader perspective, up above the clouds, unencumbered by attachment to copyright and other, older ways of doing things. What might they recommend?

They might start with the facts as they find them:

- For digital information, trying to count and control copies of information in the same way that you would track inventory and distribution of widgets is madness.
- Digital information requires reading and viewing devices. It is not enough to have a copy of the work; you also need a reading device to use it.

This last point contains the seeds of a new solution to the problem, since it means that there is an additional control point beyond the release of copies of content into a distribution channel. With information on paper, once you publish and distribute something, it is gone—beyond the publisher's control except through copyright and infringement lawsuits. But for digital information, there is the potential for control *at the point of use*.

The DMCA takes this control beyond the reach of market forces, ceding complete control over the reading device to the copyright owner if that owner wishes to have it. Doing away with market controls is a bad idea, but the focus on the reading device is right. Even without the DMCA and its one-sided approach, the potential to focus on *use* rather than on *copies* opens attractive possibilities for providing an alternative to the copyright controls that have been used for physical publications.

All of this suggests a shift in focus from copyright and copy control—the traditional way of providing limited monopolies to authors and publishers—to *licensing* of rights to use information. Software, of course, already uses licensing, as opposed to sale of copies, as the preferred compensation scheme. Applied to digitally delivered music, such control over use, rather than possession, might take the form of a monthly fee to access digital recordings, perhaps scaled to volume of use. Applied to research and reference work, the approach might take the form of licensing fees to extract, quote, or otherwise reuse information—a new start-up called Ebrary is hoping to build on just such a model.

There are also, at the moment, problems and dangers associated with the use of licensing as the control mechanism for content use. Because Congress is still stuck on the idea of controlling copies and copying, it has not taken any steps toward a common framework that might constrain the reach of licensing agreements for published works. Thinking in terms of how to establish equitable, productive licensing agreements—in place of copyright controls—has simply not been on Congress's agenda. Consequently, licensing agreements can contain terms, such as restrictions on criticism or public comment on a work, that are inconsistent with the broader objective of promoting "progress of science and useful arts."

There is important work to do here, but Congress must first take a broader view of the problem than it has to date. It needs that panel of Martians.

## Implications for Business

Apart from potential actions by Congress, there are implications for business within the changes brought into view by the Napster and DeCSS disputes and by the broader consideration of how to extract and share the value in digital content. If one gets up above the legal particulars in the Napster and DeCSS cases, it is clear that they offer a glimpse of large shifts in how businesses derive value from digitally distributed intellectual property. The changes grow from the transition from a focus on content to a focus on the *process of using the content.*

### Value Moves Downstream

Perhaps the strongest message emerging from the Napster and DeCSS cases is that the locus of value is moving downstream. If Napster, with Bertelsmann's help, is successful in inventing new ways to derive value from recorded music, it will almost certainly take the form of providing a service. If Napster fails, then it will be because someone else has done a better or faster job of figuring out how to build a business model around music as the center of a service offer. The new music business will not consist simply of recording music, promoting it, and then selling copies of discs. Instead it will shift to emphasize continuing relationships with subscribers, continuing to add value and receive payment after the song is delivered.

The strength of this shift in value from content to process is even more evident when one looks at business applications that are less closely tied to traditional publishing. For example, consider contract research organizations (CROs) working within the pharmaceutical industry. CROs began by focusing on running the clinical studies that are central to new drug research and development. The obvious "product" from CROs is the clinical data. In other words, their product is *content* comprised of patient demographic data, administrative information, test results, comments by researchers and reviewers, and so on.

Over the past few years the leading CROs have moved more deeply into digital data delivery. As in music, the adaptation to digital data and delivery changed the business, shifting the center of balance to include downstream value such as worldwide, electronic access to research results and data analysis. Some CROs have followed the downstream movement to the point where they now offer the major drug companies access to specialized professional services, such as providing expertise in oncological and cardiovascular concerns. Digital content has allowed CROs to transform their business. They have expanded their services beyond the initial content- and copy-based focus on collecting and publishing results. Consistent with the direction suggested by the DeCSS case, the key to unlocking much of this added value involves use of specialized, secure delivery environments and a shift from focus on content to focus on the processes associated with using the content.

### Business Focuses on Licenses, Not Sale of Copies

A second big message about the new rules for getting value from content grows from this focus on process and downstream use: digital content is more consistent with revenue models built around licensing and the sale of services than with models depending on sale of product, particularly when the product is a copy of some published work. Once again, Napster provides a clear example of this. Rather than selling CDs for $16.98, the focus shifts to selling a license to download and play music. Similarly, rather than selling a copy of a book, the digital content service Ebrary charges a license fee to quote and otherwise reuse work.

### Value Increases through Aggregation

The third shift is toward creating value through *aggregation* of content. If I write a great book, you might buy a copy. In that case I am selling a single copy of my *product*. But if I want to move from product to service and from sales to licensing, it is important that I understand that you won't subscribe to a service unless it can aggregate many useful kinds of information over time. I need to be able to deliver a whole library of books or a steady stream of research and articles.

The connection between digital content, aggregation, and service extends far beyond the conventional boundaries of publishing. Consider, for example, the usage, temperature, vibration, and other performance data that are automatically collected by devices such as industrial engines, tractors, airplanes, centrifuges, and so on. This is a very different kind of content than music, books, and even clinical studies. But it, too, is rapidly turning into digital information, rather than readings taken from a dial and recorded on a clipboard. Taken individually, each automated digital monitoring device can create a "report" containing usage data and impending failure conditions. But additional value is available from the aggregation of these individual reports into profiles that can be used to direct maintenance procedures and buying decisions. Note also that the aggregated data opens downstream service opportunities in maintenance, inventory management, and other high-value services that extend well beyond simply providing the content as a product.

## Practice and Policy

It is easy to see Napster as a dispute about kids stealing music, made stranger by pronouncements and lawsuits coming from rappers and rock bands. It is easy to see the DeCSS lawsuit as a story of hackers and the motion picture industry, with color commentary provided by the always quotable Jack Valenti. Such views miss the broader significance of these disputes: they are important early indicators pointing to the looming, enormous impact of the shift from physical content to digital content.

The transition to digital content will touch the operations of every business. It will change the way that companies extract value from content. Looking carefully at these early disputes, seeing them within the context of the businesses in which they occur, is an important first step to understanding the broader changes that are taking place. Summarizing the preceding discussion, the high-level impacts include the following:

- Digital content pushes the opportunities for creating value downstream in the interaction between content creator and content user.
- Licensing and other service offers, not sale of copies, become the preferred new revenue models.
- Value increases with aggregation of content.

But these changes, important as they are, are not currently the focus of the debate concerning copyright policy. As the Napster and DeCSS cases show, the hot spots in the current debate center around the protection of existing distribution channels. This is not surprising: copyright has always been a tool to protect investment in distribution. But digital content opens up new opportunities for distribution. Copyright, used in a clumsy way, can retard our ability to take advantage of these opportunities.

What we have, then, is a political problem and a business problem. We need to find ways to engage parties that are fundamentally in conflict so that each can come out with something of value. Said more simply, we need to encourage some inspired horse trading to get ourselves through this transition.

### Starting on the Wrong Foot

Deal making has, to date, been stymied by the fact that key parties on the side of existing distribution have been generally unwilling to make deals. The entertainment industry has been enjoying a sweet deal of its own over the last twenty years. Confronted with change, this part of the business community has largely answered, "No, thank you. Life is good as it is." Rather than step outside of the walls of existing distribution channels to begin to develop new ways of doing business, the entertainment industry has decided to add a moat to the fortress and has talked Congress into giving it to them.

One result is that we are generally farther from the goal of being able to put together some inspired horse trading to ease us through this transition than we were five years ago.

Another result is that, in its zeal to strengthen copyright, Congress has changed the balance of privileges between information producers and information users in fundamental ways. This is almost certainly a bad mistake. It violates the fundamental mechanism that enables new creative activity. Although I am the one writing this book, *you* are free to use the ideas herein as you want, very possibly creating something from my book that I could not have envisioned. Congress is now putting that freedom at risk.

### Moving Forward

What would inspired deal making look like? As Bertelsmann's deal with Napster suggests, it can involve investment by established distribution interests in ventures working to solve the problems still inherent in digital distribution business models. More generally, inspired deal making will involve creating shared financial interest so that established distribution companies have ways to continue to grow as digital distribution grows up. Here are some other suggestions:

- Copyright should be viewed as a stabilizing mechanism, to protect established interests during a time of transition, rather than as a complete solution in itself. It is available now and companies must use its protections now, but it is not the best tool for moving forward.

- Companies should make increased use of licensing to supplement copyright protections.
- Congress should take steps to ensure that licensing agreements give users broad freedom and discretion regarding use, guaranteeing that licenses do not place unreasonable restrictions on access. In other words, to protect the public interest as we shift from copyright to licenses, we need legislation that guarantees that the principles behind copyright law's fair-use provisions are reflected in licensing agreements.

There is an enormous upside for businesses that can rise above the misdirected focus of the current copyright discussion and that can actually see and work with the larger issues. Changes in distribution technology, whether due to the printing press, canals, railroads, radio, or overnight package delivery, have always created opportunities for businesses able to see beyond the current business models. Grasping the opportunities involves both fundamental changes in business practice and supporting changes in the government's approach to protecting content, stimulating its production, and seeing that it is widely available for use.

The tensions in the current bad fit between copyright and digital distribution can be viewed either as a sign of danger or as an indicator of the size of the opportunity. Companies interested in pursuing the opportunity will want to use copyright as a bridge rather than as a barrier.

# Copyright: Further Reading

Association for Computing Machinery (ACM). 2000. *Intellectual Property in the Age of Universal Access.* Available from the ACM (http://www.acm.org), order #300991.

This is a collection of articles that have previously appeared in ACM publications, most often in *Communications of the ACM*. This is an excellent set of readings that touch on a variety of key issues. It also collects, in one place, key articles by Pamela Samuelson and other experts in the area of intellectual property. This slender but valuable publication is an excellent place to start if you are looking for broader commentary on copyright issues.

Boyle, James. 1996. *Shamans, Software, and Spleens.* Cambridge, MA: Harvard University Press.

*Shamans, Software, and Spleens* is an inquiry into how our society uses, values, and assigns ownership to information. It explores the thesis that the role of the "author"—conceived romantically as someone who creates new information out of thin air rather than as one who processes and refines information—is central to our conception of information rights and ownership. Boyle explores this hypothesis by applying it to four very different legal puzzles regarding information ownership: copyright, blackmail, insider trading, and the ownership of one's own biological information. Looking at the apparently different ways that we regard information in each of these cases, Boyle strives to create a unified view of information. His presentation is particularly useful in exploring the lines between public and private uses of information.

I have enjoyed reading and rereading this book. Boyle is brilliant, irreverent, amazingly well read, and a deep, demanding thinker. The result is a very demanding book. It is not an easy read, but it is a very rewarding one.

Cohen, Julie. 1997. "Some Reflections on Copyright Management Systems and Laws Designed to Protect Them." *Berkeley Technology Law Journal*, 12(1). Available in May 2001 on the Web at http://www.law.berkeley.edu/journals/btlj/articles/12_1/Cohen/html/reader.html.

Julie Cohen has written widely on the potential dangers to fair use and to the "right to read" that are posed by digital copyright management systems and by laws such as the Digital Millennium Copyright Act. She explores the issues that I present here in Chapter 3, "Control Put into Practice," in more detail. It is useful to look at Cohen's work alongside that of Mark Stefik, referenced later in this chapter.

Computer Science and Telecommunications Board, National Research Council. 2000. *The Digital Dilemma.* Washington, DC: National Academy Press.

This is the report resulting from two years of study by a wide variety of academics, business leaders, scientists, librarians, and others who took a broad look at the issues surrounding the collision of digital media and copyright. This is a committee report and, at times, reads like one. On the other hand, the book is an excellent resource for anyone who wants to think more deeply and carefully about the issues. It delves more deeply into legal issues than I do here and also deals more completely with specific technologies and problems. This is not an "answer book," but it is a good book for stimulating more thinking about the issues surrounding copyright. See also Samuelson and Davis's summary of this book, referenced on the following page.

Evans, Philip, and Thomas S. Wurster. 2000. *Blown to Bits.* Boston: Harvard Business School Press.

*Blown to Bits* is not, strictly speaking, about copyright. But it is about the differences between the economics of information and the economics of "things." These differences are at the foundation of the disputes surrounding Napster, DeCSS, and other collisions of digital information and existing physical distribution systems. The disconnection of information from physical copies is at the root of the difficulty with using copyright to protect digital information. Evans and Wurster provide a good, high-level look at the impact of the economics of information on traditional business assumptions about value.

Halbert, Deborah J. 1999. *Intellectual Property in the Information Age: The Politics of Expanding Ownership Rights.* Westport, CT: Quorum.

Halbert provides a political scientist's perspective on the history and current direction of copyright law. This book, based on her doctoral dissertation, is a very readable review of copyright history and of recent legal and political activity. More important, it is an analysis of how our society is constructing a narrative around the roles of author and hacker to make copyright laws acceptable and enforceable. Halbert's perspective gets beyond the details of copyright legislation and litigation to look at the mechanisms that are shaping policy. This book is recommended reading for anyone interested in the way that copyright intersects with politics and power, but readers should be aware that Halbert tends to see recent developments as an effort by property owners to increase their power even if at the expense of the general good.

Lessig, Lawrence. 1999. *Code.* New York: Basic Books.

Lessig is a Constitutional law scholar and well-known legal commentator on issues related to software and the Internet. In *Code* he attempts to pull together his thinking about how computer code—the architecture of the Internet and the Web—is a kind of regulator, just as powerful as governmental regulations, on how the Web will be used. As in the present book, Lessig examines the way that technical architecture, laws, and business issues interact to shape the nature of our society in cyberspace. He looks in particular at intellectual property (including copyright), privacy, freedom of speech, and the issue of the conflicting sovereignty of cyberspace and national governments.

I think it is fair to say that *Code* is a difficult book because of the scope of its concerns and arguments. It is more an inquiry than it is the formulation of an answer. It also tends in the direction of more pessimistic conclusions than I reach here—in part, I believe, because Lessig places less emphasis on the business community's ability to help effect positive change. For all of that, *Code* is a tremendously important book. Lessig's thinking was responsible, in part, for stimulating the inquiry in the present book. If you are interested in what I am saying here, you should look at *Code.*

Samuelson, Pam, and Randall Davis. 2000. "The Digital Dilemma: A Perspective on Intellectual Property in the Information Age." Paper presented at the Telecommunications Policy Research Conference '00, September 23–25, 2000, Alexandria, Virginia. Accessed at http://www.sims.berkeley.edu/~pam/papers.html in October 2000.

This presentation provides a summary of the report titled *The Digital Dilemma* that was produced by the Computer Science and Telecommunications Board of the National

Research Council (see earlier citation). This summary is very readable—a good survey of the principal issues surrounding copyright and digital media. If you are looking for a nice, concise summary of the issues, this is it.

Stefik, Mark. 1997. "Shifting the Possible: How Trusted Systems and Digital Property Rights Challenge Us to Rethink Digital Publishing." *Berkeley Technology Law Journal,* 12(1). Available on the Web at www.law.berkeley.edu/journals/btlj/articles/12_1/Stefik/html/reader.html.

Mark Stefik thinks and writes about "trusted systems"—in this case, systems that are constructed to enforce copyright protections for works that are published digitally. This article provides a good overview of the use of trusted systems in digital publishing. It also reviews many of the issues that I have explored in the preceding chapters, including the question of what is a "copy" and concerns about potential diminution of fair-use rights. Stefik's presentation goes into more technical detail than I do here. He also has a relatively untroubled view of the implications of automated copyright management systems. After reading Stefik, you should look at Julie Cohen's work, referenced earlier, for counterpoint.

Stefik, Mark. 1999. *The Internet Edge.* Cambridge, MA: MIT Press.

In this book Stefik looks broadly at digital publishing, copyright, privacy, digital wallets, and other intersections of digital technology and society. As in his other work, he also provides consideration of the role and use of trusted systems. The book provides a useful complement to the present work, considering many of the same issues and problems but approaching them more from the standpoint of technology and looking ahead at what new technologies might be able to do.

# Part two

# Patents

MANY people would argue that the greatest threat to the "nature" of the Web emerges from the area of patent law.

Like copyright law, patent law grows from the Constitution's mandate to Congress "to promote the progress of science and useful arts, by securing for limited times to authors and inventors the exclusive right to their respective writings and discoveries."

While copyright protects the particular expression of an idea, patents protect the *application* of an idea. The result is that a patent often provides broader protection than copyright, since it protects the patent holder from infringement that might come in many different forms. For example, if you held a patent on the invention of the wheel, the patent could be written to give you exclusive rights to all uses of wheels, regardless of size, color, material of manufacture, and other factors.

The range of applications that can be protected with patents has expanded dramatically over the past thirty years. In particular, during the early 1970s the U.S. Patent Office and the courts tended to treat computer software as something that could not be patented. That attitude had changed by the 1980s, and companies were then able to successfully use patents to claim exclusive rights to particular software applications. By the mid-1990s the courts began recognizing an even broader range of applications as patentable. In particular, the courts began to be more consistent in upholding patent claims on methods of doing business, in addition to the more traditional patent claims on manufacturing methods, materials processing methods, and so on.

The opportunity to use patent protection in broader, more sweeping ways coincided with the early years of new business growth on the Internet. This was a little like the setup for *The Perfect Storm*, where a Nor'easter and a hurricane combined in the Gulf of Maine to create a killer storm. The collision of the Internet business boom and changes in the use of patents was explosive. Suddenly, the Web seemed to be opening all kinds of new ways of doing business. At the same time, more liberal use of patent protection gave companies a way to stake legally binding claims on these new business domains.

Some businesspeople and commentators see patent claims on methods of doing business as a very bad thing that will stifle new business growth on the Web. Others see it as a very good thing that gives new ventures a way to protect themselves from direct competition so that they have time to grow.

It is fair to say that *all* businesses should be aware of the changes in the way we are using patents. Regardless of whether one thinks that the increased use of patents for Web business methods is a good thing or a bad thing, no one denies that it is a big thing.

I begin with the Web-related patent and lawsuit that seems to have attracted the most attention, alarm, and ire: Amazon's claim that it has the exclusive right to allow customers to complete a purchase with a single click of an on-screen button. In addition to being notorious, the Amazon 1-Click patent controversy will introduce you to most of the critical issues surrounding the more general dispute over business method patents.

CHAPTER 6

# Subdividing the Internet Frontier

In the last months of 1999 a number of Internet pioneers discovered that the rules had changed. If the Internet ever had been a wide-open frontier where pioneering developers swapped and improved ideas, sharing freely to build the framework for a new economy, it suddenly looked to some of the pioneers that those days were over. Some of their neighbors were carving the frontier up into private estates and putting up "No Trespassing" signs.

The events that best signified this sudden change arose from a patent application filed by Amazon, the Internet retailer, back in 1997. On September 28, 1999, the U.S. Patent and Trademark Office (PTO) granted Amazon a patent for its 1-Click ordering system. The claims in the patent cover any system that allows a registered customer to complete an Internet order with a single mouse click. With its new patent in hand, Amazon quickly sued its major competitor, Barnes and Noble, to force the company to stop using a one-click ordering system of its own called Express Lane. On December 1, 1999, the Federal District Court in Seattle issued a preliminary injunction ordering Barnes and Noble to remove one-click ordering capability from its site.

Tim O'Reilly, publisher of a successful line of books aimed at programmers and other technical people involved in building Internet systems, responded to this chain of events with an open letter to Jeff Bezos, Amazon's CEO. The following excerpt from O'Reilly's letter summarizes his concerns and his argument.

> The web has grown so rapidly because it has been an open platform for experimentation and innovation. It broke us loose from the single-vendor stranglehold that Microsoft has had on much of the software industry, and created a new paradigm with opportunities

> for countless new players, including Amazon. The technologies that you have used to launch your amazing success would never have become widespread if the early web players, from Tim Berners-Lee on, had acted as you have acted in filing and enforcing this patent. Because, of course, you are not the only one who can play the patent game. And once the web becomes fenced in by competing patents and other attempts to make this glorious open playing field into a proprietary wasteland, the springs of further innovation will dry up. In short, I think you're pissing in the well.[1]

## The Power of Patents

O'Reilly's concerns are grounded in the strong protection of intellectual property that patents provide. Patents protect *applications* of ideas. This is a big step beyond copyright, for example, which only protects the particular *expression* of an idea. Applied to software systems, this means that patents provide significantly broader protection than does copyright. Suppose you hold the copyright to a software application. Further, suppose that I write a new application that performs substantially the same functions as your application, but I do not have access to any of your source code and am careful not to copy your user interface ("look and feel"). The odds would be excellent that I have not infringed on your copyright. But, if you held patent rights rather than just copyright, it is entirely possible that my new program would infringe on your patent, since the patent protects the full application of the idea, not just one single instantiation.

Just as important, patents protect an application against infringement whether or not the other party knows about the patented invention. If I write a story that is very much like a story that you wrote, but I write it independently, without access to your story, I am not violating your copyright. I can still sell my story. But if I build a machine or process that is similar to your machine or process, I am infringing on your patent whether or not I had access to your work. Patents provide strong protection of intellectual property for a period of 20 years. It is no wonder that they are important intellectual assets. It is also no wonder that they are contested.

## Why Have Patents at All?

When Tim O'Reilly talks about playing "the patent game" and about the Web becoming "fenced in by competing patents," it is easy to come away with the impression that patents are a very bad thing. After all, O'Reilly says that in pursuing patents for Amazon, Jeff Bezos is "pissing in the well." That's clearly very bad.

In the face of such assertions about how bad patents are, it is important to ask whether patents serve some useful purpose other than self-interest on the part of the companies that apply for them. Why do we have them in the first place?

Congress's authority to grant patents to inventors comes from Article I, Section 8 of the U.S. Constitution, which provides Congress with the power "to promote the progress of science and useful arts, by securing for limited times to authors and inventors the exclusive right to their respective writings and discoveries." So, as with copyright, the rights granted through a patent are not absolute rights like free speech but are contingent on providing benefit to society as a whole. The inventor gets limited exclusive rights and society gets the benefits of the inventor's know-how.

The pharmaceutical business provides a good illustration of how this is supposed to work. Drug companies make very large investments in research and development of new drugs; patent protection gives them a reasonable hope of making a return on this investment. Society benefits not only from the discovery and sale of the new drugs but also from the fact that the know-how to produce the drugs is placed into the public domain. Once the patent runs out, generic drug manufacturers have the information they need to make the drug available to the general public inexpensively.

## Basic Rules

The desire to make sure that inventors are protected and that the invention is fully described for later use by others is reflected in the laws and regulations controlling patents. Having at least a high-level understanding of the rules concerning patents is important to your ability to follow the discussion of how patents are being applied to the Internet.

Who Can Get a Patent? Patents are reserved for the *inventor(s)* of an invention. The significance of this for most software, information, and financial services companies without strong traditions of using patents is that the company must be sure to get an assignment of the patent from the inventor. This is, of course, easiest *before* the invention is created.

What Kinds of Things Can Be Patented? The legislation controlling patents says that patents may be granted for "any new and useful process, machine, manufacture, or composition of matter, or any new and useful improvement thereof."[2] These four categories, process, machine, manufactured good, and composition of matter, are sometimes referred to as "statutory" or "patentable" subject matter. The categories are historically important in software patents because early challenges to software patents claimed that software did not fit into any of these categories.

What Conditions Must Be Met? The invention must be "new." This means not only that there cannot already be an existing patent but also that the invention cannot be merely an instance of "prior art"—which is to say that you cannot patent something that has already been in use by others. The invention must also be "non-obvious." A patentable invention should not be obvious to someone of ordinary skill who is a practitioner in the subject area affected by the patent. Granting patents on obvious things would harm society and impede progress rather than promote it. The patent must be specified in a way that would enable someone familiar with the subject matter to build the invention covered by the patent. The patent must disclose the *best* means of implementing the invention; inventors cannot share a third-rate implementation with society and keep the best one secret. Further, the scope of the enabling description must be reasonably related to the scope of what is claimed as property under the patent. For example, if I were to discover one cure for the common cold, I could not use my single discovery to claim *all* cures, including ones that I had not yet discovered and could not describe.

## Amazon's 1-Click Patent

Given this high-level view of the reasons for patents and of the rules that are supposed to govern their issue, we can return to Amazon's patent 5,960,411 (the '411 patent), which claims exclusive rights to one-click ordering over a communications system such as the Internet. Why did this patent cause such an uproar? What does the uproar mean for you and your business?

The Amazon patent is pretty easy to understand, despite the fact that it contains 26 claims that cover details such as the potential for using a remote control from a TV to place an order. The primary claim is on a method for placing an order on a system that can display the item and then, with only a single action by the buyer, send the order, along with a user identifier, to a server. On the server side, previously stored information about the buyer is used to generate a purchase order and to fulfill the order, all without the use of a shopping cart or other required actions by the buyer.

In practice, as implemented over the World Wide Web, displaying the item involves publishing it on a Web page viewed with a Web browser. The "single action" by the buyer is a click on a button or link that sends a page request, along with a "cookie," to the Web server. Once the order has been sent to the server it is a simple matter to use the identifying information in the cookie to look up the buyer's billing information in a database and send the order.

The problem with this invention, from the standpoint of its critics, is that it is doing some pretty obvious stuff that uses capabilities already built into other tools. Web browsers are already set up, apart from Amazon's invention, to send cookies automatically with any page request to a server that sets a cookie. This is a routine use of cookies. To many, this doesn't look like much of an invention.

When the Amazon system gets the cookie along with the order request, it then uses the ID from the cookie as a lookup key for a database. Nothing novel there—what else would you do? And then Amazon ships the order. Yep, that's what you'd want to do, right? Any competent programmer told to implement a system for completing an order from a single click on a Web browser page would do it that way. In fact, given the simple nature of the basic protocols that connect Web browsers and servers, it is not clear that a programmer would have any other choices: this is *the* way to implement a one-click ordering system.

What is new, then, if anything, is the very idea that Amazon is shipping the order on the basis of the single click, without any shopping cart, validation, or "Are you sure?" steps to add extra clicks. Once you decide to ship on a single click, the rest of the steps are obvious and necessary.

From the standpoint of its critics, Amazon just placed a 20-year property claim on the ability to complete an order with one button press, while adding nothing at all to the public's know-how. The problem, critics would assert, is that the method is perfectly obvious. Society appears to be giving away a valuable exclusive claim and getting nothing in return.

## What's So Obvious?

Remember that in order to be eligible for a patent an invention must involve patentable subject matter, must be new, must not be an obvious extension or application of prior art, and must meet requirements for definiteness and completeness of disclosure. We will look at some early software patent disputes a little later and will see that, just a few years ago, it was not clear that software and business methods were patentable at all. But such questions are now pretty much settled. So now the argument moves to finer-grained questions that are specific to each invention. Is this really something new? Is it obvious?

The question of what is obvious is, obviously, a particularly difficult one. Once something has been invented it can often seem obvious in hindsight. This is the "Why, of course! Why didn't I think of that?" phenomenon. Patent office procedures are set up to protect inventors from this kind of after-the-fact obviousness.

James Glieck, writing about the Amazon 1-Click patent for the *New York Times*, tells how Demetra Smith, a patent examiner working on the Amazon patent, struggled with the problem of obviousness in reviewing the 1-Click application. As is typically the case with software and Internet patents, the Amazon 1-Click application did not include extensive references to earlier patents or to articles in professional and academic journals. Ms. Smith had to work from what she could learn from other patent applications and from articles gathered from the trade press. She could see that cookies were a well-established mechanism for identifying visitors. On the other hand, no one seemed to be using them to completely bypass shopping carts. Still, the 1-Click idea seemed to be something less than a new departure; Lucent Technologies, for example, had already filed for a patent covering the use of customer identifiers in order to provide personalized services. Personalized ordering seemed to fit into that general mold. So, in her initial ruling Ms. Smith wrote, "It would have been obvious to one having ordinary skill in the art at the time the invention was made to include various command mechanisms for a single user action in order to execute the user's request."[3] In using the language, "obvious to one having ordinary skill in the art at the time the invention was made," Ms. Smith is referencing the PTO standard for non-obviousness. So, at first, Amazon's 1-Click invention looked too obvious to deserve a patent.

But patent examiners cannot reject applications just because the invention looks pretty obvious to the examiner. The examiner must be able to show, using references to earlier patents and to the literature, that an invention fails to pass the non-obviousness test. Without a rich literature of prior art to reference, making the case about obviousness was tough in the case of the Amazon patent, as it is for many Internet patents. Amazon's lawyers were able to argue and negotiate with the patent office until Amazon was able to produce an amended application that was acceptable to the examiners.

It's important to understand that the real test of a patent's validity can come only in the courts. The patent examiner's job is to screen out inventions that are not patentable because of clear prior art or other problems. But because patent examination is necessarily done in secret, the examination process does not provide any opportunity for other parties who might be adversely impacted by the patent or who might have better information about prior art to speak against the patent. So it is only in court that the industry as a whole gets a chance to bring evidence of prior art not available to the examiner and to challenge decisions about what "one having ordinary skill in the art at the time the invention was made" might find as obvious. It turns out that when a patent is challenged in the courts, the odds are no better than even that it will withstand the challenge. Of this relatively large proportion of challenged patents that are shot down, one study looking at patent decisions between 1989 and 1996 found that 42 percent of the time the fatal bullet was a finding that the patent was obvious. Obviousness was, by far, the most common reason for deciding that a patent was invalid.[4]

The Amazon '411 patent, like most of the patents that concern people worried about the future of Internet business, has not yet been subjected to a full court test. It was first used, successfully, to get Amazon's rival, Barnes and Noble, to stop offering one-click shopping. This action, in the form of a preliminary injunction against Barnes and Noble, took place at the district court level in December 1999. Then, more than a year later, the patent ran into some trouble at the appeals court level, where the preliminary injunction was lifted. The patent might first receive a full examination in court in the fall of 2001.

But that is getting ahead of the story. My first objective is to look at the Amazon patent controversy as one particular instance of a broader class of patent activity that has a large number of people concerned that patents might stifle innovation on the Internet. Why do these patents seem so threatening to some people? What are the counterarguments? What is the bigger picture? Looking at these questions through the lens of the Amazon '411 patent requires turning the clock back to late 1999.

According to a *New York Times* article published right after the Federal District Court's ruling on December 1, 1999, against Barnes and Noble, "the judge ruled that Amazon's case 'demonstrated a reasonable likelihood of success on the basis of merits.' Moreover, she wrote that Amazon would face 'irreparable harm' if it did not have exclusive use of the one-click feature during the holidays."[5] Commenting on the ruling, Patent Office Commissioner Q. Todd Dickinson observed, "A federal judge found that the patent was sufficiently valid to issue a preliminary injunction, which is a rather extraordinary thing, right in the face of the Christmas holiday season. I thought that was kind of amazing, to be honest, and tends to suggest that the patent has validity."[6]

## Where's Alice?

On the one hand we have a lot of programmers who have "ordinary skill in the art at the time the invention was made" who think that the Amazon '411 patent is troubling because it claims something obvious, something that they feel anybody should be able to use without needing permission from Amazon. Even Paul Barton-Davis, employee number 2 at Amazon back in 1994 and a key member of the technical staff that built the original Amazon site, is deeply troubled by the patent. "Both Amazon's patent application and now legal enforcement of the patent is a cynical and ungrateful use of an extremely obvious technology," according to Barton-Davis. "1-Click is a simple, logical and obvious use of the cookie system pioneered by Netscape and others. It did not deserve to be patented, and the patent does not deserve legal upholding, let alone enforcement."[7]

Then, on the other hand, we have a federal judge who felt that there was a reasonable chance that Amazon would be able to defend its patent and succeed in restraining Barnes and Noble from infringing with a competing one-click ordering system. The judge was then joined by a PTO commissioner who was amazed and apparently pleased with a sequence of developments that so troubled the programmers.

Have we fallen down the rabbit hole into Wonderland? From either side of the argument the other side's viewpoint looks either ignorant or willfully disingenuous.

Sorting this out is a little easier if you realize that the different players are looking at the question with different *breadths* of viewpoint. Sometimes the breadth is so different that the question actually changes. For example, it would be easy to make too much of the federal judge's ruling in issuing the preliminary injunction—viewing it as a complete review of the Amazon patent or perhaps even as some kind of general vindication of the whole class of patents of which Amazon's '411 patent became the most visible example. The judge was *not* (yet) dealing with a complete examination of the validity of Amazon's '411 patent when she issued the order. Instead, the immediate question before her was much narrower: does the Barnes and Noble one-click system probably infringe on the Amazon patent, if we assume that patent to be valid? And has Barnes and Noble raised substantial questions concerning the validity of the patent? If the judge decided that infringement was likely and that there were no substantial concerns about validity, she then had to decide whether the infringement would have a high probability of harming Amazon.

The judge decided that, since the essence of Amazon's patent is one-click ordering, and since Barnes and Noble's Express Lane advertised one-click ordering capability, it was likely that, in a full trial, the court would conclude that there was infringement. The judge also concluded that Barnes and Noble's challenges to the validity of the patent lacked sufficient merit to be a reason to set aside Amazon's concern about infringement. (This is where, a year later, an appeals court saw things differently.) Given all this, the judge decided that harm was likely, so she issued the preliminary injunction.

The judge was *not* making a decision about the validity of Amazon's '411 patent, much less about the desirability of business method patents for the Internet in general. She was, instead, simply trying to deal with the much narrower questions that were actually before her.

The people arguing against the Amazon patent, on the other hand, are looking at the problem very broadly. Quoting from O'Reilly's letter, the Amazon patent opponents are worried about matters like turning the "glorious open playing field into a proprietary wasteland" and drying up "the springs of further innovation."

Barton-Davis, like O'Reilly, is not considering the problem narrowly when he writes that "Amazon.com's early development relied on the use of tools that could not have been developed if other companies and individuals had taken the same approach to technological innovation that the company is now following."[8]

Pioneering programmer Richard Stallman argued that

> if this were just a dispute between two companies, it would not be an important public issue. But the patent gives Amazon the power over anyone who runs a Web site in the United States (and any other countries that give them similar patents)—power to control all use of this technique. Although only one company is being sued today, the issue affects the whole Internet.[9]

The programmers on the one hand and the commissioner and the judge on the other are not participating in the same conversation, a fact that is unchanged by all the yelling.

## Postscript

As was the case with the Napster lawsuit in the discussion of copyright issues, the Amazon 1-Click story is an ongoing one. In the months that elapsed between the completion of this chapter and taking the book to press there were a number of important, or at least interesting, developments.

October 2000 The debate over the Amazon 1-Click patent took an interesting turn when both Jeff Bezos, Amazon's founder and CEO, and Tim O'Reilly, vocal opponent of the 1-Click patent, made investments in BountyQuest, an Internet-based service that offers rewards for information about prior art related to patents. O'Reilly got the ball rolling by offering a $10,000 bounty for information that would lead to invalidating the 1-Click patent by showing that it had been done before or that it was an obvious extension of existing practice.[10]

February 14, 2001 The U.S. Court of Appeals for the Federal Circuit lifted the preliminary injunction that Amazon had won against Barnes and Noble in December 1999. The appeals court agreed with the district court that there was substantial likelihood that Barnes and Noble's Express Lane infringed about Amazon's '411 patent claims. But, unlike the district court, the appeals court ruled that Barnes and Noble had, in fact, raised a substantial challenge to the validity of the patent. One earlier system discussed at some length in the appeals court opinion was Compuserve's "Trend" system, offered in the mid-1990s, which allowed users to order a stock chart, for a surcharge, with a single mouse click. In summarizing its survey of prior art, the appeals court wrote:

> When the heft of the asserted prior art is assessed in light of the correct legal standards, we conclude that BN has mounted a serious challenge to the validity of Amazon's patent. We hasten to add, however, that this conclusion only undermines the prerequisite for entry of a preliminary injunction. Our decision today on the validity issue in no way resolves the ultimate question of invalidity. That is a matter for resolution at trial. It remains to be learned whether there are other references that may be cited against the patent, and it surely remains to be learned whether any shortcomings in BN's initial preliminary validity challenge will be magnified or dissipated at trial. All we hold, in the meantime, is that BN cast enough doubt on the validity of the '411 patent to avoid a preliminary injunction, and that the validity issue should be resolved finally at trial.[11]

March 14, 2001 Tim O'Reilly and BountyQuest split the $10,000 bounty for prior art on the 1-Click patent among three bounty hunters. One of the patents uncovered by the bounty offer, a European patent issued to Thomson Consumer Electronics in 1995, appears very similar to the Amazon '411 patent.[12] It uses a permanent, separate means for storing customer identification and payment information in order to enable ordering of merchandise "by simply pressing one button on the TV remote control." Other things turned up during the bounty hunt included a *Doonesbury* cartoon from 1993 that made fun of something very much like one-click ordering.

It is interesting that the upshot of all this bounty hunting was a stronger sense in O'Reilly's mind that Amazon really was breaking some new ground with its 1-Click system, even if it was not something that should have received a patent. In yet another open letter, O'Reilly wrote: "The breadth, depth, and quality of the prior art documents that my Bounty turned up does, in fact, indicate that 1-Click shopping on the Web wasn't nearly as obvious as we all assumed it was."[13]

Finally, it is interesting to note that all the prior art that O'Reilly recognized in awarding the bounty was in the form of publicly available patent records. In the chapters that follow we will look more closely at the need for stronger, more effective ways to uncover prior art and involve opposing parties early in the patent process.

If Amazon and Barnes and Noble don't settle the suit beforehand, it will go to trial in September 2001. It is worth noting that if the courts do ultimately decide to invalidate Amazon's patent or significantly narrow its scope, it will very probably be because there was already an earlier patent that covered much of the same ground. Such a finding doesn't really argue against O'Reilly's initial concern, subsequently echoed by so many others:

> Because, of course, you are not the only one who can play the patent game. And once the web becomes fenced in by competing patents and other attempts to make this glorious open playing field into a proprietary wasteland, the springs of further innovation will dry up.[14]

All that O'Reilly has done with his BountyQuest exercise is find another fence, one that predates Amazon's, confirming that Amazon is not the only one who can play the patent game, fencing the glorious open playing field. The broader questions raised by the 1-Click patent still remain, whether or not the court decides that there was an earlier claim on the field.

## What to Make of All This

The Amazon 1-Click patent is truly just the tip of the Internet patent iceberg. It is one of scores of patents that claim exclusive rights to some method of doing business on the Internet. If you are managing a company that does business on the Internet, the Amazon patent is significant as an instance of this broader trend in the claiming and defending of patents. Its value lies in its ability to help in identifying some important questions.

- How widespread is the effort to lay exclusive claim to particular Internet business methods? What are the possible effects of widespread use of patents to claim exclusive rights to business methods?
- What is patentable? What is required in order for an invention to be new and non-obvious? If you are interested in patenting your inventions, this question becomes a way of evaluating the patent-worthiness of your intellectual assets. If

you are concerned about the effect of patents on the health of Internet business, the question becomes one of understanding what others might lay claim to and lock off from the general public.

- Just how broad can a business method claim be? If you are wanting to build up a collection of patents as assets, this question becomes, "How much of the 'glorious open playing field' can I claim?" If you are concerned about the patent claims made by others, the question looks more like, "Can my neighbor claim such a large estate that it leaves me homeless?"
- Is all of this good for business in general?
- Does the ability to patent Internet business methods open up any interesting new business opportunities?
- How did we get here and where are we headed? How does one steer a business through all of this change?

These are not simple questions. At the same time, managing a business without knowing the answers to these questions is a clearly uncertain and potentially even perilous proposition. The following chapters address these questions, one at a time.

## Notes

1. From an open letter dated January 5, 2000, from Tim O'Reilly to Jeff Bezos of Amazon, regarding the Amazon 1-Click patent. In May 2001 the complete letter was available on O'Reilly's Web site at http://www.oreilly.com/ask_tim/amazon_patent.html.
2. From 35 *U.S. Code*, Section 101, "Inventions Patentable."
3. As quoted by James Glieck in "Patently Absurd," *New York Times Magazine*, March 12, 2000.
4. John R. Allison and Mark A. Lemley, "Empirical Evidence on the Validity of Litigated Patents," *Social Science Research Network Electronic Library* (http://www.ssrn.com). Accessed at http://papers.ssrn.com/paper.taf?ABSTRACT_ID=118149 on August 15, 2000.
5. From Saul Hanshell, "Amazon Wins Court Ruling in Patent Case," *New York Times*, December 3, 1999.
6. As quoted by Glieck (cited above).
7. Paul Barton-Davis, from a letter published on his personal Web site. Accessed at http://www.op.net/~pbd/amazon-1click.html on August 15, 2000.

8. Ibid.
9. From Richard Stallman, "Boycott Amazon," *Linux Today,* December 22, 1999. Accessed at http://linuxtoday.com/stories/13652.html on August 15, 2000.
10. BountyQuest (http://www.bountyquest.com) is an interesting attempt to bring market forces to bear on patents and on the problem of finding prior art that would invalidate patent claims. The idea behind BountyQuest is that it often might make good business sense to pay $10,000 or more for information about prior art to invalidate a patent claim that you are trying to contest—or, for that matter, that you are thinking about filing yourself. Further, someone on the Web who happens to have such information will often be delighted to trade the information for the money. So, BountyQuest has set up a Web meeting place between people who are willing to pay for information and people who might have it.

    BountyQuest's critics point out that there are numerous potential purchasers for information about prior art and that BountyQuest invites "runaround" and possible collusion. If there is a posted bounty of $10,000 for information that would invalidate company XYZ's patent, this is an invitation to someone having such information to go directly to XYZ's lawyers to negotiate a better deal. Alternatively, the person posting the bounty could pay the bounty and then go to XYZ with the information. So long as there is sufficient potential upside from keeping the patent on the books, there is an incentive to negotiate an agreement that will do so. BountyQuest simply sets the lower bound of the asking price. The ease of creating such collusive arrangements suggests that perhaps only the PTO could administer a bounty system that would have the desired effect of weeding out invalid patents. It is an interesting idea.
11. From *Amazon.Com, Inc.* v. *Barnesandnoble.Com, Inc.* U.S. Court of Appeals, Federal Circuit (No. 00-1109). Accessed in May 2001 on the Web at http://www.law.emory.edu/fedcircuit/feb2001/00-1109.wp.html.
12. EU patent number EP680185A2, titled "A distributed computer system."
13. From an open letter dated March 14, 2001, from Tim O'Reilly. In May 2001 the complete letter was available on the O'Reilly Network site at http://www.oreillynet.com/pub/a/policy/2001/03/14/bounty.html.
14. From O'Reilly, January 5, 2000 (cited above).

# CHAPTER 7

# Patent Sprawl

As Richard Stallman noted in his comments on the Amazon 1-Click patent, the Amazon controversy would be just a tempest in a teapot if it were an isolated case. But all parties to this debate, ranging from former PTO Commissioner Dickinson on the one hand to Tim O'Reilly and Richard Stallman on the other, agree that Amazon's success in patenting 1-Click ordering is just one example among many of the ability to make a property claim on an approach to Internet business. Having some sense of what all this might mean for you and your company requires having at least a general idea of the scope and nature of this patent activity. So, let's look briefly at some examples of recent patent claims on Internet business methods.

## Some Recent Internet Patents

**Amazon's Patent on Using the Last Digits of Credit Cards** We'll start with another Amazon patent, numbered 5,715,399. This patent covers an invention that consists of using a computer displaying the last few digits of a customer's stored credit card information, potentially on a Web page or via e-mail, as a way to let the customer indicate which credit card should be used while communicating over an unsecured network. It is probable that any other business displaying the last few digits of a credit card over a nonsecure network in order to verify payment preferences is infringing on Amazon's '399 patent. Interestingly, it appears that the patent applies only to nonsecure communications systems.

This is another good example of a patent that covers something that many developers might judge to be obvious to one having ordinary skill in the art at the time the invention was made.

**DoubleClick's and 24/7 Media's Patents on Methods for Delivering and Targeting Online Advertising** DoubleClick received patent number 5,948,061 on September 7, 1999, for a method for targeting and delivering advertising over a network such as the Internet. What the company patented was the kind of linked coordination of different servers used to deliver online advertising, wherein advertising space on a company's Web pages are linked back to a central advertising server that can call out to other servers, managed by the advertisers, to supply the actual ads. The central advertising server can use information about visitors in order to select an appropriate advertisement for display. As with the Amazon '411 patent, the fact that the Web uses very simple protocols for requesting content from servers means that a developer does not have a lot of choice in setting up such a system. If you want to use a central ad server to select and deliver ads, supplied by advertisers on their servers, for delivery to other companies who provide the ad space, the method described in the DoubleClick patent covers it.

Like Amazon, DoubleClick quickly began using its new patent to attack competitors using the same broadly defined methodologies. In mid-November 1999, the company filed suit against L90, charging that L90's product, adMonitor, infringes on the DoubleClick patent. Since L90 was just then preparing for an IPO, the suit came at a difficult time for L90. Then, in December, DoubleClick sued Sabela Media, yet another ad-serving and -tracking service. Despite the lawsuit, Sabela was acquired by 24/7 Media, a yet larger media and advertising firm, in January 2000.

The picture became even more complex when the PTO issued patent number 6,026,368 on February 15, 2000, to 24/7 Media for another method for delivering targeted advertising. Although this patent was issued after the DoubleClick patent, its filing date of July 17, 1995, actually predated DoubleClick's October 29, 1996, filing by more than a year. 24/7's patent, like DoubleClick's, makes broad claims on fundamental methods for choosing ads on the basis of visitor profiles and then delivering them.[1]

Not surprisingly, 24/7 Media used its newly issued patent to strike back at DoubleClick. 24/7 filed a suit against DoubleClick on May 5, 2000, charging infringement against the '368 patent. Then, on May 18, 24/7 also filed a countersuit against DoubleClick on behalf of its new Sabela Media subsidiary. In the countersuit 24/7 and Sabela alleged that DoubleClick violated federal antitrust laws by failing to provide information about prior art to the PTO in the '061 patent application.

That same week L90 filed a separate suit against DoubleClick, striking back at DoubleClick's initial suit against L90. The L90 suit alleged that DoubleClick was using unfair business practices and, like the Sabela suit, accused DoubleClick of fraudulent behavior in acquiring its patent. L90 asserted that the DoubleClick patent should be declared invalid.

This tangle of suits and countersuits certainly shows how complicated and expensive patent litigation can be. Sorting out the question of who owns what and who is infringing on whom could easily cost many millions of dollars in these cases.

Priceline's Patent on Reverse Auctions on the Internet Patent number 5,794,207, assigned to Walker Asset Management Limited Partnership, claims ownership of an invention that enables reverse auctions on the Web. More precisely, the patent claims an invention that allows a potential buyer of some good or service to use a computer to make a purchase offer for the good or service at or below a certain price, along with information about how the buyer intends to pay. The invention then makes the purchase offer available to sellers, allows a seller to accept the offer, and then arranges payment for the seller using the information that the buyer has provided.

The invention claims ownership of this method at essentially the broad level of detail that I have just described. Any system in which a buyer uses a computer to make a conditional purchase offer by credit card that permits sellers to respond and be paid electronically would very probably infringe on this patent, regardless of what is being bought or sold. Walker Asset Management is associated with Walker Digital, which in turn owns Priceline, the online, name-your-own-price reverse auction company. The result is that Priceline essentially has a patent on its business model.

This is yet another patent that has become the subject of a series of lawsuits. In January 1999 a company named Marketel brought a suit against Priceline, claiming that Priceline's '207 patent is based on an invention that is actually owned by Marketel. Marketel alleges that it provided Priceline's founders with information about the reverse auction invention under nondisclosure and that Priceline then used this confidential information as the basis of its business and of its patent. Marketel's suit seeks to correct the '207 patent by naming Marketel employees as coinventors or as sole inventors. The suit encountered jurisdiction problems but is still pending.

In the meantime Priceline sued Microsoft and its Expedia subsidiary for infringing on its patent by using the reverse auction technique to allow buyers to bid for hotel rooms. *USA Today* reported that

> In meetings from November 1998 to last July, Priceline and Microsoft executives explored various partnerships, including whether Priceline might send customers to Microsoft's Expedia travel Web site, Priceline officials say. Priceline provided Microsoft "detailed confidential information" during the meetings, the company says. In July, when Priceline founder Jay Walker suggested a deal, Gates "asked why he simply could not take" Priceline's model and use it on Expedia, Priceline says in a summary of its lawsuit. When Walker said Priceline had a patent, "Mr. Gates became very agitated" and said "he would not allow U.S. patents to stand in the way of Microsoft's business objectives."[2]

In December 1999 Microsoft moved to dismiss the Priceline suit, or to join Marketel to the suit, because Priceline failed to include Marketel in the suit in the first place. The basis of Microsoft's motion is the assertion that a decision in *Priceline* v. *Microsoft and Expedia* would necessarily affect Marketel.[3]

The Priceline reverse auction patent is another example of a patent that covers a lot of ground, that is being used as a weapon to defend a market position, and that has inspired a fair amount of complex litigation.

**Netcentives' Patent on an Online Reward Redemption Program** Patent 5,774,870, issued on June 30, 1998, and assigned to Netcentives, Inc., claims an interactive, online incentive awards program consisting of a products catalog of items for sale online, an awards catalog describing the available awards and the number of points required to win them, and a database to keep track of the purchasing and award status for each program participant. This broad claim very probably covers most online awards programs that provide incentives for online purchases.

The '870 patent, combined with a more recent refinement described in patent 6,009,412, has not only enabled Netcentives to build an outsourcing business that serves clients such as AOL, TWA, and American Express but also allowed them to develop a patent-licensing business. Notably, patent licensees include The Sperry & Hutchinson Company, the pioneering offline rewards company that originated S&H Green Stamps.

**Intouch's Patent on Previewing Audio Samples** Intouch Group, Inc. received patent 5,963,916 on October 5, 1999, for a method that allows people to listen to prerecorded samples of music online. As with the other Internet business method patents we have reviewed, Intouch's '916 patent claims a fairly general, broad method. It includes the steps of establishing a connection between a Web browser and a central server (that's the Internet), transmitting a user identifier (once again, a cookie), selecting a prerecorded segment of music stored on the server, sending the segment back to the browser, and then previewing the segment. The patent also covers the additional, optional function of allowing the user to purchase the recording from which the segment was extracted.

Given the breadth of these claims, any company allowing identified users to preview music would probably be infringing on the Intouch patent. That's the way Intouch sees it, in any case. On April 18, 2000, Intouch announced that it had filed suit against Amazon, Liquid Audio, Listen.com, Inc., Entertaindom, LLC (a unit of Time Warner, Inc.), and Discovermusic.com, Inc. for infringing on its patent.

## Concerns Raised by These Patents

I could list dozens of other patents that could fit into this list of Internet business method claims; there really has been a great deal of activity in this area lately. But even the handful of patents that I list here share some remarkably similar characteristics. These common features are closely tied to the principal concerns voiced by the people who object to these new patents.

### High-Level Approach Rather Than Detailed Technology

In general, these patents describe a high-level approach to a problem or business opportunity. The invention consists of something as broadly defined as sending samples of music over the Internet, serving ads from a central server, or offering reverse auctions on the Web.

Consider, for contrast, the patent on a software data compression algorithm that was issued to Stac Electronics in 1991. We will look at the Stac case in more detail later (see Chapter 10) since it illustrates important uses of patents. For now it is sufficient to note that the Stac patent provides the public with a technical, low-level description of Stac's compression algorithm, which became the basis for the successful line of products that Stac sold in the early 1990s to compress files on computer disks, allowing users to fit more files on a disk. Updated to new, twenty-first-century standards, Stac might have sought to patent the entire, broad notion of real-time data compression for file storage, rather than just patenting the underlying compression technology. If the company had been able to do this, the irony is that it would have been able to claim a larger market (all uses of compression in real time to increase disk capacity) and would have actually disclosed less in the way of proprietary technology to the general public.

### Application of Traditional, Offline Approaches to the Internet

In some cases these high-level business methods are quite literally the application of well-known business methods to the new Internet environment. Reverse auctions have been around for a long time; what Priceline did that was new was to offer a reverse auction over the Web. Similarly, incentive reward programs tied to purchases have been around for a very long time; consider S&H Green Stamps. What Netcentives did that was new was offer such a program on the Internet, which means that now S&H must license the method for online incentives from Netcentives.

### The "Obviousness" Problem

Many critics of the new trends in the granting of patents feel that many of the Internet business method patents are obvious, despite the PTO's initial ruling to the contrary. There are several causes for this perceived obviousness. One is related to the high level of abstraction in the claims. For example, the idea of using a central server to coordinate delivery of advertising might seem obvious insofar as centralization of services and bookkeeping is a common way to approach nearly any distributed services problem. The devil is in the details, of course. But the DoubleClick patent does not claim one detailed and perhaps innovative implementation, but instead claims the broad architecture consisting of a central server linked to both a content provider and ad providers. Many would judge the invention to be obvious when claimed at that level.

Another powerful reason for the sense that many of these Internet business method inventions are obvious is the fact that they consist of creating Internet versions of well-known approaches to well-understood problems. As we will see in the next chapter, the Supreme Court has established a clear precedent for viewing the insertion of a computer into a familiar process as something that is patentable. But, even so, the familiarity of the basic, underlying process—such as the process of offering incentives along with purchases—does contribute to the sense that the invention is obvious.

Yet another cause for the sense of obviousness is the fact that the very simple communication protocols between machines on the Internet often result in a very limited number of ways to construct systems, when viewed at a high level. As a result, the claimed method is often the *only* method, which tends to also make it the *obvious* method.

Finally, opponents of Internet business method patents would argue that, in many cases, the flurry of litigation when patents are issued is yet another indication that the methods are obvious. Many companies develop the methods almost simultaneously. By the time a patent is issued the method is already in broad use.

Patent examiners focus on whether an invention involves patentable subject matter and on whether it is new, non-obvious, and disclosed properly. They do not make a judgment on the value of an invention. That is, of course, as it should be, since value judgments would necessarily be very subjective and, besides, would probably be often wrong. Who knows? It might turn out, for example, that patent 5,443,036—for a method for exercising a cat by having the cat chase the beam from a laser pointer as shown in the illustration from the patent in Figure 7–1—could become the basis for a successful product and new market opportunity.

It is equally true that the granting of a patent is not tied in any way to the amount invested in creating and perfecting an invention. A pharmaceutical company will invest tens of millions of dollars in developing a new drug; someone else might discover, while watching TV and playing with a laser pointer, that his cat is fascinated with the laser's red dot of light. Both inventions are patentable.

But, even acknowledging all of this, it might still be useful for us, if not the patent examiners, to consider the broader economic questions of cost and incentives that sur-

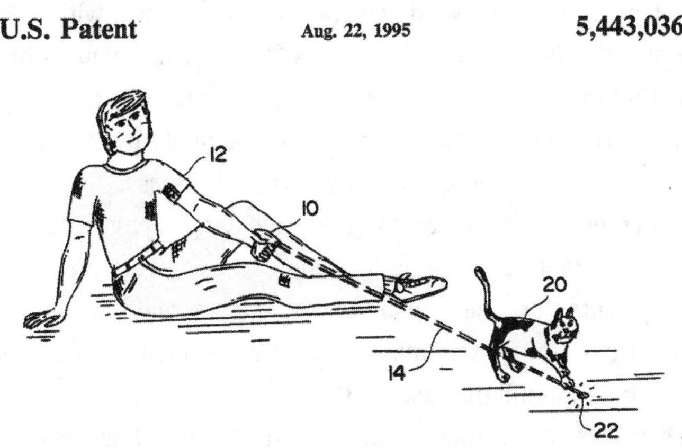


*Figure 7–1* Illustration of a patented cat-exercising method.

round the use of patents. Since we are concerned about questions of patent policy, we do not need to limit ourselves to factors that a patent examiner might use in evaluating a patent application.

The Constitution authorizes the use of patents "to promote the progress of science and useful arts, by securing for limited times to authors and inventors the exclusive right to their respective writings and discoveries." The inventor shares the invention with society as a whole, thereby promoting progress, and society gives the inventor a 20-year monopoly on the use of the invention. It is fair to ask whether society as a whole is making a good trade in the case of Internet business patents.

Framing the question this way, the problem with many Internet business methods is that they disclose very little and claim a lot. The problem grows from the issues that we have already identified: the claims are made at a high level of abstraction, they are in some cases simply extensions of well-known methods to the Internet, and the methods appear obvious to many people with ordinary skill in the art.

Opponents of Internet business patents argue that the patents are a bad deal for society. The companies owning the patents receive valuable claims to property, claims that are so broad that they can confer significant market advantage. What is society in general and the Internet business community in particular getting in return?

### Impediment to Innovation

If you are building a Web business unit and you ask customers to select a credit card by showing them the last four digits, you may be infringing on Amazon's '399 patent. If you offer rewards for purchases on your site, you may be infringing on Netcentives' '870 patent. If you allow customers to order a product with a single mouse click, you are probably infringing on Amazon's '411 patent. If you let buyers make a purchase offer that sellers can then accept or decline, you could be infringing on Priceline's '207 patent. There are scores of others that you might have to step around, depending on what you are trying to do in your Web business.

Critics of Internet business patents argue that having to pay license fees to so many patent owners or, alternatively, finding new approaches to work around the broad claims in these patents slows new business development and innovation. Since e-businesses are often working with thin margins, the need to do a lot of licensing just to get the business running can kill the case for the business.

The critics will also argue that small, thinly funded new businesses have been at the center of much of the innovation on the Internet over the past five years. Turning business methods into private property makes things much more difficult for such smaller players. It is as if, in starting a lemonade stand, you find that someone has a patent on putting a sign above the stand, another kid has a patent on the use of a card table, and someone else has patented the use of a pitcher to hold the lemonade. Like many e-businesses, the margins in the lemonade business are too slim to leave room for a lot of licensing costs, which means that patenting the methods would be a good way to keep others from entering it. This might be exactly what the "lemonade method" patent owners would have in mind, but it is not at all clear that it is the best outcome for the world of lemonade drinkers or for the economy in general.

## Not Necessary for Growth

In his dissent in an important software patent case before the Supreme Court—one we will look at a bit more closely in the next chapter—Justice John Paul Stevens observed that, "Notwithstanding fervent argument that patent protection is essential for the growth of the software industry, commentators have noted that 'this industry is growing by leaps and bounds without it.'"[4] His observation applies to the Internet business community today. Once again, this is not an argument that would affect the decisions by patent examiners; instead, it is a plea for a rational consideration of policy by Congress. The right to receive a patent is not the same kind of fundamental right as free speech. It is a conditional arrangement that has been constructed to address the problem of ensuring that there is enough exchange of information to ensure progress in the useful arts. Although the disclosure of inventions so that others may study them may still contribute to information exchange and progress in some industries, many would argue that the idea that patents are an important medium of information exchange for Internet business is absurd. Given a rapidly expanding area of innovation that is already exchanging information and learning quickly, why impose the unnecessary and very possibly damaging structure of patents?

## Intellectual Property Time Bombs for Internet Businesses

Critics of Internet business method patents contend that not only do these patents contribute nothing to the disclosure and exchange of information but, worse, they also obscure information and add to business uncertainty. Typically, two to five years elapse between the time that a patent application is filed and the time that the patent is granted. That is a very long time on the Internet, and, because the inventions are often not difficult (perhaps even obvious), by the time the patent is issued there are often many companies using the suddenly patented method. As evidence of this, consider the flurry of infringement suits and other litigation as many of these patents are granted. The result is that, as a company develops its Web business, it is very possible that it is infringing on future patents that are still working their way, in secret, through the process within the patent office. This is yet another way in which Internet business method patents could discourage rather than encourage new development and growth in Internet business.

### Burdensome Expenses of Litigation

Finally, critics of Internet business method patents point to the cost of defending patents and defending against infringement claims as a significant additional expense that changes the business development environment. Estimates vary, but it is generally agreed that the median cost for preparing a patent infringement suit through the discovery phase approaches a million dollars and that the median cost to both parties if the case goes to trial is well in excess of a million dollars. Complicated cases can often involve costs of several million dollars.[5] These kinds of expenses can kill an Internet start-up working with a few million dollars of venture capital investment. The effect of the rapid expansion of patent claims over Internet business methods and the consequent increase in litigation costs is to shift the advantage to larger companies that can afford such costs of doing business.

## Making Sense of the Dispute

Parties on both sides of the dispute over patents agree that business method patents are changing the fundamental nature of business development for the Internet. The patents allow companies to claim ways of doing business on the Internet as property. The claims can be relatively broad, including things such as ordering a product with a single click or offering incentives for purchases. As we will see in chapters that follow, there are people who view this change as an inevitable maturation of Internet business, as a movement beyond the wild early days of the gold rush to a more ordered environment where companies can own things and demand that others pay for their use. In this chapter, however, we have looked at the arguments raised by others who view such fencing off of the Internet as a huge mistake, even as a tragedy.

The causes of this alarm have a number of roots. One is that the claims made in these patents are sometimes pretty broad, effectively staking out an entire area of business as a company's private domain. Another problem is that the patents are sometimes for methods that seem obvious to many, despite the fact that patents are not supposed to be issued for obvious extensions of prior art. Another related concern is that many of these patents seem to be all about staking claims and much less clearly about disclosing anything of real value. It seems in these cases that society is getting very little in return for grants of exclusive privilege to inventors. Worse, some might add, is the additional burden on young companies that is imposed by licensing costs and defense against patent infringement. Carving up the Internet into private estates favors the status quo; part of the value of Internet business up until now is that it has provided useful, important alternatives to the status quo. The argument against patents, then, is that we are destroying something valuable in order to lock in gains for a few, carving up our economic future and receiving cynical, obvious, worthless disclosures in return.

One of the striking things about this debate is its vehemence. People opposed to patents on Internet business methods see the actions by Amazon, Priceline, and other companies as a conscious, malicious attempt to grab market advantage without regard to the general good. Tim O'Reilly's strong phrase, "pissing in the well," captures this distaste and vehemence. The critics of these recent patents see their use as selfish, reckless, unconscionable, and perhaps immoral behavior.

The view from the other side looks, if anything, even weirder. Companies that have been paying attention to patent law developments surely know that it is now possible to lay claim to business methods. If knowledge and key business methods are becoming property, any business with serious hopes for the future ought to claim some. Being an Internet business five years from now without any intellectual assets to license, sell, or trade looks like a loser's game. Given all of that, what on earth can you make of someone who is morally outraged by your rational pursuit of obvious self-interest, all within the bounds of established law? They are either hopelessly out of touch, dangerously imbalanced, or both.

Disagreement is normal, but disputes that spread this wide, so that one side cannot understand, much less respect, what the other side is trying to say, are not at all normal. Such disputes can potentially show us something new. It is clear that both sides are trying to say something that is important and that is probably "true" in some sense. Your ability to choose the best path forward for your own business is enhanced by being able to extract what is useful and important from both sets of truths.

The first step toward sorting through the increasingly divergent points of view on Internet patents involves understanding what caused the divergence in the first place. How is it that each viewpoint can look reasonable, internally, and so absurd or malicious to the other side? What is the source of such differences? These are the questions pursued in the next few chapters.

## Notes

1. The DoubleClick '061 patent and the 24/7 '368 patent do not necessarily conflict with each other. DoubleClick's patent focuses more on the linking system that coordinates the actions of the ad server and the servers actually containing the ads in response to user action on the content server. The 24/7 patent addresses itself more to methods for keeping track of actions and queues of ads within the ad server. Both systems make use of profile information for targeting, but each, taken as a whole, potentially address different dimensions of the ad-serving problem. The precise relationship of the two patents will be for the courts to figure out. However, it is very likely that any ad-serving implementation would make use of the methodologies described in both of these patents. If the patents do turn out to be independent and complementary, it could be that 24/7 and DoubleClick are each infringing on the other's patent in the regular operation of their businesses.
2. From Paul Davidson, "Priceline.com: Microsoft Violated Patent," *USA Today Tech Report*, October 14, 1999. Accessed at http://www.usatoday.com/life/cyber/tech/ctg424.htm on August 20, 2000.
3. As reported in an Expedia press release, "Civil Action No. 3:99 CV 1991 (AWT), December 20, 1999: Memorandum of Law in Support of Motion to Dismiss," about the motion filed by Microsoft. Accessed at http://www.expedia.com/daily/service/press/releases/memorandum.asp?FromServerName=www.expedia.com&MSID=6256680F6FB011D4B75800508B676C21 on August 20, 2000.
4. From *Diamond* v. *Diehr,* 450 U.S. 175 (1981).
5. Cost estimates for patent litigation are from the American Intellectual Property Law Association (accessed in May 2001 at http://www.aipla.org/) and from Internet sources such as Dr. Karl F. Jorda, "Patent Infringement Litigation: the U.S. Experience," speech presented at the Indonesian Intellectual Property Society Meeting, Jakarta, March 23, 1999 (accessed on August 20, 2000, at http://www.ipmall.fplc.edu/pubs/speeches/jorda_03_23_99.htm).

CHAPTER 8

# What Is Patentable?

THERE are three concepts that managers, marketers, and even sometimes attorneys and judges get all mixed up. The first has to do with patentable subject matter: is the topic or focus of the patent one that is patentable in the first place? The second concept has to do with the requirement that inventions be new and non-obvious. (The PTO and the courts don't even consider the novelty and non-obviousness requirements if the subject matter is not patentable.) The third concept has to do with whether the patent is good for the industry, promotes progress and growth, and is in other ways a generally good idea. The PTO and the courts generally don't consider such issues at all, even though they are the central focus for many of the people who are most concerned about patents for Internet business methods. Such policy issues are properly the business of Congress and of us, the public, as we are represented through Congress.

These distinctions seem simple and sensible: subject matter, novelty and obviousness, and policy. It would appear that it should be easy to keep them straight. But even a casual reading of the history of patent litigation shows that, in practice, keeping the different considerations separate has been anything but simple.

Part of the problem is related to the issue of breadth of vision that we discussed earlier. You might have broad reasons for wanting to attack a patent, but the approach you take in your attack will often necessarily focus on narrow details where the patent is vulnerable. Consequently, court decisions typically focus on such narrow questions. However, once the narrow legal decision is rendered the victors tend to make the broadest possible claims in press releases and marketing literature. All of this can make it difficult for a manager to keep track of just what has really been decided, what is patentable, and what is not.

Paying careful attention to these three distinctions is critical to your success in developing a patent strategy, understanding patent trends, or attacking a competitor's patent claims. To assist with these distinctions, this chapter looks at the way that the PTO and the courts have changed their thinking about what constitutes patentable subject matter, and it looks at how decisions on subject matter have intersected with questions of novelty and policy. This brief look back in history will give you a strong sense of where things stand today and where they are headed over the next few years.

## Software

Patent law for software got off to a confusing start. Businesspeople are still coping with the effects of that confusion today, thirty years later.

*Gottschalk* v. *Benson*, a case that came before the Supreme Court in 1972, was the first software patent case considered by the Court. For new, relatively untested areas of law the Supreme Court serves the important function of setting the direction for lower courts to follow. The matter of patents for software was typical in this regard. What was more unusual was that the Court's decision turned out to be more of a puzzle to be solved over the next thirty years than a clearly articulated precedent.

The invention that was the subject of *Gottschalk* v. *Benson* was a method for converting binary coded decimal (BCD) numbers into pure binary numbers. Although the patent application stated that the invention was intended for use on general-purpose digital computers, the patent did not restrict use to any particular computer. In fact, the algorithm could be performed with pencil and paper, without use of a computer.

The question before the Court was not whether the invention was new but whether the subject matter was patentable at all. Scientific truths and the mathematical expressions of such truths are not patentable subject matter. Newton would not have been able to patent gravity (think of the royalties!), and Einstein would not have been able to patent $E = mc^2$. But Newton *could* have patented bungee jumping, since inventions that make use of a scientific truth are most certainly patentable.

In *Gottschalk* v. *Benson* the Court was faced with the question of deciding whether the inventor, Benson, was trying to patent a scientific truth or an application of such a truth. This was a tough call that was made even more difficult by the fact that the proposed invention involved no physical gadgets and looked a lot like a mathematical algorithm. It was also clear that a decision in favor of the patent would set an important new precedent that could change the nature of software development, since, up until that time, important software breakthroughs such as B-trees, new sorting algorithms, new hashing schemes, and so on were published and freely shared, critiqued, and improved upon.

The Court decided that the subject matter was not patentable. The problems encountered in the following years did not arise so much from the fact of this decision, which was, after all, consistent with contemporary practice, but instead from the arguments that Justice William O. Douglas, who wrote the opinion, offered as an explanation.

> Here the "process" claim is so abstract and sweeping as to cover both known and unknown uses of the BCD to pure binary conversion. The end use may (1) vary from the operation of a train to verification of drivers' licenses to researching the law books for precedents and (2) be performed through any existing machinery or future-devised machinery or without any apparatus.[1]

Notice that Justice Douglas is breaking one of the rules set down at the start of this chapter: while considering whether the subject matter is patentable he is wandering off into speculation about social consequences and policy. Supreme Court justices are entitled to break these rules, if anyone is, since the Court's rulings are, in fact, often a blend of law and policy. The problem is that other jurists, attorneys, and inventors have picked up on Justice Douglas's mixing of questions of patentability and policy and amplified it over the years. As we will see, the mixing persists today. It is a great question for general public discussion but makes a poor basis for attacking patents in the courts.

Justice Douglas did not stop there in constructing an opinion that would take decades to untangle. Aware that he was writing the first Supreme Court opinion dealing with the question of patents for software inventions, he was careful to state that it was not the intent of the court to preclude patents for any "program servicing a computer." It would seem that this would have left the door open for other software patents to be considered apart from the shadow of *Gottschalk* v. *Benson*. But unfortunately Douglas went on to muddle the matter by also suggesting that perhaps Congress should take up the issue if it wanted to allow patents for software. The end result was that the PTO interpreted the ruling to mean that software was not patentable. They didn't stop there. The PTO began treating any application that used the word "algorithm" as suspect.[2]

## Adding a Computer to a Known Process

It seemed clear throughout the 1970s that getting a patent for software was either pretty difficult or impossible. Despite Justice Douglas's apparent desire to not shut the door on software patents, the rest of the *Gottschalk* v. *Benson* ruling did just that. But what about getting a patent for the use of a computer in some other process?

Two inventors, James R. Diehr and Theodore A. Lutton, decided to try to do just that for the use of a computer program in a rubber-molding process. The overall rubber-curing process was old and well established, as was the mathematical formula used to calculate the curing time. What was new was that Diehr and Lutton inserted a computer into the process that measured temperatures, did the calculations using the formula, and then sent a signal to automatically open the mold when curing was complete.

The PTO approached the application by dismembering it, throwing out all the steps that used computers on the continued assumption that computer processes were not patentable. What was left, of course, was the well-known method for curing rubber. That wasn't patentable, since it had been invented long ago. So the PTO rejected the patent application.

After a series of appeals the case reached the Supreme Court in 1981 as *Diamond* v. *Diehr*. The case set a very important precedent. It was the first case in which the Supreme Court ruled in favor of a software patent application. It also showed potential applicants how to get a patent approved. If we have *Gottschalk* v. *Benson* to thank for our continued tendency to confound questions of patentable subject matter with questions of social impact, we have *Diamond* v. *Diehr* to thank for the idea that by stirring a computer into an existing process you can produce something patentable. It provided the prototype for many of today's Internet business patents.

The question before the Court in *Diamond* v. *Diehr* was whether the subject matter of the invention was patentable as opposed to whether it was new or obvious. The answer to that question depended on what you saw when you looked at the patent. Five members of the Court, represented in an opinion written by Justice William H. Rehnquist, saw a process for curing rubber—clearly a patentable topic, as illustrated by the fact that Charles Goodyear received a patent for such a process a long time ago. Four members of the court, represented in an opinion by Justice John Paul Stevens, saw things differently:

> The patent application filed by Diehr and Lutton . . . teaches nothing about the chemistry of the synthetic rubber-curing process, nothing about the raw materials to be used in curing synthetic rubber, nothing about the equipment to be used in the process, and nothing about the significance or effect of any process variable such as temperature, curing time, particular compositions of material, or mold configurations. In short, Diehr and Lutton do not claim to have discovered anything new about the process for curing synthetic rubber.[3]

What the dissenting members of the Court saw was a software algorithm masquerading as a physical process. In this quotation Stevens is arguing that, if the invention were really dealing with the curing of rubber, the patent application would have something novel to say about the process. But as an algorithm, the invention was no different than Benson's invention of a BCD-to-binary conversion system and so, according to the *Gottschalk* v. *Benson* precedent, the patent should be rejected on the basis of its subject matter.

Notice in reading Stevens's complaint—that the Diehr and Lutton patent does not teach anything about the process of curing rubber—that one could make similar observations about many of the Internet business method patents. The Netcentives patent teaches us nothing about incentives programs. It merely takes a well-understood process and adds the Internet. Priceline's patent teaches us nothing new about how to conduct a reverse auction; it merely claims use of reverse auctions on the Internet. These new patents are consistent with the successful approach taken by Diehr and Lutton.

*Diamond* v. *Diehr* made two important contributions to the development of the laws for software patents and, later, Internet patents. The first was simply that it established that the use of software and computers within a patent application would not automatically, inevitably, guarantee that the invention was not patentable. The second contribution was that it established that patent applications were to be considered as a whole, rather than being dissected into old and new claims and considered piecemeal. Justice Rehnquist wrote that "a new combination of steps in a process may be patentable even though all the constituents of the combination were well known and in common use before the combination was made."[4] The idea that a process or method was to be considered as a whole became an important building block for later establishing the potential patentability of business method claims.

James Thurber used to draw cartoons in which horses showed up in living rooms, behind curtains, and in other surprising places. The humor came from the fact that the well-dressed people in these cartoons never paid attention to the horse and sometimes denied its existence. The horse in the living room throughout *Diamond* v. *Diehr* is the question of whether Diehr and Lutton had really created anything new. That was actually the really interesting question. Does adding a computer to a known process create a new invention worthy of patenting? Or is it just an obvious combination of well-known techniques to create a process that is most certainly an improvement but not really anything new? But—and this is the key thing—in *Diamond* v. *Diehr* the question before the Court *did not have anything to do with novelty* but with whether the subject matter was patentable. In fact, Justice Rehnquist, in upholding the patent, wrote:

> In this case, it may later be determined that the respondents' process is not deserving of patent protection because it fails to satisfy the statutory conditions of novelty . . . or nonobviousness. . . . A rejection on either of these grounds does not affect the determination that respondents' claims recited subject matter which was eligible for patent protection.[5]

But the Diehr and Lutton patent was not subsequently challenged on questions of novelty. Despite the critical importance of the question whether Diehr and Lutton had actually created anything new, the question was never raised in a serious way, much less examined and answered. Notwithstanding this failure to press on the question of novelty, the *Diamond* v. *Diehr* case has gone on to become a precedent cited in most software and Internet business method patent decisions.

## Software Patents at the Start of the Internet Boom

*Gottschalk* v. *Benson* and *Diamond* v. *Diehr,* supported by a number of other cases echoing similar themes, established the trend line for software patents and, later, Internet patents. *Benson* established the idea that software was clearly different than physical engineering and design and that it was more like mathematics or scientific truth, and therefore not patentable in itself. The way around this, as *Diamond* v. *Diehr* demonstrated, was to patent a software application. As computers began to replace manual or mechanical controls and processes, this opened up large new realms for patent activity. The formula for generating new patents looked like this: take an established method or system, automate it by using a computer to perform manual or mechanical steps, and apply for a patent on the entire process.

Looking back from today's vantage point, when it is possible to patent a whole area of business, such as the serving of advertisements or offering online incentives, the *Diamond* v. *Diehr* decision was a big step in the direction of establishing today's business environment, but it still left a couple of important things undone. The problem was that *Diehr* addressed production processes and technologies that, though important, covered only a part of an overall business model. From the standpoint of someone wanting to use patents to stake claims on a new market, it would be much better if you could patent the entire business method, rather than just the most technical parts of it. These kinds of questions became especially interesting in the last years of the 1990s as Internet business began heating up. Here was a vast, new, unclaimed space that promised phenomenal growth for the companies that could stake early claims. In 1998, just as the valuations of Internet companies were beginning to climb rapidly, the United States Court of Appeals for the Federal Circuit handed down a decision that showed how one could use patents as part of that claim-staking process. That ruling is the subject of the next chapter.

## Notes

1. From *Gottschalk* v. *Benson,* 409 U.S. 63 (1972). This decision is widely available on the Internet.
2. In a case called *Application of Chatfield,* 545 F.2d 152 at note 5 (CCPA, 1976) the Court of Customs and Patent Appeals had to take pains to explain to the PTO that algorithms were, in fact, a step-by-step process and not necessarily a bad thing in a patent.
3. From *Diamond* v. *Diehr,* 450 U.S. 175 (1981). This decision is widely available on the Internet. The opinions are well written and make lively reading. Stevens's dissent is a particularly useful summary of software patent activity up to the time of this case and does a good job of articulating many of the same issues that concern people who are uncomfortable with current trends in Internet business method patents.
4. Ibid.
5. Ibid.

# CHAPTER 9

# Claiming More: Business Method Patents

STATE Street Bank and Trust is a very large financial services company that specializes in serving institutional investors, such as mutual fund companies. In 1998 State Street was handling about 44 percent of the total value in the U.S. mutual fund market.[1] It is the 800-pound gorilla in the market for management services for mutual funds, with over $700 billion in assets under management as of mid-2000.

One of the services that State Street provides to mutual fund companies is the ability to pool investments with other funds within a partnership. This gives State Street's mutual fund clients the advantages of scale that come with the ability to make large investments. At the same time the pooling, which is treated as a partnership for tax purposes, provides an attractive tax structure. But managing the pooled investments requires a significant amount of bookkeeping. Doing the books right, crediting all the funds with gains and losses as individual investors move in and out of the funds and as the values of investments rise and fall, is a requirement of the business.

In the early 1990s Signature Financial Group was a very small competitor to State Street in the mutual fund management market. Signature trademarked the term "Hub and Spoke" to describe the kind of mutual fund investment arrangements that they and State Street offered. Signature developed an attack on State Street's dominant market position that was built around a software system for doing the accounting within the pooled funds. The company filed a patent application titled "Data processing system for hub and spoke financial services configuration," claiming the data processing system for managing such Hub and Spoke services as an invention. Patent number 5,193,056 (the '056 patent) was granted in March 1993. The claims made in the patent were broad—so broad that Signature later admitted in court testimony that "any data processing system designed to perform book accounting for a multi-tiered fund arranged in a Hub and Spoke configuration likely would infringe the '056 Patent."[2]

With $38 billion in mutual fund investments under management and 25 clients,[3] Signature appeared positioned to use its new intellectual property assets to improve its market position.

## An Initial Setback

Signature informed State Street that an accounting system for State Street's pooled investment system would very probably infringe on the '056 patent. In response State Street attempted to negotiate a license to use Signature's patented system, but negotiations broke down. In 1994 State Street decided to take a different path around the problem and filed a suit in the U.S. District Court in Massachusetts that sought a declaratory judgment stating that Signature's patent was invalid and unenforceable. As was true in *Diamond* v. *Diehr* and in *Gottschalk* v. *Benson*, the attack on the patent claimed that the subject matter was not patentable, rather than asserting that the invention was not new or was obvious.

The District Court judge, Patti B. Saris, ruled in favor of State Street in March 1996, deciding that the invention claimed by Signature was not a patentable process. The judge found two problems with the '056 patent. The first was the familiar concern that, as software, the patent described a process that was a purely mathematical algorithm. After all, it was bookkeeping, taking numbers in and putting numbers out.

The second problem that the District Court had with the Signature patent was that it claimed a "business method" as an invention. The idea that business plans and business methods—bookkeeping, for example—are not patentable extended back through a series of cases to 1908 and had emerged in the courts as the "business method exception." Judge Saris's opinion does a good job of summarizing the reasoning behind the business method exception:

> If Signature's invention were patentable, any financial institution desirous of implementing a multi-tiered funding complex modeled on a Hub and Spoke configuration would be required to seek Signature's permission before embarking on such a project. This is so because the '056 Patent is claimed sufficiently broadly to foreclose virtually any computer-implemented accounting method necessary to manage this type of financial structure. . . . In effect, the '056 Patent grants Signature a monopoly on its idea of a multi-tiered partnership portfolio investment structure; patenting an account-

ing system necessary to carry on a certain type of business is tantamount to a patent on the business itself.[4]

Note that the judge is echoing the approach that Justice Douglas took in *Gottschalk* v. *Benson*, mixing the question of patentable subject matter with broader questions of how broad the patent is and how it might impact the market. Like Tim O'Reilly and others looking at Internet business method patents, the judge is examining larger policy issues at the same time she is considering narrower questions of law.

According to contemporary news reports this ruling against Signature was devastating for Signature. It lost two of its larger clients to State Street Bank during the summer that followed the ruling and began looking for financial assistance in the form of a merger in order to keep operating.[5] The company also, however, appealed the District Court ruling.

## Expanding the Scope of Patents

By 1998 the U.S. Court of Appeals for the Federal Circuit reviewed the *State Street* v. *Signature Financial Group* decision and, in late July of that year, reversed the District Court's decision, ruling in favor of Signature Financial Group and its patent.

This decision continued the strong trend toward increased scope for patent coverage that had begun in the early 1980s. Just as important, it made those trends visible and explicit. The reason for the case's impact and subsequent notoriety was not tied so much to the particulars of the *State Street* suit as to the reasoning and viewpoint expressed in the Court's opinion. The ruling elicited commentary that used words such as "seismic"[6] and "madness"[7] and had the effect of making other companies much more aware of the potential for using patents to claim new territory.

In reading through the ruling, one finds that the Federal Circuit Court quickly disposed of the mathematical algorithm objection by declaring that, insofar as the result of the calculations was a final share price, the calculations produced a useful, tangible result. Hence the use of an algorithm in Signature Financial Group's invention was an *application*, and therefore patentable subject matter, rather than pure mathematics. Things had clearly come a long way since *Gottschalk* v. *Benson*. The *State Street* decision effectively put an end to the mathematical algorithm exception that loomed so large back in 1972. As one commentator wrote, "If calculating a share price for a trade is adequately 'tangible' for patentability . . . then all functioning software must pass this 'tangible' test."[8]

The Federal Circuit Court then turned to the second objection raised by the District Court, which was that business methods comprised a special class of subject matter that was not patentable.

> We take this opportunity to lay this ill-conceived exception to rest. Since its inception, the "business method" exception has merely represented the application of some general, but no longer applicable legal principle. . . . Since the 1952 Patent Act, business methods have been, and should have been, subject to the same legal requirements for patentability as applied to any other process or method.[9]

In short, according to *State Street*, business methods are no different than any other kind of process for which one might seek a patent and therefore should receive no special consideration, either for them or against them. In the context of the *State Street* case, this meant that State Street could not challenge Signature's patent on the basis of the subject matter that it addressed. If there were going to be a challenge, it would need to be on other grounds, such as that it was not really new or that it was an obvious extension of existing art.

State Street Bank sought review of the Federal Circuit Court's decision before the U.S. Supreme Court, but in January 1999 the Supreme Court declined to review the case. The decision by the Federal Circuit Court stands as written.

## The Impact of *State Street*

The timing was right for the *State Street* decision and contributed to its impact. The case was decided on July 23, 1998. The e-commerce boom on the Internet was just then beginning. *Business Week*, for example, had just published an annual report on information technology, titled "Doing Business in the Internet Age," intended to introduce businesspeople to key e-business issues. It contained articles with titles like "The New Supply Chain" and "You Ain't Seen Nothing Yet." Stock prices provide other evidence that the *State Street* decision occurred at the very start of the e-commerce boom. Adjusted for subsequent splits, Amazon and Yahoo were both trading in the low 20s on the day of the *State Street* decision. Investors buying these stocks on the day of the decision would be able to realize 500 percent gains over the next nine months.

Just as important, patents directly related to e-commerce had been filed in the months and years preceding the *State Street* decision, and these patents began reaching the end of the review process and attracting notice in the business press. For example, on August 11, 1998, Cybergold received a patent for a system for paying people to look at ads on the Internet. On that same day Priceline received its patent for a method of using reverse auctions on the Internet. In September 1999 Amazon received its 1-Click patent.

The application for each of these patents was made before the *State Street* decision, but their appearance along with other, similar patents in the year following *State Street* communicated the clear message that the PTO was now issuing patents that covered methods of doing business on the Internet. The *State Street* decision brought these trends together and articulated the clear message that you can now receive patent protection for a business method and, effectively, for a position in a market.

## Subject Matter and Breadth

There is one more aspect of the *State Street* decision that is worth a closer look before setting the case aside and moving on.

One of the noteworthy things about Internet patents is that they can effectively turn a segment of the market into one company's property. Companies building business strategies around Internet patents view this as an important feature of these patents. They answer complaints about "fencing in" the Web by pointing out that the creation of fences is what patents are supposed to do. When, for example, Eli Lilly patented the antidepressant drug Prozac it built a fence around a big segment of the market for antidepressant medications. That is precisely what was intended.

Opponents of Internet business method patents might reply by arguing that, on the Internet, the fences encircle even broader domains. Prozac is one antidepressant in a market that contains a number of such drugs. The patent on Prozac, though tremendously valuable, does not lock other companies out of the market. But a patent on a *business method*, as opposed to a technology or a formulation of a drug, can do just that.

This was the problem that bothered the District Court judge in the *State Street* case. She wrote that "patenting an accounting system necessary to carry on a certain type of business is tantamount to a patent on the business itself." As noted above, she was mixing the narrow question of patentability with broader questions about the public good, but her motive for doing so was the same as the motives of many who object to Internet business method patents today: the claims look so broad as to be dangerous to the health of the market. And she could point to no less an authority than Justice William O. Douglas as a precedent for importing such policy concerns into a legal deliberation.

The Federal Circuit Court, however, wasn't buying any of that. In a few terse sentences the Circuit Court informed the District Court judge that she was making an elementary mistake and was guilty of offering opinions that were irrelevant to the case at hand:

questions about whether claims are too broad have nothing at all to do with whether subject matter is patentable. Reading the Circuit Court opinion is reminiscent of Lloyd Bentsen's famous response to Dan Quayle in the 1988 vice presidential debates, but would be paraphrased in this case as "Judge, you're no William O. Douglas."

Apart from the judicial one-upmanship, the Federal Circuit Court is saying a couple of important things here.

- As in other cases, the court prefers to deal with questions in narrow, precise terms. The courts are the wrong place to consider broad questions such as whether business method patents, in general, are a good or bad thing. If you are concerned about such issues, write your congressperson.
- It is possible to attack the breadth of a particular patent application, but you cannot do so by attacking the patentability of the invention's subject matter. Instead, you need to show that the breadth results in conflicts with prior art or results in an invention that is obvious. One must deal with the specifics of the individual patent rather than with questions about what kind of patent it is.

This is a frustrating verdict for people who feel that business method patents are threatening the very nature of Internet business. Once again, we are faced with a difference in breadth of viewpoint. To the people who see the new patent policies as an imminent, dangerous threat to innovation on the Web, it must seem as if the courts are myopically following detailed precedent to detailed precedent without any sense that they are heading off the edge of a cliff. To those who are trying to maintain the current system or build businesses based on Internet patent claims, it must seem that the opponents of Internet patents want to substitute their own rules and prejudices for an orderly, careful, and deliberate process that has been unfolding in the same general direction for twenty years.

## State Street in a Nutshell

The Federal Circuit Court was sending a number of strong messages in the *State Street* decision that are very important both for companies that want to defend their Internet business method patents and for those who would attack such patents.

- The days of being able to attack an Internet or software patent on the basis of the patentability of the subject matter are over. If you decide to pursue such an attack, be sure that the inventor really is claiming rights to gravity or $E = mc^2$.

Otherwise, understand that software and business methods have now been determined to be patentable subject matter. Case closed.

- If you think that an invention does not deserve a patent, then in most cases you should be able to show that the invention is not new and is already in use or that it is an obvious extension of prior art. If you are coming from the other side and want a strong patent, make sure that you are not vulnerable in terms of prior art.
- Do not waste your time or the court's time attacking the invention because you think it is bad for the industry. The courts should not deal with such questions.
- Patenting a business method that is central to the operation of a particular line of business or marketplace can be an excellent way to establish and defend a position in that market.

This last point was not lost on the other companies, like Amazon, Priceline, DoubleClick, Cybergold, and many others that had patents in the works in the second half of 1998. The *State Street* decision signaled to the PTO that such patents should not be rejected on the basis of subject matter and sent the message to the assignees that, once the patents were granted, there was a good chance of being able to use them aggressively to claim and defend Internet market decisions. As we have seen, that is just what they did.

The Federal Circuit Court's clear statement in *State Street* that it was not going to become involved in broader questions of policy does not, of course, mean that such questions are not important. Concerns that business method patents are damaging the Web as an environment that nurtures experimentation, rapid exchange of information, and adaptation of and improvement upon freely circulated ideas are very serious matters. All Internet businesses will be affected, for better or for worse, by the trend toward more aggressive patent use that the *State Street* decision represents. The question of whether the outcomes will be good or bad is, in the long run, much more important than questions of novelty and obviousness for any particular patent. These broader questions are the focus of the next chapter.

## Notes

1. From William T. Ellis and Aaron C. Chatterjee, "Shakeout on State Street," *IP Magazine*, November 1998. Accessed on the Web at http://www.ipmag.com/98-nov/ellis.html in November 2000.

2. From *State Street Bank & Trust Co.* v. *Signature Financial Group, Inc.*, 927 F. Supp. 502, 38 USPQ2d 1530 (D. Mass. 1996).
3. From Beth Healy, "On State Street: Signature Financial in Tough Times," *The Boston Herald*, August 15, 1996.
4. From *State Street Bank & Trust Co.* v. *Signature Financial Group, Inc.* (cited above).
5. From Healy (cited above).
6. From Ellis and Chatterjee (cited above).
7. From Brenda Sandburg, "Madness in PTO's E-Commerce Method?" *IP Magazine*, August 27, 1998. Accessed on the Web at http://www.ipmag.com/dailies/980827.html in November 2000.
8. From Stephen C. Glazier, *e-Patent Strategies for Software, e-Commerce, the Internet, Telecom Services, Financial Services, and Business Methods*, LBI Institute, 2000, p. 31.
9. From *State Street Bank & Trust Co.* v. *Signature Financial Group, Inc.*, 149 F.3d 1368, 1374-75, 47 USPQ2D (BNA) 1596, 1602 (Fed. Cir. 1998).

CHAPTER 10

# Predicting the Impact of Internet Patents

PAMELA Samuelson, MacArthur fellow and professor of law at the University of California at Berkeley, has focused her career on the issues surrounding intellectual property, software, and the Internet. She suggests that "We'll find out over the next decade or so whether or not patenting software really does promote innovation."[1] In her view the possibilities are too numerous to permit firm conclusions today about whether the ability to patent software and business methods will help or hinder overall technical and economic progress.

But it would be nice to get at least some hints, to sketch out the likely alternatives. Particularly in the area of Internet business methods, where the field is still young and the use of patents is still taking shape, it would be nice to know more about the likely high-level impacts of providing stronger, broader patent protection. Ten years from now, when the effects will be more evident, we will also have put in place a substantial legal and financial infrastructure around Internet patents that will be resistant to change. If we want to shape the interaction of patent law and Internet business, now would be the time to begin.

But Professor Samuelson is right to be cautious. As we have seen in the preceding chapters, the issues are complex and the viewpoints are different in kind, not just in degree. Fortunately, the very strength of these differences actually gives us a way to sketch out a few of the broad scenarios for how the current trends in patent law might affect Internet business development. This kind of sketching exercise is valuable because it can help clarify the thinking behind the different viewpoints and can ultimately aid in thinking more clearly about patent strategy and patent policy.

I begin by looking at a market that developed without patent protection. This is an exercise in hindsight, in "What if?" The idea is to use what is known about the way this market actually did develop to consider what might have happened if it were developing today, given today's changed patent environment.

## A Market without Patent Protection

In the spring of 1978 Dan Bricklin was sitting in room 108 of Aldrich Hall on the Harvard campus, working on his MBA. But he was thinking about other things. The paper and blackboard spreadsheets that he was using in business school were difficult to construct and difficult to change. So Bricklin daydreamed about a heads-up display, like in a fighter plane, tied to a calculator that was also a pointing device. He daydreamed about "flying" around the virtual spreadsheet, punching in numbers and automatically generating results.[2]

Bricklin brought his daydream down to earth. After all, he really did have to work with spreadsheets, even if the heads-up display was out of the question. Over the course of a weekend, Bricklin created a prototype of an electronic spreadsheet program, written in Apple Basic and running on an Apple II. He decided that he had something interesting.

He teamed up with a friend, Bob Frankston, who could help him create a production version of the spreadsheet. He then got together with Dan Flystra, who owned a software publishing company called Personal Software. In early January 1979 Bricklin and Frankston incorporated a company called Software Arts and began work in earnest on the product, with Frankston doing most of the coding in an attic apartment in Arlington, Massachusetts. The product name, VisiCalc, was coined during a meeting at a Cambridge eatery, and in May 1979 the first advertisement for the product appeared in the back pages of *Byte* magazine (early vaporware).

Over the summer Bricklin and Frankston showed VisiCalc at a number of computer shows and conferences. By July it had attracted the attention of Ben Rosen, then of Morgan Stanley, who wrote, "So who knows? VisiCalc could someday become the software tail that wags (and sells) the personal computer dog."[3]

Rosen's prediction turned out to be true. VisiCalc was the first application that allowed nonprogrammers to develop business applications on a PC. Sales started off slowly because the application was new and many buyers didn't understand what it could do. But once people familiar with paper spreadsheets began using the product, sales took off. VisiCalc sold more than 700,000 copies over its product lifetime. In 1981 the Association for Computing Machinery recognized Bricklin's innovative contribution to computing by presenting him with the Grace Murray Hopper award, its prize for the outstanding young computer professional of the year.

Also during 1981, the IBM PC first appeared, accelerating the growth of the PC industry and taking it in new directions. VisiCalc was ported to the PC, but by then it had a lot of competitors. The April 1982 issue of *Personal Computing* magazine listed 18 spreadsheet products. The most expensive product in the list was Context M.B.A., which combined the spreadsheet with graphic displays, word processing, and other features.[4] The integration of features in Context M.B.A. was interesting, but the product was slow.

In 1983 yet another competitor appeared in the form of Lotus 1-2-3. This product took the Context M.B.A. idea of integrating spreadsheets with graphics and data manipulation and really made it work. Lotus 1-2-3 was fast since it was written in assembler and bypassed the DOS operating system for critical functions, writing directly to the screen to display results. Perhaps equally important, Lotus launched the product with a multimillion-dollar rollout, spending about four times as much to launch the product as to develop it.[5] Lotus 1-2-3 quickly became the leading application on the IBM PC during its early years, and the IBM PC became the leading personal computer platform. In 1985 VisiCorp, the renamed company that had started out as Personal Software and that published VisiCalc, filed for bankruptcy. Bricklin and Frankston sold Software Arts and the VisiCalc product to their competitor, Lotus Development. Lotus stopped selling and supporting the old product. VisiCalc, the first "killer app," was dead.

This is not the kind of story that encourages would-be inventors. The inventors of the spreadsheet had a good ride for a few years but then were displaced by a firm that was better at marketing and better at business execution. It looks like the kind of situation where patents might have made a difference.

### What If?

The great new benefit enabled by Bricklin's electronic spreadsheet invention was the ability to ask "What if?" It is a question we can apply to this case. We already know, from our earlier survey of key Supreme Court cases, that Bricklin and Frankston had an extremely remote chance of getting a patent on their electronic spreadsheet invention back in 1979.[6] It is also clear that, if they had invented the electronic spreadsheet today, it's very probable they would be able to patent key parts of the application and perhaps even the entire invention. What if the changes to patent law had come earlier, and what if Bricklin and Frankston had patented the electronic spreadsheet in 1979?

What would have happened differently? It seems clear that the outcome would have been better for Bricklin and Frankston, but what about the rest of us? Would society at large have benefited? Would the software industry have benefited?

### The Argument against Patenting

Perhaps the most compelling argument against increased use of patents is that they interfere with the market's ability to do its work. Lotus 1-2-3 was outselling VisiCalc by October 1983, less than a year after its initial release. VisiCalc was trying to support too many platforms, was therefore slow in responding to market threats, and was offering a product that ran more slowly on the IBM PC. According to contemporary reviews in computer magazines, Lotus 1-2-3 was a clearly superior product. The market responded rapidly, and Lotus 1-2-3 reaped the rewards of dominant market share.[7]

Market evolution didn't stop there. In 1985 Microsoft, writing for the Macintosh platform, used the Mac's windowed graphical user interface (GUI) environment to approach electronic spreadsheets in a new way. The new product was Excel, which was first available only on the Mac. In 1987 Microsoft ported Excel to the new Windows environment. Adoption was slow at first because Windows required more hardware than most users had available, but from early on, reviewers understood that the GUI environment offered new possibilities and capabilities. As early as 1987 many reviewers were saying that Excel was a product superior to Lotus 1-2-3. Borland also produced a strong competing product called Quattro Pro, which many reviewers ranked ahead of Lotus 1-2-3 in terms of features and capability.

Because of its large installed base, Lotus continued to enjoy market dominance for awhile. But, like VisiCalc before it, Lotus 1-2-3 was now available in too many versions to allow it to adapt and innovate rapidly. In particular, Lotus was slow to bring out a strong offer for the Windows platform, which was growing in popularity as more powerful hardware became more readily available. By 1992 Excel surpassed Lotus 1-2-3 in market share.

Spreadsheet users benefited enormously from this competition for market share. Product capabilities and ease of use advanced quickly. In addition, the market competition steadily brought the price of spreadsheet programs down. Looking at the average price received by each manufacturer from 1990 on, it is clear that Lotus sold its products less expensively than did Microsoft for most of these years, probably in an attempt to address its declining market share through pricing. The consumer was the big winner. In 1990 the average revenue received by Microsoft and Lotus for each copy of spreadsheet software sold was in excess of $250. By 1997 this figure had dropped to around $50.

The argument against patent protection in such a vibrant market is that it serves no general positive benefit. Yes, Bricklin and Frankston would have come out better, perhaps much better. But broad patent protection for the electronic spreadsheet invention would have given Software Arts and VisiCorp complete control over the use of the invention. Arguably, their ability to use legal means, rather than market competence and product excellence, to protect their market share would have slowed the pace of innovation. Lotus, and later, Microsoft, would have needed to find a way to either license the invention from Software Arts and VisiCorp or would have needed to find a way to invent around the patent. It is almost certain that more time and investment would have been spent in the courts challenging and defending claims, and this activity very probably would have slowed the pace at which new products came to market.

Perhaps most important of all, the patent would very probably have slowed the decline in spreadsheet product cost to the public. Consider, for example, the difference in the price of drugs before and after patent protection ends.

In short, the argument against use of patents for innovations such as the electronic spreadsheet is that the ability to control the market through contract and litigation, rather than through continued innovation and pricing, can result in more expensive, less functional offers to users. This line of argument contends that, in such a case, patent protection would produce greater benefit for a small group—Bricklin, Frankston, Software Arts, and VisiCorp—at the expense of spreadsheet users and of other firms who could better meet the needs of those users.

### The Argument for Patenting

Justice Stevens noted in his dissent in *Diamond* v. *Diehr* that people and companies involved in creating and inventing things can reasonably take a favorable stance toward patents out of self-interest. A patented intellectual asset is generally worth much more than one that is not patented. If you are a software innovator like Software Arts and VisiCorp, you may want patent protection because it helps you defend the markets that you create and increases your company's value.

On the other hand, if you are an innovator like Lotus—a company that can take an idea and improve on it and bring it to market more effectively—you may be less interested in patents. Unless, of course, you can own the patent. Lotus did, after all, eventually buy Software Arts and the rights to the VisiCalc software product. If Software Arts had had a patent for the electronic spreadsheet invention, Lotus very probably would have acquired that, too. Lotus would have paid more for Software Arts and its intellectual property (IP), but that would have been fine, since the IP would have also been worth more. Perhaps Lotus could have used it to fend off the competitive assault from Excel.

As Justice Stevens suggested, such arguments from self-interest are not broadly compelling. Obtaining a limited monopoly over use of an invention is of course appealing to those who could own that monopoly. But such a line of reasoning avoids the large and important question of whether the market and the overall software industry benefit as a whole, over time. From a policy standpoint and even from a long-term business standpoint, the question about broader benefits is the more interesting one.

The general argument in favor of patents follows directly from the language of the Constitution: we need to give inventors a limited monopoly over their inventions "to promote the progress of science and useful arts." In other words, without the ability to benefit from an invention, inventors will be less likely to invent, and we will all be poorer and make less progress as a consequence.

Someone arguing against patent protection for software would say that it is difficult to see how the absence of patents stood in the way of progress in the useful art of spreadsheet design. Software Arts, VisiCorp, Lotus, Microsoft, and the investors behind each of these companies were apparently quite willing to continue research, continue investment, and take risks without patent protection. But this argument misses the point. VisiCalc had already demonstrated that the electronic spreadsheet was a "killer app" and a highly profitable market segment. Once Software Arts and VisiCorp had made the initial investment and taken the initial risk to prove the market, of course everyone else wanted in.

The point of patents is that they encourage the initial investment and risk taking required to establish a new market in the first place. The VisiCalc example makes a compelling demonstration of how the people who make the early investments and take the initial risks often do not enjoy the rewards when there is no patent protection in place. Now let's look at an example where, with patent protection, the initial inventors were able to continue to pursue the market created by their invention.

## A Market with Patent Protection

In 1989 Douglas Whiting, Glen George, and Glen Ivey of Stac Electronics applied for a patent for a "Data compression apparatus and method." On May 14, 1991, the PTO granted patent number 5,016,009 for the invention, with rights assigned to Stac Electronics. The PTO's willingness to patent software had clearly come a long way in the decade since 1979, when the electronic spreadsheet was invented. The "apparatus" in the Stac patent application consists solely of hash tables, lookup tables, pointers, and other elements of a software algorithm.

The important qualities of the data compression algorithm described in the Stac patent were that it could achieve good compression on a wide variety of input data without a lot of computational overhead. This made Stac's compression scheme ideally suited for real-time use in tape backup applications, which was the initial focus of Stac's business.

Stac soon discovered that there were applications of the patent that were more lucrative than tape backup. In 1990 Microsoft announced Windows 3.0, the first version of Windows to gain serious market acceptance. Windows, and applications running on Windows such as Microsoft Word and Excel, took up more disk space than had the previous generation of software tools. The problems faced by computer users were compounded by the fact that the magnetic storage industry had not yet caught up with the need for high-capacity, low-cost disks. So Stac introduced Stacker, a utility that could run on the DOS operating system (which was the foundation for Microsoft Windows), compressing files as they were stored on the disk and decompressing them as they were called up for use.

Stacker was a very successful product, emerging as the leading compression utility for DOS and winning *PC Magazine*'s Technical Excellence Award, *Windows Magazine*'s WIN 100 Award, *PC Magazine*'s Editor's Choice Award, and *PC Computing*'s Most Valuable Product Award, to name just a few of Stacker's many awards for excellence and usefulness.[8] The effect on Stac's revenues was as impressive as the industry awards: Stac grew from revenues of less than $1 million in 1989, when the patent application was filed, to over $33 million in 1992, with a net income of more than $8 million.[9] Stac's stock reached a price of over $60 a share in 1992. Stac appeared to be a software company on its way to bigger things.

## A Potential Deal with Microsoft

Stac's success in solving an important problem for Microsoft's DOS operating system naturally attracted Microsoft's attention. In 1991 Microsoft began shipping DOS 5.0 and partnered with Stac and other companies to provide the market with both the basic operating system and with utilities to do things like compress files, check for viruses, and repair disk errors. Once DOS 5.0 was shipping, Microsoft began thinking about the next version. It decided that DOS 6.0 should include many of these support functions as built-in capabilities of the operating system.

According to the complaint that Stac later filed in court, Bill Gates met with Stac's president at the Fall Comdex show in 1991 and said that Microsoft was thinking about including data compression in the next version of DOS and that Microsoft did not intend to build that capability internally. Subsequent to the conversation with Gates, Brad Chase, who eventually became Microsoft's general manager for MS-DOS, began discussions with Stac about licensing the Stac compression technology.

### The Deal Goes Sour

From Stac's point of view, the problem was that Microsoft wanted a fully paid-up, flat-fee, worldwide, perpetual license for the technology rather than a license that continued to pay Stac royalties over time. Further, Microsoft made it clear that if the company could not acquire the technology from Stac, Microsoft would find it elsewhere. Stac representatives reminded Microsoft that Stac had a patent on its approach to compression and that they would defend that patent.

Brushing aside the concerns about patent infringement, Microsoft stressed that the inclusion of any competing compression technology in the next version of MS-DOS would undercut Stacker's viability as an independently marketed product. Microsoft even produced spreadsheets to show Stac how bad things would be. Stac broke off negotiations in April 1992. In June Microsoft informed Stac that Microsoft had, indeed, acquired compression technology from another source.

In November 1992 Brad Chase contacted Stac once again because Microsoft had determined that its new MS-DOS 6.0 compression utility, DoubleSpace, would infringe on Stac's patent. Chase wanted a license for use of the patented technology. Stac invited Microsoft to make an offer.

It turned out that no offer was forthcoming. In early January 1993 Stac received a beta version of MS-DOS 6.0 along with a note from Chase advising Stac, "Don't worry about the patent stuff. We are just going to keep with our changed code which does not infringe." But Stac engineers working with the beta release determined that, changed code or not, Microsoft's DoubleSpace feature was using Stac's patented technology. Stac took Microsoft to court later that month. On March 30, 1993, Microsoft began shipping MS-DOS 6.0, including the disputed DoubleSpace feature.

### The Patent Works

The interesting thing about the *Stac* v. *Microsoft* case, from an intellectual property perspective, is that the patent protection made the difference for Stac. Stac's lawsuit alleged patent infringement, copyright infringement, and trade secret violation. The judge ruled against Stac on both the trade secret and copyright allegations. It turned out that Microsoft, like most companies with strong internal policies on IP, was able to make sure that it was not violating copyright or trade secrecy laws. But they were not able to use parts of Stac's "Data compression apparatus and method" without infringing on the patent.[10]

On June 8, 1993, the District Court in California ordered Microsoft to stop shipping products that included the infringing DoubleSpace feature. This forced Microsoft to produce a version 6.21 of MS-DOS that switched the DoubleSpace feature off and contained a sticker on the package telling users to disregard all references to the DoubleSpace feature in the documentation.

On June 13 the court awarded Stac $120 million in damages for Microsoft's infringement.

On June 21 Microsoft and Stac reached a cross-licensing agreement in which Microsoft paid Stac $1 million dollars a month for a license to use the patented Stac technology in the Microsoft DoubleSpace product. The agreement stipulated that the license payments would continue for 43 months, until December 1997. In addition, Microsoft agreed to make a $39.9 million investment in Stac.[11]

### Financial Outcome, Thanks to the Patent

Had Stac not patented its compression algorithm, it seems very likely that it would have experienced a rapid falling off in product revenues, just as Microsoft predicted. Microsoft's inclusion of DoubleSpace within the MS-DOS product, coupled with the rapidly increasing size and decreasing cost of disk storage, effectively killed the market for disk compression software. Stac discontinued development work on the Stacker product in early 1996 and stopped sales of the product on September 1, 1997.[12]

Fortunately for Stac, it had $16 million a year in patent-licensing revenues from Microsoft and IBM. This didn't make the company rich, but it did give Stac time to diversify its product line through acquisition of other companies and through continued internal research. It developed a line of hardware-based compression and security devices and spun this hardware subsidiary off in late 1998 to create a new company called Hi/fn. As of mid-2000 Hi/fn was profitable and had revenues in the range of $45 million annually. The software side of Stac was also still operating into the year 2000, renaming itself as Previo and addressing the market for networked support systems for end-user devices.

VisiCalc, on the other hand, was dead after six years. The advantages of patent protection for the pioneering companies in new markets seem clear. Patents can provide real protection for early market developers from others who come into the market once the pioneers have paved the way.

## Pros and Cons: Patent Policy

These stories help bring the arguments for and against Internet business method patents into sharp focus. The people arguing against patent protection contend that patents distort and impede the action of the marketplace. Sure, it would have been nice if the inventors of the spreadsheet could have turned out to be the market leaders, but they failed to keep pace with new features and new performance demands. They made the common mistake of focusing too much development investment on marginal platforms, and they paid the price. Interfering with market action by giving the inventors a monopoly would have resulted in less functional, slower spreadsheet products that would have cost more and, consequently, been less broadly available to the public.

The people arguing in favor of increased patent protection contend that the market, unassisted by patents, tends to undervalue innovation. Naive market models assume the information flows efficiently and uniformly to buyers; in short, the model builders look at the market once it is up and running. Creating such an information flow, so that there is a well-functioning market, is precisely the problem that innovators must surmount. Without patent protection, well-established companies can wait until an innovator has identified and established a market and then move in to dominate the market before the innovators can realize a return on their investment. This is like eating your own seed corn rather than preserving it so that you can plant new crops again. As the *Stac* v. *Microsoft* case shows, patents don't prevent technologies from getting broad distribution at low cost; they simply even up the sides in a negotiation so that the innovator can get a fair shake.

Each of these arguments says something true about innovation in the Internet marketplace. The trends in patent law at the start of the twenty-first century favor the second argument over the first. The PTO is increasingly willing to grant patents for software applications and Internet business applications, and the courts seem increasingly willing to respect and defend those patents. Returning to Professor Samuelson's observation at the start of this chapter, we will really understand whether this was the right course only in hindsight, ten years or so down the road.

I have sketched the competing viewpoints in this dispute over the value of software and Web business method patents in stark, black-and-white terms. My intent has been to make it easier to see that each viewpoint has merit. I also want to help you see that patents and patent policy really will have an impact on the "nature" of the business environment surrounding the Internet. As in the Napster dispute over the relative merits of protecting copyrights and opening up new distribution channels, businesspeople need to get above the details of the dispute to see the bigger issues and opportunities that are at stake.

Developing an effective approach to patents that works for your business requires that you have a number of things. First, you need a broad sense of what is at stake. This chapter and the ones that precede it provide you with that big picture. You also need the following:

- The outline of an approach to making use of patent policy as it exists today
- An overview of what Congress has done with regard to patent policy and what it is likely to do in the next year or two
- An idea of how all the pieces—the courts, the PTO, Congress, and business interests—fit together to determine the shape of patent policy over the next few years

The next three chapters address these requirements, one at a time.

## Notes

1. As quoted by Beth Lipton Krigel in "Floodgates Open for Patent Cases," *CNET News.Com*, August 28, 1998. Accessed on the Web at http://news.cnet.com/news//0-1005-200-332689.html?tag=st.cn.sr.ne.1 on August 8, 2000.
2. Dan Bricklin's Web site at http://www.bricklin.com/ provides an entertaining history, complete with photos, of the early days of VisiCalc.
3. From Ben Rosen, *Morgan Stanley Electronics Letter*, July 11, 1979. Accessed in November 2000 at http://www.bricklin.com/.
4. From Stanley J. Liebowitz and Stephen E. Margolis, *Winners, Losers & Microsoft: Competition and Antitrust in High Technology* (Oakland, CA: Independent Institute, 1999).
5. From W. E. Pete Peterson's *Almost Perfect*, chapter 4. Accessed on the Web at http://www.fitnesoft.com/AlmostPerfect/ap_chap04.html in November 2000.
6. Dan Bricklin has found that people routinely ask him why he didn't patent the electronic spreadsheet. Personal Software (later VisiCorp) actually retained a patent attorney to meet with the teams from Personal Software and Software Arts and to advise them with regard to patenting the electronic spreadsheet invention that was the basis for VisiCalc. The counsel retained by Personal Software suggested that there was a less than 10 percent chance that Bricklin and Frankston could get a patent for the electronic spreadsheet invention. The inventors decided to try to protect themselves, instead, through copyright and trade secrecy. Bricklin has written a short essay describing his experiences and his current thinking on patents. It is available on his Web site at http://www.bricklin.com/patenting.htm.

7. Margolis and Liebowitz include a detailed and fascinating account of the development of the spreadsheet market in *Winners, Losers & Microsoft* (cited above). The portrayal of the spreadsheet market used in constructing my argument here is taken from their research.
8. Information in this section and data about Stac's market position are taken from Stac Electronics' patent infringement complaint against Microsoft Corporation filed in the United States District Court, Central District of California, on January 25, 1993. Accessed on May 15, 2001, at http://www.vaxxine.com/lawyers/articles/stac.html.
9. From Stac, Inc.'s 10K report filed with the Securities and Exchange Commission on December 23, 1996. Accessed in May 2001 at http://www.sec.gov/Archives/edgar/data/1003513/0000936392-96-001225.txt.
10. From Stephen C. Glazier, *e-Patent Strategies for Software, e-Commerce, the Internet, Telecom Services, Financial Services, and Business Methods* (Washington, DC: LBI Institute, 2000), pp. 6–9.
11. "The Tale of MS-DOS 6," which appeared in August 1994 in *ITSC PC News* VIII(2) (published by The Chinese University of Hong Kong), is an interesting and useful contemporary account of the case and its effect on customers. Accessed in November 2000 at http://www.cuhk.edu.hk/itsc/publications/pcnews/vol8n2/dos6.htm.
12. Information about Stacker is from the Stacker product support page on the Stac Web site, accessed in November 2000 at http://support.stac.com/policies/Stacker/default.shtm.

CHAPTER 11

# The Business of Inventing

DAN Tedesco noticed two things while standing in front of the vending machine down the hall from his desk. First, the machine was once again sold out of Snickers bars and, once again, still held a stack of Mounds bars. Second—and this was the thing that bothered him—Snickers bars and Mounds bars both sold for the same price. On this particular day this seemed particularly wrong.

Incongruity is the mother of invention. Dan Tedesco is an expert in something called "revenue management." He works at Walker Digital, the parent company that created and spun off Priceline, the reverse auction company. Priceline's original focus had been on selling seats on airplanes that would have otherwise stayed empty. Prospective travelers offer to buy seats between, say, Chicago and Phoenix at some price that they are willing to pay. Then the airlines flying between Chicago and Phoenix survey the offers from different buyers and decide whether they have seats that look like they will otherwise go unfilled and whether the offers look attractive. If it looks like accepting an offer will produce some additional revenue (the plane is flying in any case, with or without customers in seats), the airline sells a seat at the offered price. Consumers think of Priceline as a way to fly on the cheap. But airlines think of Priceline as one component in their broader programs for revenue management. Tedesco knew all about those programs.

Why couldn't you use revenue management to make vending machines more profitable? Why should candy bars, chips, and the other products in vending machines always sell for fixed prices rather than in response to the preferences of the local market that the vending machine serves? Many new vending machines have microprocessors;

why not use the machines as point-of-sale devices in an overall revenue management system? Tedesco went back to his office with a candy bar that he didn't really want and began thinking about these questions.

Tedesco works in an environment that takes such questions very seriously. His business card says that his title is "Inventor." Walker Digital has developed a set of procedures to help inventors determine whether questions such as Tedesco's have answers that might lead to useful inventions.[1]

The first step in the Walker Digital process involves making a quick determination as to whether the inventor really has a new idea. Have other people been thinking, talking, or writing about applying revenue management to vending machines? If so, even if it is a great idea, it may be difficult to protect. Walker Digital is not interested in business ideas that are just going to be copied as soon as they are introduced. Instead, Walker is interested in inventions that are unique enough to receive patent protection.

In the course of assessing the "protectability" of his potential invention, Tedesco surveyed the structure and the state of technology in the vending machine industry. His objective was to determine, first, whether the idea looked viable from the 35,000-foot level. For example, if he had found that digitally controlled vending machines were having a hard time finding acceptance and that the industry was moving back to mechanical machines, that would have been a cause for concern (and perhaps an indicator that there was another potential invention lurking in the background).

What Tedesco found was reassuring. Microprocessors were being used in increasing numbers of vending machines, but the focus was on bringing down costs, on performing basic accounting, and in some cases on enabling purchases against a debit card rather than requiring change. In other words, the vending machine industry was still thinking of the machine's function in the same way that it had for the last fifty years, as a dispensing and collection device. Nobody was thinking in terms of the machine as a point-of-sale device within an inventory and revenue management system. So, Tedesco's insight might really be a new one, which is to say a protectable one.

Having established that the potential invention was worth a closer look, Tedesco's next step was to arrange a "knockout" search. At Walker Digital the small group of inventors is complemented by a small group of top-notch patent attorneys. Since the potential value of an invention depends both on its solving a business problem and its being protectable, attorneys and inventors work together as a team from the outset. At Walker there is no throwing an invention over the wall to "legal" to start the patent process; the legal and business objectives are pursued in parallel. The purpose of the knockout search, which involves an average of 10 hours of patent and literature searching, is to uncover any prior art that might weaken or constrain the invention's patentability and value.

Dan Tedesco's vending machine idea made it through the knockout search without a hitch. That meant it was potentially valuable enough to bring before the entire group of inventors at Walker for consideration, brainstorming, and critiquing. The working group of inventors, led by founder Jay Walker, is small, numbering between a half dozen and a dozen people. The size varies as inventors move from the working group out to individual projects and back and as the group looks at different technologies and businesses.

The inventors are generalists who have acquired lots of specific knowledge over time. They proceed by asking questions. Why hasn't revenue management been thought of before in the vending machine industry? How is ownership and control of vending machines distributed: who would make the buying decisions? How would the cost of the management compare with the expected revenues?

The objective is not to answer all the questions but instead to ensure that there are no immediately negative answers—no slapping of a palm against the middle of a forehead. The questions, of course, also push and extend the inventor's thinking. If the questions raise only interesting possibilities, and if the impact and value of the invention looks large enough, the group authorizes further investment in developing and patenting the invention. Everybody at Walker Digital, attorneys and inventors alike, has an equity stake in the outcome; everybody wants to develop a portfolio of inventions that builds value, and nobody wants to waste time on marginal inventions.

Tedesco received authorization to proceed with developing his potential invention. This meant weeks of intense research and work to define the scope of the invention, develop and describe an implementation, and evaluate the business case behind the invention's use. The research required analyzing the structure of the vending machine industry and understanding current revenue flows and bottlenecks. The analysis looked both for horizontal applications across the different industry segments and for rich, vertical starting points. Tedesco looked beyond U.S. practice to understand how the vending business works in Japan and other countries where vending applications are radically different than they are in the United States. He focused on understanding how the patent would become an opportunity for Walker Digital to make money.

The research took about a month. Tedesco had been working with the patent attorneys assigned to the team from the outset; now it was time to develop the disclosure statement that would be used as the foundation for the patent. The research team had been continuing its search for prior art and for possible evidence that the invention might be obvious. At Walker Digital the average amount of time invested in patent and literature research for a patent application is 26 hours, in addition to the time spent on the knockout search. Outside of Walker the average amount of time spent searching for prior art related to an invention is more like 8 hours. The investment that Walker makes in its research is a reflection of its focus on protectability. Walker intends to make money by enjoying a protected monopoly on important ideas. It wants its monopoly position to be a sure thing.

Walker Digital constructs its invention process around the fact that the U.S. patent system grants patent rights to the person who is the "first to invent" something, rather than first to file a complete patent application. This means that Walker moves quickly once it has an interesting idea. It also means that Walker is careful to document each step of the process, starting with the initial idea and going forward. All documents are notarized. If it looks like it will take more than a few weeks to define the claims that will be made in the patent and to reduce the invention to practice, Walker will sometimes file a provisional application, which requires only a description of the invention but does not require claims. The purpose of the provisional application is to establish an early filing date to support the other evidence that a Walker Digital inventor was, in fact, the first to invent.

In the case of Tedesco's vending machine invention, the Walker team was able to prepare an initial patent application after several months of work. But filing the application, complete with claims, was in no way an end point. Walker Digital is a business methods laboratory. The company's value is tied to the value of its inventions. That value is determined, in part, by ensuring that inventions can be protected. Protectability is what drives the company's focus on rapid development of inventions and of patent applications. But the other key determinant of an invention's value is its scope and its ability to either increase a business's revenues or decrease costs. Walker Digital wants inventions that are not only protectable but that also have a big impact.

It would be very unusual to have developed the maximum scope and impact of a new business method in just a few months. So, after the initial application filing, Tedesco continued to study the vending machine industry. He also began looking hard at the more general issues associated with revenue management in retail sales. He began thinking about ways to sell slow-moving inventory, or inventory that is reaching the end of its shelf life, by changing things other than price. What would happen if, instead of dropping the price, you offered package deals that bundled slow-moving products with ones that were in more demand? In other words, the initial patent application was not an end point but a beginning. Dan Tedesco had a lot more work ahead of him.

## A Business Method Laboratory

Dan Tedesco and the company that he works for, Walker Digital, approach business method patents from a different direction, with different objectives, than Amazon, Signature Financial Group, and most other companies that we have looked at in the preceding chapters. Walker is not selling books or managing funds but is actually focused on inventing new ways to do business. Its inventions center around the way that networks, distributed computing, and encryption create new opportunities to access and use information. Tedesco's vending machine invention is a good example: the key to the invention was the realization that the vending machines with microprocessors (and perhaps with an address on the Internet) have access to information that is not currently being put to productive use.

At Walker Digital the process of invention is not a complement to the primary business; it *is* the business. Success is measured in terms of the company's ability to create inventions that can be spun off into new companies or that can be licensed to other companies and perhaps traded for equity in those companies. Patents are central to the Walker Digital strategy: Walker is counting on receiving a limited monopoly that protects its exclusive right to exploit its inventions.

Monopoly is a familiar game for Jay Walker, the company's founder and driving force.[2] As a student at Cornell University he took on the task of mastering the Parker Brothers game of that name and, within a couple of years, won the world championship. To describe the situation using one of Jay Walker's favorite metaphors, he unraveled the DNA of Monopoly. Naturally, he decided to profit from his research, and so, continuing the metaphor, he published a book that contained the DNA sequencing for Monopoly, titled *1,000 Ways to Win Monopoly Games.* One might have expected Parker Brothers to see such a book as free promotion for the game—a good thing. But instead the company reacted as if Walker really were publishing Monopoly's DNA sequencing and, before the book appeared, sued Walker to stop publication. Walker hired attorneys and fought the suit, arguing that Parker Brothers was attempting to exercise prior restraint against his right to publish freely. He won the case and ended up using the proceeds from the book to pay for his legal expenses.

After graduating from Cornell, Walker started a number of publishing ventures, including a magazine that focused on coupons and other promotions for retail businesses. It seemed that every time he got a new idea, he started a new business. By the early 1990s he had started more than a dozen of them. Some didn't work out, but others, such as the businesses that grew from his idea about ways to automate magazine subscription renewals, made a fair amount of money.

In the early 1990s Walker began reading about encryption and the truly revolutionary invention by Ron Rivest, Adi Shamir, and Leonard Adleman of a way to exchange encrypted information without first exchanging encryption keys. (This is the RSA public key cryptography algorithm, U.S. patent number 4,405,829. I provide an overview of this algorithm and its uses in Part III as part of the description of electronic signatures.) Walker had been thinking about casinos, and it struck him that encryption provided a way to create a hand-held casino that would be immune from cheating and deception. But along with this insight came a problem: his model for making money from his ideas had always been to build a business around them. He wasn't going to open a casino. Besides, it seemed to him that the idea of encryption was so powerful and had the capability of transforming so many businesses—not just casinos—that he felt suddenly overwhelmed by opportunity. He could not possibly start and successfully manage the scores of businesses that corresponded to all the applications that he could see for encryption. Was there some way to ride above the details of all these individual businesses and make money just by developing the ideas? Walker began reading up on patent law. In an interview with *Strategy+Business* published in mid-2000, he described what happened next:

> I hired some lawyers and said, "Let me see if I've got this right. If I invented the credit card and was able to describe it as a 'periodic billing system for transaction charges,' I would have been able to own the credit card?" And the patent lawyers said, "Yeah." I said, "If I invented the frequent-flyer program as a 'rewards points tracking system,' I could have owned any frequent-flyer program?" "Sure, of course," they said.
>
> And I said, "Does it strike any of you as odd that nobody owns those things?" And they said, "Business does that all the time. They invent things and they don't realize they could own them." . . .
>
> So I started raising and investing millions of dollars on the basis that I could invent new solutions that were indeed ownable. If they were useful, they'd be valuable. And if they weren't useful, I would just own something useless. The only question was: Was I going to own land in Montana or own land on Park Avenue. That's about the quality of invention, not the quality of patents. It turns out I can own land on Park Avenue.[3]

In short, when Jay Walker understood that he could patent business methods, he realized that he had found just what he was looking for: a way to own a new business idea, such as the idea to apply revenue management to vending machines, just like he could own a car or land. If he could own enough really critical, valuable patents, it would be just as good, maybe better, than owning a lot of midtown Manhattan. In the past year Walker Digital has applied for around 150 patents, each one a piece of conceptual real estate located somewhere between Montana and Park Avenue.

The most well-known Walker patents are the ones associated with Priceline. In the case of these patents Walker fell back to his old model of starting a business as a way of getting a return from his inventions. Walker describes this as a kind of bootstrap strategy—a way to generate some immediate cash flow while he waits for his other investments in inventions to mature. The intent over the longer run is to demonstrate to established businesses how they could benefit from the inventions. Once Walker Digital sells a company on the value of a new invention, Walker and the partner company can work together to find ways to cooperate and share in the upside. The options range from equity partnerships to simple licensing agreements.

In summary, Walker Digital is playing a long game. It typically takes two to three years to receive a patent, and in most cases Walker Digital will want to wait until the patents are in place before beginning the sales, demonstration, and negotiation process. Full patent protection increases Walker's leverage in negotiations about licensing and ensures that anyone who decides to simply copy the ideas and infringe on Walker's patents will be facing treble damages. It's just like Monopoly: you want to make sure, if possible, that you have hotels built on Boardwalk and Park Place before the other players land on them.

## Inventing from Value and Extending Value

One of the key ideas at Walker Digital—an idea that other companies might usefully emulate (it's not patented)—involves focusing on the value of inventions. There are two parts to this idea. The first has to do with where ideas come from. The second has to do with how the ideas grow and extend.

For many companies the value is centered in the technology. Stac Electronics, discussed in the preceding chapter, is a good example of how this works. Stac invented a nice, fast compression algorithm. Stac's managers are astute businesspeople and so they have been diligent in finding new markets for compression technology, starting with tape backup, extending to real-time disk compression, and most recently moving into network support systems. But the applications have emerged from the technology. It is as if Stac has an answer, and the answer is real-time compression, and the company has spent the last decade looking for questions to which it can apply this answer.

Walker Digital reverses this process. It begins by looking for things that seem broken or wrong. Sold-out candy bars when a vending machine is still full of other brands of candy bars looks wrong. Starting with the business problem, Walker begins its research to find whether a solution to the problem looks protectable, whether good solutions are likely to exist, and whether there is enough value in the solution to provide Walker with property on Park Avenue rather than property in Montana. In short, Walker has identified the value and potential licensees even before it reduces the invention to practice.

Even so, inventions at Walker Digital are not rifle shots; when someone is thinking about a business problem, one thing leads to another. That is what happened with Dan Tedesco. Working with the rest of the Walker team, he filed the patent application for his vending machine invention, titled "Method and apparatus for dynamically managing vending machine inventory prices." But once he began seeing the retail inventory problem in vending machines, he began seeing it everywhere. That is one of the important functions of the brainstorming and inventing sessions at Walker Digital—important business insights often reveal other opportunities to create value.

For example, Tedesco's vending machine work came together with other work on revenue management at Walker Digital to extend the thinking about revenue management from vending machines to fast foods. As Jay Walker describes it, a typical fast food franchise might have profits of around $300K per year. But that same franchise will give millions of dollars in change back to customers. Why? Do the customers want all of those quarters, dimes, and nickels? Walker's bet is that they don't. They'd rather have fries, or maybe a cookie for dessert.

The Walker Digital team saw a convergence of several problems and opportunities. In the simplest case, suppose a customer has 43 cents of change due. If the order did not include fries, the customer might find the offer of a bag of fries that normally sells for 79 cents to be an attractive alternative to receiving the change. If the actual cost of fries to the vendor is only 22 cents, the proposition makes sense for the vendor, too.

Things are more complicated if the restaurant has a policy of discarding fries after they have been on the hot table for more than 20 minutes. If the fries are 18 minutes into their shelf life, it might make sense to the vendor to offer them to a customer in return for change even when the amount of change is only 15 cents. The customer gets a great deal, and the vendor avoids losing the entire value of the product.

The problem with such complicated offers is that the cashier, who is the point of contact with the customer, could not possibly keep track of all the offers and revenue enhancement possibilities without assistance. So, the Walker Digital team devised a system using databases, order information, and information from timers used for quality control to dynamically calculate the most interesting offers and opportunities for revenue enhancement. The system then turns these opportunities into prompts that the cashiers can read from the point-of-sale terminals. "I see that you have 43 cents in change coming back to you. We have a special promotion where I can offer you our 79-cent fries in place of that 43 cents. Would you like the fries?" The result is an invention that was awarded patent number 6,119,099, titled "Method and system for processing supplementary product sales at a point-of-sale terminal." A prototype is in use in the Burger King across from Walker Digital's offices.

What is interesting about this invention from a patent processing point of view is that Walker applied for this new patent by making use of a U.S. Patent Office procedure called "continuation-in-part" (CIP). A CIP is filed while an original, parent patent is still pending. Here is the reference to the parent and applications presented in the '099 patent:

> The present application is a continuation-in-part application of co-pending patent application Ser. No. 08/822,709, entitled "System and Method for Performing Lottery Ticket Transactions Using Point-of-Sale Terminals" filed on Mar. 21, 1997, incorporated herein by reference.[4]

Notice that the earlier patent is still pending. The CIP provides Walker with a way of mixing old claims with new ones. Here is an even more dramatic example of use of the CIP procedure—this one is from patent 6,138,105, an invention that represents more of Dan Tedesco's work on vending machines and related revenue management ideas (don't worry about the details here—just skim this to get a quick sense of what is going on—the sequence of "begats" is almost worthy of the Old Testament Book of Genesis):

> This is a continuation-in-part of commonly owned, co-pending U.S. patent application Ser. No. 09/012,163 entitled "Method and Apparatus for Automatically Vending a Group of Products" filed Jan. 22, 1998, which is a continuation-in-part of commonly owned, co-pending U.S. patent application Ser. No. 08/947,798 entitled "Method and Apparatus for Dynamically Managing Vending Machine Inventory Prices" filed Oct. 9, 1997, and a continuation-in-part of commonly owned, co-pending U.S. patent application Ser. No. 08/920,116 entitled "Method and System for Processing Supplementary Product Sales at a Point-of-Sale Terminal" filed Aug. 26, 1997, which is a continuation-in-part of U.S. patent application Ser. No. 08/822,709 entitled "System and Method for Performing Lottery Ticket Transactions Using Point-of-Sale Terminals" filed Mar. 21, 1997, the entirety of each being incorporated herein by reference.[5]

Notice that both the '099 patent and the '105 patent start from the same root on the "family tree," a March 1997 patent application dealing with lottery tickets. The CIP procedure gives Walker a way to associate earlier dates with patents, making them easier to defend: even though the '105 patent was not filed until May 1998, it has, in part, claims that go back more than a year earlier. Even more important, notice how the CIP provides Walker Digital with a way to organize its patents that actually reflects its internal process of continual development, refinement, and extension.

As Jay Walker learned during his first years at Cornell, the way to win at Monopoly is to keep improving your properties, adding value so that they are worth even more when another player lands on them.

## Walker Digital's Big Idea

Just as the general debate over business method patents is polarized, so is the view of Walker Digital polarized. Some people see innovation and genius. They think that, just as Gideon Gartner invented a new kind of business when he created Gartner Group as a decision support and industry analysis service in 1979, so is Jay Walker creating a new kind of business with Walker Digital. Inventing is hard, requires different internal processes, and demands a different focus than most companies can afford to maintain as they manage the patterns and disciplines of their core businesses. It's like architecture. Most companies don't have architects on the staff; they hire them when they want to build a new building. Perhaps someday they will also hire a business method laboratory when they need to renew or reinvent their business processes.

Other commentators view Walker Digital as something closer to the work of the devil. They suspect that Walker is consciously using the weaknesses in the patent system to engineer a massive intellectual property land grab, providing very little value in return for a frighteningly large monopoly on business methods. They assume that, given enough property, Walker Digital will be able to litigate its way to wealth.[6]

Still others just see Jay Walker as the "guy with the patents."[7] Not a threat, and not the harbinger of a new business model either. The tendency to write Walker Digital off as being an odd company of no real significance has been particularly strong since the fall of Priceline's fortunes, and stock market value, in the last months of 2000. Priceline's stock fell to less than 1 percent of the value that it had earlier that year. Because Priceline was a key component of Walker's strategy for bootstrapping Walker Digital, the enormous change in Priceline's value has had a big impact on Walker Digital's immediate operations. But it is a mistake to confuse the two businesses or to equate Priceline's troubles with a judgment on the value of what Walker Digital is doing.

My own take is that Jay Walker and Walker Digital have picked up on a really important new idea. Time will tell whether they can build on the idea, how they will make money from their portfolio of patents, and how other companies will respond to offers from a business methods laboratory—but the big new idea is right.

The idea is that we are reaching the end of interesting ways to use computers, technology, and better access to information to reduce costs and increase efficiency. We have been automating business processes for almost half a century and have been reengineering the enterprise for over a decade. It's over—we are chasing diminishing returns. Applying Web technologies to existing business methods to wring out more costs and save more time is a fine thing to do, if its cheap, but it's a thin play. It is certainly not the foundation for a "New Economy."

Having said all of that, I believe that the Web really does hold out the promise of creating new value. Getting at the new value involves inventing new ways to do business. With more information available more cheaply, the big win is not to find ways to use the information to improve efficiency; instead it consists of using the information to create new value. We are reaching the end of the time when rewards go only to speed and execution and are entering a time when rewards will be attached to thinking deeply and creatively to make something new.

That's the big idea. It is a hopeful, optimistic idea. Walker Digital understands it and believes it. We will see what they do with it.

## Learning from Walker Digital's Practices

At the more mundane level, Walker has, of necessity, figured out some useful, innovative approaches to working with patents, particularly business method patents. Any company interested in using patents to protect its assets can learn from Walker's example. Here are the key points:

- Invent starting from value rather than technology. This typically means focusing on a business problem that, when solved, opens up new opportunities for creating value. This advice is most important for business method patents.
- Notarize and log everything as you go.
- Understand that business methods *can* be patented. Even if, for some reason, you choose not to pursue a business method patent, understand that some other company might do so. This means that keeping careful track of development work, complete with dates and notarization, is important even if you do not intend to seek patents: it provides you with a defense against patents by others.

- Recognize that the return that you can receive for your investment in an invention is a function both of its value to those who use it and your ability to protect it from copying. Patents are, of course, an excellent way to address the second concern.
- Because protectability is so important, you should take the search for prior art very seriously. There may not be much point in developing an invention that you cannot own (and perhaps cannot use without infringing on someone else's patent).
- Patent attorneys and inventors should work together from the outset of creating an invention. Don't do the work and then hand it to the legal department.
- Consider use of a provisional patent application if it looks like developing the full application might take awhile.
- Keep extending the value of your patents. View the patent application as a way point in a longer journey rather than an end point.
- Consider use of continuation-in-part applications as a way to formalize and recognize your continuing efforts to refine and extend your inventions.
- Repeat: start from the value, not from technology.

As always, the usual disclaimer applies: this is not legal advice. If you are developing patents you should be working as closely as possible with good patent attorneys.

Walker Digital is a wonderful example of a company that is making the most of current patent policy as it has emerged through the courts and in the hands of the PTO. Congress, of course, can change patent policy. In the next chapter I look at what Congress has been doing and at what it is likely to do next.

## Notes

1. Information about Walker Digital's internal processes was collected during a set of e-mail exchanges and from a site visit to Walker's facility in November 2000. Chief Counsel for Intellectual Property Dean Alderucci was particularly helpful in explaining processes and in reviewing a draft of this chapter.
2. Biographical information about Jay Walker comes from interviews that I conducted at Walker Digital on November 21, 2000, and from an article in *The Industry Standard* (December 18, 1998) by David Noonan titled "The Priceline.com is Right."
3. As quoted by Randall Rothenberg in "Jay Walker: The Thought Leader Interview," *Strategy+Business,* 19(2), 2000, pp. 87–94. This interview provides a good synopsis of Jay Walker's thinking about patents, technology, and the future of the Web.

4. From the text for patent 6,119,099, accessed in May 2001 at http://164.195.100.11/netahtml/srchnum.htm.
5. From the text for patent 6,138,105, accessed in May 2001 at http://164.195.100.11/netahtml/srchnum.htm.
6. For an article that develops this darker view of Walker Digital, see Mark Gimein's "Jay Walker's Patent Mania," in *Salon* magazine (August 27, 1999). Accessed at http://www.salonmag.com/tech/feature/1999/08/27/priceline/index.html in December 2000.
7. From James J. Cramer, "Jay Walker Has Left the Room," *TheStreet.com*, October 6, 2000. Accessed at http://www.thestreet.com/comment/wrongtactics/1114317.html in December 2000. This is a good example of a viewpoint that looks only at current financial performance of Walker properties, in particular, Priceline. I would argue that the more interesting things about Walker Digital are still below the surface and won't show up in immediate financial performance.

CHAPTER 12

# Congress and Patents

THE last chapter took today's patent environment as a fact of life—as the hand you have been dealt. Looking closely at Walker Digital provided insight into practices and approaches that you can use to play that hand most effectively. For decisions that you are making now, where key impacts are focused on the next two years or so, the "play the hand as dealt" tactic is clearly the way to go. You have no other choice.

But you will also be in business five years and ten years from now. In those longer timeframes it makes sense to look beyond your current hand to some of the broader questions I examined in the earlier chapters: what kind of patent policies will most contribute to the health of Internet business? Are we on the path to such policies? What steps should your company be taking now to ensure that patent policy, over the long run, stimulates Internet business growth?

Congress is inevitably a key player in framing the answers to such questions. As Justice Douglas wrote in his 1972 opinion in the very first Supreme Court case looking at patents for computer programs,

> It may be that the patent laws should be extended to cover these programs, a policy matter to which we are not competent to speak. . . . If these programs are to be patentable, considerable problems are raised which only committees of Congress can manage, for broad powers of investigation are needed, including hearings which canvass the wide variety of views which those operating in this field entertain. The technological problems tendered in the many briefs before us indicate to us that considered action by the Congress is needed.[1]

Only now, nearly thirty years later, is Congress beginning to act on the Justice's advice. In November 1999 Congress passed the American Inventors Protection Act of 1999, the most comprehensive review and revision of the laws governing patents since 1952. In our effort to understand the dynamics that shape and create patent law policy, the American Inventors Protection Act is the place to begin.

## Scope of the American Inventors Protection Act

Over the course of the preceding chapters I have identified a number of big questions and problems concerning the current course of patent practice and policy.

- Are business method patents such as Amazon's 1-Click patent a good thing for Internet business as a whole?
- How should we deal with the fact that business method patents such as the 1-Click patent, Priceline's reverse auction patent, and Netcentives' patent on offering incentive programs on the Internet seem obvious to many observers, despite the fact that they are apparently not obvious within the definition of current patent policy?
- There is concern about the breadth of business method patents, as expressed by the lower court judge in the *State Street* case: "patenting an accounting system necessary to carry on a certain type of business is tantamount to a patent on the business itself."[2] It may be, as the appeals court decided, that this is an inappropriate matter for the courts to consider in this case. But it is still an important issue for someone to consider.
- Does simply adding a computer or the Internet to a recipe for an otherwise well-known method make something that is patentable? The answer is apparently "Yes" today, but this seems unfair to companies that have spent years developing the bulk of these methods apart from the Internet and then cannot use them in the Internet environment because someone else has claimed the rights there.
- How do we balance the goal of providing incentives and protection for inventors while still obtaining the broader public benefits that come from wide application and competition of ideas and their implementations?
- Does the "fencing" of Internet application know-how into patented, privately owned domains hurt small businesses and stifle innovation? Does it discriminate against smaller, start-up companies?

Although the 1999 Act is the most comprehensive effort to come to terms with patent policy issues in a long time, it only begins to touch on the edges of big questions such as these. Briefly summarized, the American Inventors Protection Act deals with:

- Protection of inventors from unscrupulous promoters offering services in securing patents
- Reduction in patent and trademark fees
- A "First Inventor Defense" that protects prior users of business methods from infringement claims
- Adjustments to the length of patent terms
- Requirements for domestic publication of patents that have been filed abroad
- An alternative procedure that can provide a way to settle disputes about the validity of a patent without going to court
- Reorganization of the U.S. PTO to give it more autonomy
- Miscellaneous issues dealing with matters such as electronic filing of patent applications, commissioning a special study, and so on

Even a brief comparison of these two lists, attempting to match up the concerns in the first list with the key elements of the legislation in the second one, shows that Congress is not yet addressing the kinds of broad issues that have been the focus of the preceding chapters.

But what Congress has done is a start. Some of the provisions in the Act, such as the creation of a less expensive mechanism for challenging patent validity, begin to at least touch on some of the issues implied by the broader questions.

## Congress Meets *State Street*

Viewed through the lens of the policy concerns that we have identified, the most interesting part of the American Inventors Protection Act is Subtitle C, which describes the First Inventor Defense. This part of the bill was Congress's first response to the *State Street* decision and to the sudden, notable increase in applications for broadly claimed business method patents. As Senator Charles Schumer said while speaking in favor of adoption of the final bill,

> In the wake of *State Street*, thousands of methods and processes that have been and are used internally are now subject to the possibility of being claimed as patented

> inventions. . . . The patent law was never intended to prevent people from doing what they are already doing.[3]

Clearly, members of Congress were hearing from constituents about *State Street* and were hearing some things that caused concern. The response by Congress, embodied in the First Inventor Defense provisions, addresses one concern in particular. It appeared to Congress that the new, more permissive attitude toward business method patents might allow a company to file a patent on methods long known and used by a competitor and perhaps treated as a trade secret by that competitor. Such a maneuver could force the competitor to either cease the use of long-established processes or to pay a kind of ransom fee in order to continue in business. To some observers, it looks like this was exactly what Signature Financial Group was doing to State Street Bank.

The First Inventor Defense undercuts such use of patents as an offensive marketing weapon by giving the alleged infringer a way to protect itself. If the accused company can show that it reduced the business method to practice a year in advance of the patent filing and that it put the method into commercial use before the filing date, then it is insulated from infringement claims. Use of the defense does not invalidate the patent. The protection from infringement claims is also limited in scope to the person or assignee that can demonstrate the prior use of the method; it is not possible for another company to buy the right to that protection by, say, buying the First Inventor company and then using acquired rights to create an end run around the patent by expanding the unlicensed use of the business method.

Perhaps the strangest limitation of the First Inventor Defense is that it does not provide a definition for a "method of doing or conducting business"—which is, after all, the focus of the legislation. Remember that the Appeals court, in rendering the *State Street* opinion, argued that there was nothing special or unique about "business methods." Is adapting well-known incentive programs to the Internet a business method? Is Amazon's 1-Click patent a business method? Or are these, in fact, software patents? Because the First Inventor Defense does not define its terms, the answers to such questions are not at all clear. It seems very likely that anyone trying to construct a defense of their current practices using the First Inventor Defense will find that the plaintiffs simply contend that the infringement does not concern a business method and that the defense is therefore not applicable. Given the vague wording of the statute and complex legal precedents regarding business methods, resolving such a dispute will not be straightforward.

## A Limited, Adapted Response

Apart from the matter of not defining terms, this is the legislative equivalent of a surgical strike on a problem. Although Congress is to be commended for responding so quickly to *State Street*, anyone who has thought very long about all the issues surrounding business method patents must see the First Inventor Defense as a strangely limited response. The patent claim, despite use of a First Inventor Defense, is still valid for all future uses of the business method. So, even though the new law might ensure that patents do not "prevent people from doing what they are already doing," the patent is still completely effective at preventing any new entrants from using a method that was already, before the patent, in use by other companies. This is clearly an important concern for early patent claims in an expanding area such as the development of Internet businesses. One might reasonably ask why we would want to ever allow such patent claims in the first place.

Further, it is clear that Congress is still some distance from coming to terms with the question raised by the lower court judge in the *State Street* case: isn't patenting an accounting system necessary to carry on a certain type of business tantamount to a patent on the business itself? How could Congress deal with only such a small piece of what is clearly a large set of patent policy questions?

Part of the answer to this question is that Congress knows that it is not addressing the whole problem and in fact simply adapted some earlier legislation to a new purpose. Tracing a bit of the history of this bill provides insight into how Congress, perhaps pragmatically, often uses what it has at hand rather than taking on the much harder, more time-consuming task of looking for a fresh, more comprehensive approach.

The First Inventor provisions first showed up in proposed legislation in early 1997 as a very broad change to patent laws to protect anyone from liability for infringement if they could show that they had made use of the patented subject matter before the filing date of the patent. The initial versions of this legislation were not limited to business methods but covered all patents. In this broad form, the provision would address some of the concerns about breadth and novelty that have been the focus of our discussions in the previous chapters. If I were using some process, product, or business method before the filing date of your patent, then I would be immune from any infringement claims you might subsequently file against me, regardless of the breadth or claims made in your patent.

An important question here is, "Why wouldn't my prior use simply invalidate your patent?" The answer, which illuminates the focus of the early proposed legislation, is that I might have been trying to protect my use of the technology as a trade secret, rather than as a patent, which would mean that there would be no public disclosure of prior art. The idea behind this initial proposed language was that, in this kind of a face-off between my trade secrets and your patents, we could both win. This arrangement could be particularly attractive with regard to software development, where the use of patents is a relatively recent development and where most companies have traditionally relied on trade secrecy laws for protection.

This initial proposal ran into a lot of opposition. One of the strongest objections was that this language undermined one of the most fundamental reasons to have patents in the first place, which is to provide inventors with an incentive to disclose and share their inventions. As Representative Dana Rohrabacher said in a strongly worded argument against the early language,

> We simply cannot champion trade secret protection over patent protection for clearly patentable subject matter. We cannot betray our Founding Fathers by abandoning the foundation upon which our patent system is based. We cannot allow state-based rights [laws governing trade secrecy] to trump long-standing Federally created intellectual property rights [patents]. We cannot openly advocate secrecy when our patent system calls for us to vigorously promote the progress of science through the sharing of critical technology information.[4]

Other legislators and professional organizations argued, on the other hand, that patents are prohibitively expensive for small companies with many inventions to protect and that trade secrecy was indeed the most reasonable way for such companies to protect their intellectual property. Such companies should not lose the use of their trade secrets just because someone subsequently patents the technology.

Seeking compromise, subsequent drafts of the proposed bill limited the scope of the First Inventor protection. It was turned into possible "defense" rather than a release from liability, shifting the burden of proof to the person accused of infringement. Other compromises to limit the scope of the protection included changes to time-limit requirements and restrictions on expanding the scope of the unpatented use.[5]

By this time it was late spring 1999. The *State Street* decision had come out in July of the previous year and began receiving substantial notice by fall. Given the need to limit the First Inventor provisions in some way and the need to find a way to respond to *State Street*, the combination was irresistible. The form of the First Inventor Defense that eventually became law emerged out of the need to limit scope to something everyone could agree on.

## Looking Forward

It is important to realize that the First Inventor Defense provision was one of the most ambitious, controversial components of the American Inventors Protection Act of 1999. At the same time, we can see that this provision was, at best, a way of backing into addressing just a small part of a much larger problem. Testimony before final passage of the bill shows that at least some legislators knew that they had only begun addressing the problem. They said things such as, "I would hope that beginning early next year that the Judiciary Committee will hold hearings on the *State Street* issue, so that Senators can carefully evaluate its economic and competitive consequences."[6] Such sentiments are a hopeful sign that Congress might be just beginning consideration of the kinds of issues raised in this book. On the other hand, just getting the First Inventor Defense passed was a difficult fight. When companies have so much to gain or to lose from adjusting patent laws, deadlock and minimal action is not a surprising result.

In the very last months of the 106th Congress, coinciding with the last months of 2000, Representative Howard Berman introduced H.R. 5364, titled the "Business Method Patent Improvement Act of 2000." Berman knew that a bill introduced so late in the session during an election year had no chance of passage. His intent, instead, was to float some ideas and start a discussion about approaches to dealing with business method patents. His ideas are interesting and warrant attention from the business community.

Berman's bill would make the following changes to patent law:

- **Definition of business method**: Unlike the First Inventor Defense provision, Berman's bill does include a definition of "business method," as follows:

  (1) A method of—
  (A) Administering, managing, or otherwise operating an enterprise or organization, including a technique used in doing or conducting business; or
  (B) Processing financial data;
  (2) Any technique used in athletics, instruction, or personal skills; and
  (3) Any computer-assisted implementation of a method described in paragraph (1) or a technique described in paragraph (2).[7]

- **Identification and publication**: The bill requires the PTO to determine, within 12 months of the filing date, whether a patent application is for a business method. If the determination is positive, the PTO would be required, with a few exceptions, to publish the patent application within 18 months of filing. This is a substantial change from current policy, which keeps patents under wraps until they are issued. The idea is to make business method patent applications available for public review and comment.

- **Administrative opposition**: The proposed legislation would create a panel of at least 18 "administrative opposition judges" and would create procedures enabling administrative review of arguments submitted against a business method patent application. Oppositions could be filed up to nine months after the date of a patent's issue. The idea is to make it easier for citizens and companies to become engaged in the critical review of business method patents by providing other, less expensive arenas, in addition to the courts, for challenging patent applications.
- **Decreased burden of proof**: The Berman bill proposes lowering the burden of proof for legal and administrative challenges to a business method patent's validity. Rather than requiring "clear and convincing evidence"—the usual standard—the bill would change the standard to the less demanding "preponderance of the evidence." This change would decrease the likelihood of granting an overly broad or obvious business method patent, while accepting more risk of rejecting business method patents that, under the more rigorous standard of proof, might have received a patent. Berman's calculation, clearly, is that granting too many business method patents presents a greater threat to the health of business than does the risk of granting too few.
- **Presumption of obviousness**: This is an interesting provision that speaks directly to the matter that was left unresolved in *Diamond* v. *Diehr*: the proposed bill states directly that if a business method merely mixes a computer into some combination of otherwise familiar techniques, it will be considered an obvious extension of prior art and therefore ineligible for a patent. This is another big change from current practice. The current assumption is that a patent is not obvious unless the examiner can make the case that it is. When a business method patent is nothing more than an application of computers to known practices, the Berman bill would shift the burden of proof to the applicant.
- **Requirement to disclose prior art search**: Consistent with the focus on requiring that business method patents be more than just a rehash and computer automation of known methods, the Berman bill would require that an applicant for a business method patent fully disclose the extent of the search for prior art.

Taken all together, these provisions single out business method patents for particularly close scrutiny and make it easier to challenge them. The bill recognizes that the work that Walker Digital and other companies applying for business method patents are doing may be valuable and deserving of patent protection. But it also recognizes that the cost to the business community will be substantial if the PTO grants patents for business methods that are merely a rehash of known practices. Consequently, the bill would submit business method patent applications to more testing and challenges than is usual for other kinds of patents.

As one might expect, the Berman proposal has generated a fair amount of discussion and criticism.[8] Some of the criticism deals with important but somewhat technical legal issues, such as how administrative opposition rulings fit together with proceedings in courts and how they constrain opportunities to bring issues up again. But other criticisms are at a higher level and deserve consideration by businesspeople concerned with patent law.

Perhaps the most general criticism is that business method patents should not be singled out for special attention. Some commentators argue that the same requirements for disclosure of prior art, publishing, and administrative opposition should be applied to all patents, not just to business method patents. Critics are also concerned that the effect of the bill will simply be to cause patent attorneys to find ways to draft patent applications so that they will not look like business method applications. For example, Greg Aharonian, a well-known commentator on patent policy, has suggested the effect of the bill would simply be that Amazon's 1-Click patent would have been named "Method for minimal interactions when using a graphical interface" rather than "Method and system of placing a purchase order via a communications network."[9]

Stimulating discussion and criticism was Representative Berman's objective in introducing H.R. 5364. The bill pulls together a powerful collection of substantive patent reforms into a single, coherent proposal. For both businesspeople and Congress, H.R. 5364 is a useful place to start when thinking about how to balance the valuable protection that patents provide against the potential that patents have to constrain useful market activity.

The goal is to get the upside from patents—increased innovation—without the cost of granting limited monopolies for little or nothing in return. Notwithstanding Representative Berman's proposal, Congress has been notably inactive in pursuing this goal to date. Perhaps that is because the members figure we are already headed in the right direction. The next chapter explores that possibility.

## Notes

1. *Gottschalk* v. *Benson,* 409 U.S. 63 (1972). The case is widely available on the Internet.
2. From *State Street Bank & Trust Co.* v. *Signature Financial Group, Inc.*, 927 F. Supp. 502, 38 USPQ2d 1530 (D. Mass. 1996).
3. Testimony of Sen. Charles Schumer, *District of Columbia Appropriations Act, 2000—Conference Report—Resumed* (Senate, November 19, 1999).
4. Testimony of Rep. Dana Rohrabacher, hearings on patent reform and PTO reauthorization, House Courts and Intellectual Property Subcommittee, Committee on the Judiciary, March 25, 1999.
5. The restrictions on expansion grew from concerns that a small early developer, using trade secrecy as protection, might acquire immunity from infringement claims and then sell itself, and the immunity, to a much larger producer who could use this acquired right in place of licensing the patented invention.
6. Schumer (cited above).
7. From the text of bill H.R. 5364.
8. Professor John R. Thomas, of George Washington University, wrote a useful paper titled "The Business Methods Patent Improvement Act of 2000: An Overview and Analysis of H.R. 5364." As the title states, it is an analysis of the bill. It was reprinted in Gregory Aharonian's *PATNEWS* newsletter as issue !20001108 on November 9, 2000.
9. Ibid.

CHAPTER 13

# Maximizing Benefit, Minimizing Cost

SPEAKING very broadly, the situation that businesspeople face regarding patents is similar to the one we face regarding copyright. In both cases there has been a substantial shift in the fit between law and government regulation, on the one hand, and the business landscape, on the other. In both cases technology, in the form of the Internet, new Web-based approaches to business, and digital networks in general, has exacerbated the bad fit. In both cases there is an increasingly broad consensus that things aren't working and that, by gosh, something needs to be done.

I also contend that, in both cases, the greatest threat to making good business decisions and good policy decisions comes from standing too close to the problems and seeing only trees and not the forest.

In the case of copyright, standing too close has led to the conclusion that copyright laws need to be strengthened, when, in fact, they may need replacement with something more useful. In the case of patents, standing too close makes it difficult to see just how broad the changes have been over the past thirty years and even over the past ten years. Not seeing the scope of the change leads to not being able to anticipate its impact and direction.

## Who's Behind the Change?

Not long ago, it wasn't possible to patent software. Now you can not only patent software, but you can also patent entire methods for doing business on the Internet. Patent policy has changed, and much of the change has happened just in the last few years.

Suspending judgment about whether these changes are good or bad, it is useful to ask simply about the mechanism that drives and shapes this change. Who or what is making the decisions? We know that Congress has not made any substantial additions or modifications to patent law for nearly half a century. Where is the change coming from?

By looking at the forces and the players behind the change it should be possible to understand whether the change is constrained and directed in some useful way. The goal, of course, is to have change that is responsive to the interests of business and the larger economic community.

One place to begin in trying to understand the decision process behind patent policy is with a look at the different actors. Apart from Congress, there are the courts, the Patent Office, and the businesses involved in the patent process.

### The Courts

One of the clearest messages emerging from the examination of patent litigation over the preceding chapters is that the courts usually make decisions using an intentionally narrow focus on only one or two aspects of what might be a complex question. For example, in the pivotal *Diamond* v. *Diehr* case the Supreme Court deliberately chose not to consider the question of whether adding a computer to a process created anything that was really new. That was very clearly an important question then and one that is still unsettled. (Consider Representative Berman's proposed legislation in 2000.) But the question of novelty was not the question before the Court, and so the majority set it aside. This involved some pretty fine hairsplitting—so fine, in fact, that four of the nine justices didn't go along with it, arguing instead that the question of subject matter must begin with the question of just what is being claimed as an invention, which necessarily involves asking what it is that is new.

The upshot was that the Court rendered a major decision—one that literally changed the direction of patent law for software—on very narrow grounds that were not at all well matched to the impact and reach of the decision. Justice Stevens spoke indirectly to this mismatch in his dissent from *Diamond* v. *Diehr*: "The broad question whether computer programs should be given patent protection involves policy considerations that this Court is not authorized to address."[1] Justice Stevens is undoubtedly right about the limits to the Court's authority, but in the absence of consideration by Congress, *Diamond* v. *Diehr*'s narrowly considered decision became a key turn in the road that put patent policy on the path that it still follows today.

The same tension between important, broad issues of policy and the narrow focus of the courts was apparent in the very important State Street decision. The lower court judge was concerned that, by allowing Signature Financial Group to patent a fundamental business method, the court was effectively giving Signature a government-protected monopoly on an entire area of business. The higher court took a dim view of mixing such broad policy concerns into what was, from the court's standpoint, a narrow question of patentable subject matter. Once again the courts, perhaps unwittingly and unwillingly, took a significant step toward a particular patent policy while aggressively avoiding looking at policy implications.

Although these court decisions are undoubtedly correct from the standpoint of the courts' sticking to their proper role, it is simply unrealistic to pretend that they do not shape policy direction. What one *can* say is that the resulting policy direction has not been carefully considered and is more accidental than intentional.

This is not a comforting conclusion.

## The Patent Office

Like the courts, the Patent Office is making decisions primarily on the basis of present constraints, rather than with an eye to the future. This is natural and inevitable. The PTO is a government agency charged with executing its functions within the framework established by Congress. Moreover, the PTO has some real near-term issues of its own as it copes with its increasing workload coupled with the threat of funding cuts.[2]

The narrow, near-term viewpoint at the PTO is reflected in the director's report to Congress. It is long on facts and figures regarding the number of patents processed and the availability of staff to do the work, but it speaks not at all to broader policy issues. Interestingly, while discussing increases in workload in his March 2000 report, Commissioner Q. Todd Dickinson made particular reference to the added burden due to business method patents:

> Some of the largest increases in patent filings are occurring in the area of business methods and biotechnology. With respect to business methods, the 1998 decision of the Court of Appeals for the Federal Circuit in State Street Bank and Trust Co. *v.* Signature Financial Group Inc. has had a dramatic impact on the number of applications filed with our office. In fact, the number of new cases filed in [this class of patents] more than doubled from 1,285 in FY 1998 to 2,600 in FY 1999.[3]

The lack of longer perspective is most jarringly apparent in a white paper on business method patents that the agency prepared and released in mid-2000. The white paper was issued in response to what it called "the beginning of a change in the approach to how inventors choose to describe their inventions."[4] Unfortunately, in the white paper the PTO made no attempt whatsoever to understand or describe this change except in terms of frequency counts of patent applications. It certainly made no attempt to assess the impacts of the change beyond the walls of the PTO. The paper limited its focus to noting how the need to process more business method applications changes the demands placed on patent examiners.

The PTO is clearly reacting to and accommodating changes in patent policy rather than contributing in a useful way to consideration of policy direction and impact. As is true for the courts, this lack of engagement with broader policy issues may be as it should be. But we are left with the conclusion that neither the PTO nor the courts is driving the car, and they may not even be looking out the window.

### Businesses Seeking Patents

When Jeff Bezos set about getting a patent for Amazon's 1-Click ordering application in 1997, he was focused on Barnes and Noble and on the protection of his still young business. He wasn't thinking about patent policy. He was after advantage. As we have seen, a business operating in today's patent environment, where broad business method patents are a fact of life, needs to be thinking about patents tactically.

In addition, businesspeople should also be thinking strategically, of course. The long-term effects of business method patents on the health of markets is potentially large. But most businesses are still struggling to come up to speed on the tactics, let alone look at the larger issues.

Unfortunately, broader vision and perspective will not grow naturally from our current, tactical focus on patents. It requires that companies start thinking about patents in new ways. Stimulating such thinking is, in fact, a primary reason for my writing this book.

However, as a group, we are not there yet. Most businesses are still approaching patents with a view to immediate requirements rather than in terms of broader policy. We are choosing policy direction like rats in a maze.

## An Invisible Hand?

Good policy direction does not necessarily have to emerge from the collective wisdom of judges, individual businesspeople, or other sources. It would suffice—and perhaps even be preferable—to have market constraints or other forces that interacted to ensure that the mechanism of issuing and valuing patents is in some way an optimal balance between competing interests.

There certainly are economic forces that shape the decisions companies make about patents. The decision about whether to pursue a patent or whether to protect property as a trade secret is informed by considerations of the costs of pursuing a patent and the probability of success. Such considerations kept Bricklin and Frankston from even trying to patent their spreadsheet invention in 1979.

Economic considerations also shape the decision to contest or, alternatively, to license someone else's patent. State Street Bank initially tried to license Signature's Hub and Spoke patent rights before deciding that the costs of licensing were too high and that litigation looked like the better alternative. Microsoft initially tried to license Stac's compression technology on its own terms and, when that failed, decided to bear the cost of litigation. After the litigation failed Microsoft returned to the market to negotiate a licensing agreement.

When, as in the 1999 patent legislation, Congress decides to enable alternate ways of handling patent disputes or decides to change the patent fee structure, it is trying to change the kinds of decisions companies make about patents by changing the costs and benefits of different kinds of patent activity.

It is useful to identify the constituencies that participate in and affect the economic give-and-take surrounding patents. The PTO plays in this interchange, of course, since it actually decides whether a patent is granted or not. Congress has an indirect role through the PTO in the setting of fees and in establishing basic patent approval and dispute-resolution mechanisms. Patent attorneys certainly participate, as do the companies they represent, companies that are either seeking patents or challenging them.

The striking thing is that the larger business community and society as a whole are not well represented in this economic subsystem. In its publications and in presentations to Congress the PTO frequently makes reference to its "customers." The PTO apparently sees itself as participating in a market that serves a clientele. But even a cursory reading of these publications and presentations makes it clear that these customers are limited to the inventors and the companies applying for patents. After all, the PTO's revenues come from the fees that these customers pay. The framed poster outside the PTO Commissioner's office reads, "Our Patent Mission: To Help Our Customers Get Patents."[5]

This is troubling. It is like the problem encountered when the U.S. Forest Service conceives of its mission as serving its primary fee-paying customers, the timber companies. The problem is that, like the Forest Service, the PTO was established to serve broad, national interests. When the U.S. Constitution authorized Congress "to promote the progress of science and useful arts, by securing for limited times to authors and inventors the exclusive right to their respective writings and discoveries," the focus was on benefit to society as a whole, not on benefit to inventors as customers.

One serious problem with looking to some kind of "invisible hand" to guide the patent process, then, is that the business community in general, with its broad interest in a healthy economy, is not well represented by the economic constraints that are at work. If the PTO is speaking for the companies that want to receive patents, then who is speaking for the companies that are concerned that broad use of Internet patents is a bad idea? How do constituencies with concerns about the direction of patent policy participate in the market with patent attorneys, patent applicants, and the PTO?

Ultimately, this is another problem for Congress to solve. Representative Berman's "trial balloon" bill at the close of the 106th Congress contains some interesting ideas about how to begin that work. His sense that the solution lies in the direction of enabling more participation by more of the business community seems right. This is an area that needs more thought and attention.

But it is clear that, as the system is currently structured, it would be naive to think that there is some kind of system of self-correcting constraints that will ensure that patent policy represents our collective, broad interests.

## Where We Are Headed

We have major, direction-setting decisions being made by courts that, at the same time, deny that they are dealing with policy issues and refuse to consider them at all, let alone carefully. We have a PTO that understands its mission as one of helping more companies get more patents. We have business interactions that depend on the specialized training of a relatively small group of people—patent attorneys—who are intimately familiar with PTO processes, who speak their own language, and who are not typically closely involved with normal business processes. We have a Congress that, until very recently, has been largely missing in action when it comes to patent law. We have a *de facto* decision mechanism that is almost wholly devoid of any broader external frame of reference.

In short, nobody is steering the ship, and there is no autopilot. The mildest possible conclusion is that there is no reason to believe that we will end up anyplace that we would want to be.

## What to Do?

A comparison and contrast with the problems surrounding copyright is useful in bringing patent problems into focus.

In the case of copyright law and the broader dispute over digital content distribution, it appears that there are powerful companies with a large interest in the status quo. Their successful efforts to lobby Congress and the White House have resulted in some legislation that is of very questionable value to other businesses as they move forward in the use of digital content. The objective for other businesses, then, is to ensure that their best interests are more closely aligned with exploring change rather than with preventing it. The goal, for both business and Congress, is to broker agreements that provide reasonable protection for established interests, through a transition period, and that look toward providing new mechanisms—other than simple copyright—for protecting content.

In the case of patents it seems much less clear that there is a single powerful interest group that is driving the changes in policy. To be sure, there are companies that are making the most of the changes as they happen. But the mechanism behind the changes appears to be the combined effect of many small, narrowly focused, tactical decisions, each taken without much in the way of strategic intent.

If this analysis is correct, then the challenge for the business community and for our society as a whole is to find a way to assert some control over the patent process. This is not to suggest control over individual patents but instead to speak to the need for a patent system that routinely makes use of more inputs from a broader segment of the business community. Proposals might include the following:

- Full funding of the PTO so that it can do a more thorough job of reviewing patent applications. (Currently Congress allocates a budget for the PTO that is less than the PTO earns in fees. Rather than the PTO subsidizing the rest of the government, the tremendous potential impact of patents on our economic well-being suggests that the subsidization should work in the other direction.)
- Development of a system of oppositions proceedings, perhaps similar to the Berman proposal but applied to all patents, that can economically bring more public input into the patent process.
- A clear statement by Congress that merely using a computer to automate an existing process is not novel. Again, this could usefully apply to all kinds of patents, not just to business method patents.
- Requirements to disclose the extent of searching for prior art that apply to all patents.

## Getting a Patent Policy that Works

There is a tendency—one that I certainly share—to be cautious about bringing the government and regulation into business processes. This tendency is particularly strong among Internet pioneers. As early Internet philosopher and activist, John Perry Barlow, said, "Governments of the Industrial World, you weary giants of flesh and steel, I come from Cyberspace, the new home of Mind. On behalf of the future, I ask you of the past to leave us alone. You are not welcome among us."[6]

This mindset, asserting that control of the Internet should not involve government, leads directly to the somewhat bizarre situation with which I opened this consideration of patents and patent policy. When confronted by Jeff Bezos, Amazon, and the 1-Click patent, the response from many in the Internet community was moral opprobrium. The desire to keep clear of government led to the surprising conclusion that the most useful response to the Amazon patent was a boycott, mixed with some name calling.

Patents are, of course, an *invention* of government and cannot exist apart from government. It seems likely that in the minds of people concerned about the fencing in of the Internet frontier, the intrusion of patents into cyberspace represents an intrusion of government. The solution to this problem would be, of course, to push the government back out of the picture. These pioneers do not approach this task by working with government, since that is contrary to their goal. The preferred approach is to encourage the cyberspace community, including Amazon, to reerect cyberspace's walls against governments, to do the "right thing" and refuse the seductions of patent protection and other governmental assistance.

This point of view sounds a little simplistic when boiled down this way, but I believe that it is also a reasonably fair sketch of the problem as viewed by some critics of business method patents: they're bad, don't use them. This approach is not likely to have much impact, one way or the other, on the use of business method patents.

In the preceding chapters I have tried to set aside the moral stridency of the anti-patent contingent to look at the substance of their concerns. The review of the recent history of patents and the examination of possible consequences leads me to the conclusion that at least some of the concern about business method patents is warranted. It seems likely that the recent direction in patent activity, if left to run unconstrained, will retard business development, particularly as you move your business on to the Web.

So, I have tried to help you find the handles on this problem. The solutions will not be found in the courts, and not in the PTO. Slowing down the process—moving from an Internet patent land grab back to open exploration of opportunities—will require help from Congress. In particular, businesspeople need to encourage Congress to greatly strengthen the opportunities for public input and engagement in the patent process. The ideas put forth in Representative Berman's trial balloon legislation are a useful starting point, even if imperfect, for policy deliberation.

Patents are a complicated topic. They also have the potential to dramatically impact your business's future and its value. This is not a dispute where you can safely sit on the sidelines and watch. Businesspeople need to actively work toward a policy that protects and rewards innovation while keeping markets open to competition, growth, and change. That's not the direction we're headed. Getting there won't be easy. Heck, we've hardly even started.

## Notes

1. *Diamond* v. *Diehr,* 450 U.S. 175 (1981).
2. For example, the PTO projected revenues of $1.2 billion in fiscal year 2001 from fees. Marked-up appropriations bills in mid-2000 proposed cuts to the PTO budget that would reduce funding to around $905 million, providing the PTO with only about 75 percent of the fees that it takes in. Commissioner Q. Todd Dickinson estimated that this would eliminate hiring or replacement of more than 600 patent examiners.
3. From a statement by Q. Todd Dickinson, Assistant Secretary of Commerce and Commissioner of Patents and Trademarks, before the Subcommittee on Courts and Intellectual Property, Committee on the Judiciary, U.S. House of Representatives, March 9, 2000.
4. From U.S. Patent and Trademark Office, "Automated Financial or Management Data Processing Methods (Business Methods)," July 26, 2000. Accessed at http://www.uspto.gov/web/menu/busmethp/index.html on September 9, 2000.
5. From James Glieck, "Patently Absurd," *New York Times Magazine,* March 12, 2000.
6. From John Perry Barlow, "A Declaration of the Independence of Cyberspace" (Davos, Switzerland. February 8, 1996). Accessed at http://webserver.law.yale.edu/censor/barlow.htm on September 24, 2000.

CHAPTER 14

# Patents: Further Reading

Aharonian, Greg. *PATNEWS*. Internet Patent News Service (http://www.bustpatents.com).

Greg Aharonian's day job is searching for prior art. His clients are usually trying to establish that they have a valid patent or that someone else's patent is invalid. But his very early morning and sometimes late at night job is writing *PATNEWS*, the irregular but nearly daily (sometimes including holidays) patent newsletter from Aharonian's Internet Patent News Service. *PATNEWS* covers a wide variety of topics related to patents—information about what is going on inside the PTO, pieces on approaches to drafting patents, information about lawsuits, opinions about patent policy, and so on. Aharonian has assembled a very broad collection of informants and contributors—patent attorneys, academics, and patent examiners—who help keep *PATNEWS* interesting and useful. If you are at all interested in keeping up with patent developments, *PATNEWS* is a must read. And it's usually also a good read.

Berners-Lee, Tim, with Mark Fischetti. 2000. *Weaving the Web: The Original Design and Ultimate Destiny of the World Wide Web*. New York: HarperCollins Publishers.

Tim Berners-Lee invented the Web, and this is the story of the events leading to that invention and to the Web's acceptance as a global publishing and collaboration system. This book is not about patents or intellectual property per se, but it provides important insights into the values and objectives that are implicit in much of the opposition to the use of patents to protect Web business methods. Berners-Lee's story is also important food for thought: how would things have turned out if Berners-Lee had patented his invention? This is a very readable book that is key background reading for anyone who wishes to understand how the Web came to be what it is.

Boyle, James. 1996. *Shamans, Software, and Spleens.* Cambridge, MA: Harvard University Press.

I offered my rave review of *Shamans, Software, and Spleens* in Chapter 5, "Copyright: Further Reading." The arguments and inquiry in *Shamans* are just as applicable to patents as to copyright. Questions of public and private good and of how our society establishes ownership are much of the focus of Boyle's book—questions that are clearly important to thinking in innovative ways about patents.

Durham, Alan L. 1999. *Patent Law Essentials.* Westport, CT: Quorum.

If you want to understand more about how patent law works, or about continuations-in-part, or about the various categories of infringement, this is the book. Durham provides a detailed overview of patent law, including many of its legal technicalities, that is accessible to people without legal training. Businesspeople who need to understand patent law and patent litigation in enough detail to be able to have useful conversations with patent attorneys should own this book. It is also an excellent reference book.

Glazier, Stephen C. 2000. *e-Patent Strategies.* Washington, DC: LBI Institute.

This book is one of a series of volumes that Glazier has written on patent law. In this book Glazier focuses on software, e-commerce, and business method patents. The book's objective is to get readers thinking about patents as a business tool. Unlike Durham, Glazier's books are not texts that describe patent law and litigation. Instead, using a mixture of case studies, high-level (and somewhat superficial) commentary on trends, and recommendations regarding things such as intellectual property audits, Glazier attempts to assemble a sourcebook of patent development tactics. Not at all a policy book, the focus is on using patents to make money, given the policies as they stand today.

Glieck, James. 2000. "Patently Absurd." *New York Times Magazine,* March 12.

This short, readable, entertaining article provides an excellent introduction to the potential problems surrounding business method patents. Highly recommended for anyone who needs a 20-minute overview of the issues.

Liebowitz, Stan J., and Stephen E. Margolis. 1999. *Winners, Losers & Microsoft: Competition and Antitrust in High Technology.* Oakland, CA: Independent Institute.

Well, this book does not actually deal directly with patent issues. What it does do is provide an excellent overview of the development of the spreadsheet market, which I used in Chapter 10 in my "what if" speculation about how things might have been different if Bricklin and Frankston had been able to patent their spreadsheet program. The book also provides an excellent overview of "path dependence"—the theory that systems can lock into patterns that might produce suboptimal outcomes. It is useful to apply some of the thinking about path dependence to the question of how the United States is making decisions about patent strategy.

Nichols, Kenneth. 1998. *Inventing Software.* Westport, CT: Quorum.

Nichols takes a thoughtful, careful look at the issues surrounding the patenting of software. He examines some of the peculiar problems that software inventions pose for patent law and illustrates his points with close examination of a number of software patents. Stepping back from the sometimes heated controversies over software patents, Nichols attempts to look at what software patents can add to software development as well as the ways in which patents don't fit the problem. He closes with a consideration of different policy proposals for new approaches to protecting software inventions. This book is unique in its close focus on software patent problems, but it is not an easy read. It deals with issues both at fairly high levels, as when it considers policy alternatives, and also gets down to fairly low-level considerations, as in his code examples. *Inventing Software* is perhaps most useful for programmers interested in a broader look at the software patent debate.

# PART three

# Electronic Signatures

ON June 30, 2000, President Clinton signed the Electronic Signatures in Global and National Commerce Act (the E-SIGN Act) establishing the validity of electronic signatures for interstate and international commerce. After signing the bill with pen and ink (still required for legislation, interestingly enough), he also signed it electronically.

President Clinton's use of an electronic signature for the E-SIGN Act contained symbolic messages in addition to the intended one. One side effect of the publicity surrounding this event is that we all now know the password associated with Clinton's digital ID: it is "Buddy," the name of his dog. In his choice of a weak password and his more revealing willingness to publicize it, President Clinton was telling us that he certainly is not going to be using electronic signatures himself. That's not surprising, of course. But he was also demonstrating that there are still educational and infrastructure barriers in the way of broad, routine use of electronic signatures.

There are two good reasons to take a closer look at electronic signatures and at the way the E-SIGN Act addresses the problems and opportunities that surround them. The first is that the questions of how you know whether an electronic document is valid and how you know whether a customer has really committed to a purchase are critically important for businesses that want to make more use of the Web.

The second reason to look more closely at the E-SIGN Act is that it provides a good example of how legislation can work together with market activity rather than constraining or replacing it. The policy approach taken in the E-SIGN Act provides a model that is useful in evaluating policy for copyright, patents, and privacy. In the search for useful models for the interaction of technology, law, and business, the problems associated with electronic signatures and Congress's response provide a useful, even hopeful example.

CHAPTER 15

# Matching the Legislation to the Problem

THE hype surrounding the signing of the E-SIGN Act would have people believe that they will soon be using electronic signatures to buy homes and cars on the Internet, all without paper. Turning to the ever-popular "Internet as highway" metaphor (could we legislate against that, perhaps?), Senator Spencer Abraham, a chief sponsor for the legislation, announced, "This bill literally supplies the pavement for the e-commerce lane of the information superhighway."[1] (This is enough to make one wonder about the literal meaning of *literally*.)

In fact, the problem of knowing whether you can trust an electronic signature is a difficult one. We are still a ways from having the whole road paved. On the other hand, there are sections of the road that are ready for use today.

The place to start in understanding what the problems are and how the E-SIGN Act addresses them is with a look at the Act itself.[2]

## What the Legislation Does

There are already 46 states with some kind of legislation that establishes the validity of electronic signatures. In some states, such as Utah, the legislation even specifies particular technical approaches to signatures, sets liability limits, and takes other steps toward constructing the infrastructure to support electronic signatures. But different states have passed different laws, and states cannot regulate interstate commerce or international transactions. The federal law provides a way to harmonize the different state regulations and establishes a framework for interstate commerce. The primary purpose of the law is to ensure that no signature or contract will be ruled as invalid simply because it is in electronic form. In other words, electronic signatures and records are as good as paper ones, subject to the same general questions of authenticity that apply to paper documents.

The bill does not, of course, *require* that people use electronic signatures. In fact, it makes the use of electronic records and signatures in place of paper contingent upon the active consent of all parties involved in the transaction. Moreover, the consent must be provided electronically, in order to demonstrate that each person can actually access records electronically. Congress is attempting to ensure that people without access to the hardware to sign or access documents electronically are not excluded from doing business and contracting for services.

On the other hand, the E-SIGN Act does give businesses the right to charge an extra fee for having to deal with paper rather than electronic signatures and records—choosing to use paper can end up costing the customer more. Businesses also have the right to terminate a relationship with a customer who withdraws consent to receive electronic records. As use of electronic signatures and records matures and as market tolerance for "electronic only" operations increases, these provisions will allow businesses to accelerate movement away from paper.

Although the focus of most news coverage of the E-SIGN Act has been on electronic signatures, the bill is also important because of its treatment of electronic records (to which the electronic signatures would be attached). Given the active consent of a party to receive electronic information, the Act establishes that electronic records and electronic notice can satisfy requirements for notice in writing. Further, it makes it acceptable to use an electronic record in place of a paper record in a broad class of instances where record retention is a requirement. It legitimizes electronic record keeping. Overall, the purpose of the E-SIGN Act is to establish that electronic records and signatures can replace paper for most transactions.

Another important feature of the E-SIGN Act is that it creates a class of transactions and contracts that are exempt from the effect of the Act. In other words, there are transactions for which electronic records, notice, and signatures cannot be substituted for paper. This set of exceptions includes wills, divorce and adoption documents, court orders and other court documents, eviction or foreclosure notices, notice of cancellation of life insurance or health insurance, cancellation of utility services, and product recall notices that impact health or safety.

Finally, the E-SIGN Act preempts state legislation that contradicts the federal law or that requires use of specific technologies or methods of signing or encoding electronic documents. It does allow the states to specify alternative procedures or requirements for establishing the acceptability or validity of electronic signatures or documents.

## What the Legislation Does Not Do

The most striking and important thing about the E-SIGN Act is that it does not say what an electronic signature is, other than to provide the very general definition that an electronic signature is an "electronic sound, symbol, or process, attached to or logically associated with a contract or other record and executed or adopted by a person with the intent to sign the record."[3]

Given this definition, an electronic signature could be my name, spelled in ASCII characters, at the bottom of a document. It could be a digitized image of my handwritten signature. It could be a digital signature using a public key architecture and a certification authority. It could be a biometric signature such as an electronically recorded thumbprint or a retina scan. It could be a voiceprint of me saying my name or it could be the digital encoding of the biometric factors (pressure, speed, direction) that I use in creating my handwritten signature as detected on a digital pad. Clearly, some of these signature technologies will be more secure or easier to authenticate than others. The E-SIGN Act will let the market sort out the winners from the losers.[4]

One particularly important kind of electronic signature is a *digital signature.* Digital signatures make use of powerful encryption technologies that can help increase confidence that the signature actually belongs to the person who owns the encryption key. I have discovered that most businesspeople don't have even a high-level idea of how digital signatures work. This is unfortunate since digital signatures will be used in many ways over the coming years, including use in establishing that automated, computer-to-computer interactions have not been invaded and redirected to other ends. Immediately following this chapter is a supplemental chapter, titled "A Deeper Look: Technical Background on Digital Signatures," that will give you a basic but useful notion of just what a digital signature is and does.

Consistent with the refusal to evaluate and choose technologies, the bill does not deal with any of the infrastructure needed to establish the validity of signatures, other than to state that when a notary public is required to verify identity, the notary can use an electronic signature in performance of the notarization function. Similarly, the E-SIGN Act does not deal with liability issues associated with certification authorities or falsification of signatures or documents. These issues are, as they are with paper documents, left to the states or to the Uniform Commercial Code.

## What Is the Problem to Be Solved?

Before attempting to assess the probable impact of the E-SIGN Act on the business community, it is important to step back and look at the broader question of what is required before one can have confidence in a signed document. Understanding the "big picture" issues will help in assessing how close the business community really is to actually being able to use electronic signatures. It will also help in understanding the particular approach to regulation that is exemplified by the Act: given the problems, how did Congress go about addressing them?

**Authentication** The first requirement for a useful signature is to be able to know that it actually belongs to the person who is believed to be buying the home, signing the contract, incurring the debt, and so on. In other words, we need to know that the signature is not a forgery. In the world outside of electronic signatures we use a number of systems to ensure against forgery. For frequent and typically relatively low-value transactions we keep a record of the authentic signature on file (for example, a bank's signature card). For more critical transactions we require that the signature be notarized, which is to say that we trust a third party to verify that the signature is authentic. In order to make sure that the notary does his or her job, state laws make notaries liable for damages (usually limited to some fixed amount) if the signature turns out to be a forgery. For really important transactions such as the purchase of a house we sometimes even require that the signatories be physically present for the signing or that they provide power of attorney to someone else who can be physically present. For such critical deals we still want to be able to look the other party in the eye. The ceremony surrounding the signing event signifies to all parties that the deal is done.

**Integrity** Once the document is signed we want to make sure that it is not altered. I want to be bound by the agreement that I sign, not by some other agreement. With paper documents we typically do this by giving each signatory a copy of the signed document. When documents are sent back and forth to be executed over distance, we trust that the mail or express delivery packages are not opened and that the documents are not tampered with in transit. One of the more famous literary examples illustrating the critical importance of integrity is Hamlet's opening the letter, sealed with the Danish king's royal seal, that Claudius sent with Rosencrantz and Guildenstern to the King of England giving the order for Hamlet's immediate execution. Hamlet changed the order to request the execution of the letter's bearers, affixed his father's copy of the royal seal, and sent Rosencrantz and Guildenstern to their deaths. Integrity in transit matters.

Nonrepudiation If I loan you money and you sign a note promising to repay it, I want to ensure that you cannot later repudiate your signature, claiming that it is not yours at all and that you made no promise to repay. Faced with such a claim, I could hire an expert in handwriting analysis who might be able to convince a court that the signature is indeed yours. I would be in a much better position if I had also required the signatures of witnesses to the act of your signing. Notaries can serve as witnesses, since they keep a record of each signature that they authenticate.

### Unresolved Issues

Given this outline of what is required in order to give us the confidence necessary to act on a signed document, how close are electronic signatures to meeting the requirements?

Authentication I have a digital signature of my own. It consists of a public key and a private key that allow me to send encrypted e-mail to other people with digital signatures. I can assert, through use of my private key, that a signed document came from me. Should you believe me?

I obtained my digital signature by going to the Web site of a certification authority (CA) and giving them my name and e-mail address, along with $15. That's it. Nobody looked at my driver's license, passport, or birth certificate. There is no checking mechanism that would prevent me from, say, creating a new e-mail address for my brother, Bob, and then paying another $15 to get a digital signature for Bob. The problem (or opportunity) would be that I, not Bob, would have the private key for Bob's signature. If I started using Bob's digital signature, and if companies accepted it as Bob's, I might be able to spend a lot of my brother's money.

The issue here is not the security of the actual digital signature but the nature of the certification that authenticates it. The kind of digital certificate that I can get for my e-mail, or Bob's e-mail, is a Class 1 certificate. There are other kinds of authentication and other kinds of certificates. For example, to get a Class 3 certificate from VeriSign, one well-known digital signature certification authority, one has to appear in person.[5] The point is that electronic signatures are not all alike and are not all equally worthy of your trust, even when they use the same technology for keys and encryption.

Remember what the E-SIGN Act does. It simply states that it is permissible to use an electronic signature in places where one would have used pen and ink in the past. It does not speak to the technical merits of different signature technologies, much less to the requirements for certification. It does not augment the existing authentication infrastructure with a new one that is appropriate for e-commerce. This is a critically important fact for Web businesspeople to keep in mind as they try to understand the impact of this bill. The infrastructure does not change just because of this bill.

Before electronic signatures are used in new ways, supporting new kinds of e-commerce, we need to establish mechanisms for authenticating electronic signatures. As we will see when we look at liability concerns associated with authentication, the problem is more complicated than simply having everyone get a Class 3 digital ID. The complexity and the need to allocate risk in different ways for different contexts is why it is exactly right that the E-SIGN Act does not prescribe how to authenticate signatures, leaving it to the market to figure out what works best.

**Integrity** If Claudius had ordered Hamlet's death in an e-mail sent in clear text to the King of England, Hamlet may have still been able to change it to a request for the execution of Rosencrantz and Guildenstern, assuming he could intercept the e-mail. Perhaps relying on the connections of his friend Horatio, he could have captured it using a filter placed on the primary Internet links leaving Denmark. In that case he wouldn't have even needed his copy of the king's seal.

But if Claudius had encrypted the message using a strong encryption algorithm and kept the key to himself, Hamlet would have been a dead prince much earlier in the play.

Electronic signatures, coupled with encryption, are currently capable of ensuring the integrity of a message. This is what my Class 1 digital ID does well. You may not be able to be sure just who the real person is who sent the message, but you can be sure that the message you received was the message that was sent.

The biggest barrier to message integrity at the moment is the fact that a surprising number of businesspeople do not encrypt their e-mail, even when it concerns sensitive, business-critical agreements.

**Nonrepudiation** If you cannot authenticate the identity of the sender, the issue of nonrepudiation is moot. We're back to the same infrastructure problem that underlies authenticating the identity behind a signature. However, as we will see, it is possible to solve the authentication problem for many business applications. If you can take care of the authentication, you can get nonrepudiation as well. The reason for this is that certain kinds of digital signatures act like an electronic fingerprint and can be uniquely associated with the signer. It is worth noting that there are also kinds of electronic signatures included in the broad definition of the E-SIGN Act that would not address nonrepudiation (for example, the ASCII representation of my name.) It will take awhile for the market to settle on technologies that work and to weed out the ones that don't.

Liability The electronic signatures act simply states that legal documents will not be declared invalid solely because they are in electronic form and contain electronic signatures. It does not make other changes in law or infrastructure. So nothing else should change, right?

Unfortunately, because electronic signatures are new technology, untested in the courts, the use of electronic signatures will inevitably raise new questions about who is responsible for paying the costs if something goes wrong. For example, consider the following hypothetical situation, presented and explored by C. Bradford Biddle. Biddle's scenario assumes that some company or other entity steps forward to act as a certification authority—kind of like a super notary—keeping track of digital certificates, or signatures, and vouching for their validity. In this scenario, the private key is the part of the signature that the signer uses to assert authenticity.

> Cedric, a licensed certification authority, duly issues a certificate to Susan, who accepts it. Cedric publishes the certificate in a recognized repository. Susan's private key, which corresponds to the public key in the certificate, is kept on a floppy disk. Irving, a malicious computer hacker, releases a computer virus on the Internet that finds its way onto Susan's computer. Subsequently when Susan uses her private key, the virus program surreptitiously sends a copy of Susan's private key to Irving. Irving immediately uses the private key to cash a $10,000 electronic check drawn upon Susan's account payable to a numbered, anonymous account in a state having rigorous bank secrecy laws. Irving disappears and cannot be found. As soon as Susan learns of the fraud she revokes her certificate.[6]

Who covers the $10,000 loss? Susan's first hurdle if she wants to avoid the $10,000 loss is to repudiate the false signature. The new Electronic Signatures Act doesn't say what the standard for nonrepudiation should be. Some states, such as Utah, have set up more specific rules to deal with such issues. Under the Utah law a document containing a person's electronic signature is presumed to have been signed by that person unless he or she can present "clear and convincing" evidence that he or she did not, in fact, sign the document. So, if she lived in Utah, Susan would need to start out by hiring an attorney as well as someone with the technical expertise required to meet a high standard of proof in convincing the court that she did not sign the check.

However, even if Susan gets past that hurdle, she may still be liable for the loss. The Utah law makes the person who owns the electronic signature completely responsible for any loss due to a failure to exercise "reasonable care" in safeguarding the private key. If Utah were making the laws for the United States, Bill Clinton would already be headed down the slippery slope for letting us all know that his password is "Buddy." Susan, too, may be in trouble. Wouldn't "reasonable care" include use of a virus protection program? The Utah law doesn't say, so Susan would be left with the task of convincing the court that her inability to detect the virus was within the bounds of "reasonable care."

Biddle notes that under the Utah digital signature law Susan accepts much greater risk than she does by using her credit card, where consumer liability in the case of fraud is capped at $50. If she kept using only handwritten signatures she would have no liability, since one cannot be bound by a fraudulent handwritten signature. Biddle observes that "no rational consumer would agree to accept this level of risk in a marketplace transaction. The benefits of having a certificate simply do not outweigh the very real possibility of facing extraordinarily large unreimbursed losses."[7]

But if we don't want to hold Susan responsible for the loss, who should get stuck holding the bag? The certification authority? If the CA is a third party that is not involved in the transaction, but only in validating the signature key, this could be quite a burden. Such a company would have no way of knowing whether the signature was tied to a micropayment of a few cents or tied to the purchase of a home. Unbounded liability for transactions to which you are not a party sounds like a great way to go broke.

The third alternative is to make the party who accepted the signature liable for the loss. In Susan's case, this would be the bank making the payment. In such a case, the bank might want to do away with the services of a third-party CA, establishing its own records of signatures and its own rules for accepting them. The bank might, for example, set a limit on how much risk it is willing to take on the authenticity of an electronic signature, requiring additional evidence of authenticity for amounts exceeding that limit. Note that the bank, as a party to the transaction, is in a better position to assess risk than would be a third-party CA.

My point here is not to resolve these issues or to argue for a particular solution. The examples and detailed discussion of liability are intended to drive home the idea that authentication is not a technical problem, but it is sometimes a legislative problem and *always* a business problem. There is overhead and expense associated with authentication—electronic signatures do not make that expense go away. The amount that you spend to reduce the probability of fraud needs to be balanced against the costs of fraud. If you are engaged in transactions where your worst-case loss can be held to a few dollars, you may be willing to make signatures quick and easy, accepting some loss in order to do more business. If you are, however, incurring substantial exposure, you will want to make the investment required to buy substantial assurance of authenticity.

Existing State Laws The new federal law is catholic (some might even say indiscriminate) in its embrace of electronic signature technologies and infrastructures. Its approach is to let the market do the work of sorting things out. Some state laws, such as Utah's, prescribe particular approaches to electronic signatures. The federal law preempts state laws that "require, or accord greater legal status or effect to, the implementation or application of a specific technology or technical specification."[8] How will this affect the law and the use of the digital signature infrastructures that are already in place in Utah and in other states? This is a complicated question that will take time, and perhaps additional action on the part of state legislatures, to answer.

## Summary of the E-SIGN Act Approach

The E-SIGN Act addresses one part of a much larger problem. Here is a summary of what it does. This summary will be useful in trying to evaluate the E-SIGN Act as a model for other approaches to policy.

- **Removes barriers**: The E-SIGN Act deals broadly with the use of electronic documents. Its intent is to ensure that, with a few exceptions, no contract, signature, or other legal document is invalidated solely because it is in electronic form. In short, it focuses on removing legal impediments to electronic signature use.
- **Provides transition from current practice**: The Act provides for a relatively small number of exceptions in which a signature, notice, or agreement can still be required to be in paper form. So, while looking forward to new practice, it protects established practice.
- **Lets the market sort out the technologies**: The new law relies on the market to decide what kinds of electronic signatures are useful. The definition of an

electronic signature in the E-SIGN Act is broad enough to cover any conceivable approach to recording electronic signatures. In other words, the Act does not second-guess the market.

- **Lets the market sort out the infrastructure issues**: Before companies will accept electronic signatures they need to know when to trust them as authentic and when not to. The Act leaves it to the market to develop useful mechanisms for validating signatures and establishing trust in electronic documents.
- **Lets the courts, states, and market sort out the legal details**: There are important questions about liability associated with the use of electronic documents and signatures that are not clearly resolved by reference to existing laws and regulations concerning paper transactions. The E-SIGN Act does not touch on these. This is consistent with the decision not to prescribe details of signature technologies or authentication and trust mechanisms. But it does mean that there may be potentially large liabilities associated with the use of electronic signatures until there is more experience, legal precedent, and, possibly, legislation dealing with electronic signatures and records.
- **Recognizes that the Web is a national infrastructure**: The E-SIGN Act preempts state laws to the extent that they are not consistent with the federal law and to the extent that they exhibit preference for particular technologies. In other words, the E-SIGN Act regards the framework for business on the Web as a national concern rather than one that should be solely the province of the states.

## Notes

1. As quoted by Christopher J. Dorobek in "Agencies Expect E-SIGN Law to Spur e-gov." *Government Computer News*, July 10, 2000. Accessed in July 2000 at http://www.gcn.com/vol19_no19/news/2407-1.html.
2. A copy of the full text of the bill was available in May 2001 on the Library of Congress's "Thomas" service (http://thomas.loc.gov/). Search for bill number S.761.ENR under the legislation passed by the 106th Congress.
3. From Section 106(5) of bill S.761.ENR (cited above).
4. From the viewpoint of a computer scientist or a Web businessperson, anything moving on the Internet is necessarily in digital form, and so any kind of signature sent across the Internet would be a digital signature. Attorneys and legislators, however, prefer to reserve the term *digital signature* for applications that use public encryption keys and matching private encryption keys to transmit documents

securely and to "sign" them. The broader term *electronic signature* includes this more restricted class of digital signatures as well as other kinds of electronic signatures that do not use public key encryption.

5. For more information about VeriSign's classes of service, see the *VeriSign OnSite 4.0 Administrator's Handbook*, section 12.1.1, available on the Web in May 2001 at http://www.verisign.com/onsite/doc/adminBook/adminBook/.
6. From C. Bradford Biddle, "Comment: Misplaced Priorities: The Utah Digital Signature Act and Liability Allocation in a Public Key Infrastructure," 33 *San Diego L. Rev.* 1143 (1996). Accessed in January 2001 at http://www.acusd.edu/~biddle/mp.html.
7. From C. Bradford Biddle, "Legislating Market Winners: Digital Signature Laws and the Electronic Commerce Marketplace." *World Wide Web Journal* (Summer 1997). Accessed on January 9, 2001, at http://www.w3journal.com/7/s3.biddle.wrap.html.
8. From Section 104(b)(2)(C)(iii) of bill S.761.ENR (cited above).

# Technical Background on Digital Signatures

THIS section provides some technical background about digital signatures—a special kind of electronic signature—for readers who are interested in knowing more about how digital signatures work. Readers who do not care about the details of the technology can skip to the next chapter.

*Electronic signature* is a broad term that encompasses many different approaches to establishing identity in electronic communications. Used in this broad way, electronic signatures include digitized images of signatures (as on faxed documents), biometric approaches to identification (for example, retina scans, thumbprint scans), and the use of special encryption keys known as *digital signatures*. This last category, digital signatures, is what many people have in mind when they talk about electronic signatures. Because digital signatures will see broad use, it is useful to have a high-level idea of how they work.

Digital signatures were invented as one part of a solution to a larger problem. The larger problem had to do with encrypting messages so that they could be transmitted securely over public networks such as the Internet. Good encryption technologies had been around for a long time, but they were all "symmetric" in the sense that the key used to lock (encrypt) a message was also the key used to unlock (decrypt) a message. This meant that secure communication depended on shared copies of keys. Whether the encryption system was the "Enigma" machines used by the Germans in World War II or the Data Encryption Standard

(DES) that was widely used within the financial and information processing communities in the 1970s, the extent to which anyone could communicate securely was limited by the extent to which they could safely distribute keys. For computer networks, this meant that you needed to find some way to communicate that was *off* the network—usually by secure private couriers—before you could communicate *on* the network. Clearly, secure communications with people that you have never met—something that we now take for granted on the Internet—was impossible.

The solution to this problem was first outlined by Whitfield Diffie and Martin Hellman in the mid-1970s.[1] Their insight was that it would be possible to get around the key distribution problem if you could invent a way of locking things that used two keys. Unlike symmetric encryption, in which the sender and the receiver use the same key to lock the message and then to unlock it, Diffie and Hellman proposed the use of an asymmetric encryption scheme, in which the locking and unlocking functions are split apart. A "public" key would be used to encrypt a message. The locked message could be decrypted only through use of an associated "private" key. Assuming that you could find a way to create such public/private key sets, you could then distribute public keys widely, publishing them. If I wanted to send you a message, I would go to a directory where I would look up your public key. I would then use that key to encrypt the message and send it to you. Since you would be the only person with the corresponding private key, only you could decrypt and read the message.

The public/private key idea was slick. The only problem was that, for awhile, nobody could find a way to create an encryption scheme that used such asymmetric keys. Finally, though, Ronald Rivest, Adi Shamir, and Leonard Adleman came up with an encryption algorithm—later named RSA after the inventors' initials—that did the job.[2] Understanding something about how they solved the problem is useful, even for businesspeople, because it helps in understanding how digital signatures work.

Rivest, Shamir, and Adleman knew that if they were going to build an asymmetric locking scheme they would need to focus on mathematical operations that are, themselves, asymmetric and one-directional. Most mathematical operations are symmetric and two-way. For example, if you add numbers together, it is just as easy to reverse the operation and subtract them. But there are a number of mathematical operations that are very difficult to run backwards. One of these is the factoring of a large number into its prime components. Prime numbers are numbers that are divisible only by themselves and 1. The numbers 1, 2, 3, 5, 7, 11, 13, and 17 are primes. The number 15 is not prime because it can be broken apart into its prime factors of 3 and 5. What is interesting about primes and factors from an encryption point of view is that while it is very easy to multiply two large prime numbers to create their product, it is extremely time consuming, given the product, to figure out the original primes. This fact became a critical component of the RSA algorithm.

The RSA encryption scheme multiplies two very large prime numbers to create an even larger number, which is then used as the *public* key to the encryption scheme. Constructing the *private* key depends on knowing the two prime factors. If you pick numbers that are sufficiently large, millions of computers working together for hundreds of years will not be able to recover the prime factors, given the public key.

Suppose that Joe wants to submit a sealed bid on property that Kathy is selling. Ed would like to eavesdrop on Joe's bid so that he could outbid him while still spending as little as possible. Kathy has published her public key—an enormously large number—for use by all bidders. Joe uses Kathy's public key to encrypt his bid. Once he has completed the encryption, there is no one, including Joe himself, who can read the encrypted message without knowing the prime factors of the public key. Because finding the prime factors by trial and error is extremely time consuming, Ed is locked out of the communication and only Kathy, who possesses the private key that expresses the factors, can read the bid.

But how does Kathy know that the bid really came from Joe? How does she know that this isn't an artificially low bid submitted in Joe's name by Ed? And, if she accepts the bid, how can she prove that Joe really made the offer, keeping him from repudiating the bid? In other words, how can all of this encryption be used to create a signature that is known to be authentic and that cannot be repudiated?

The answer lies in the fact that the unique linkup between a private and a public key works in either direction. For purposes of secure communication, Joe uses Kathy's public key, which means that only Kathy can unlock the message, since only Kathy has the matching private key. But suppose that Joe also has a public/private key pair of his own. He can then use his own *private* key to encrypt a message (as opposed to using the recipient's public key). This encrypted message will be readable only if a receiver has Joe's *public* key. Of course, since Joe's public key is published and freely available, that means that the message is available to anybody. But—this is the signature part—since only Joe has Joe's private key, anyone decrypting this message with Joe's public key can be sure that it was sent by someone with Joe's private key—presumably Joe. If Joe tries to repudiate the message, denying that he made the bid, he is in the difficult position of having to explain how and why someone else has his private key.

A digital signature, then, is asymmetric encryption used in reverse. The sender uses his or her private key to encrypt a message. Anyone with the sender's public key can read it, but such readers can be sure that the message really was sent by someone in possession of the sender's private key—presumably the sender.

For communications that are both signed and secure, the messages are doubly encrypted. Going back to our example, Joe would first encrypt the message with his own private key—"signing" it—so that Kathy can be sure that the message is from Joe. Then Joe would encrypt the message again, this time using Kathy's public key, so that he can send it and be sure that only Kathy can read it. When Kathy receives the message she first uses her private key to unlock the outer layer of protection and then uses Joe's public key to establish that the message was really signed by Joe.

Where do all of these public and private keys come from, and who keeps track of them? It is possible to do all of this encrypting and signing without any central authority, which is the approach taken by a program known as Pretty Good Privacy or PGP.[3] In the PGP model, each computer user generates his or her own keys and is responsible for getting the public keys out to people with whom he or she wants to do business.

Obviously, managing and circulating your own public key and keeping track of the public keys of everyone else who send you things is a lot of work. So, the more frequently used approach is to use a central certification authority (CA) that generates the big prime numbers, issues the keys, keeps track of who has them, and makes a directory of public keys available to anyone. Most common e-mail packages are set up to automatically make use of the keys issued by CAs such as VeriSign both for purposes of creating signatures and for encrypting mail.

The CA keeps track of the certificates and is responsible for validating them. If you receive a signed document, the CA tells you who signed it. For the most commonly used classes of signatures, however, the CA will only validate that a particular signature is associated with a particular e-mail address. Although this is useful, it is very different than asserting that a particular individual person did the signing. As explained in Chapter 15, obtaining real certainty about the actual identity of a sender depends on the same techniques as any other identification process, ranging from passwords to personal appearances. The advantages gained from having a given degree of certainty about the identity of a signer must be balanced against the costs of obtaining that degree of certainty.

If you are interested in more information about digital signatures and about encryption in general, you might enjoy reading *The Code Book* by Simon Singh (Doubleday, 1999). It provides a readable, entertaining history of cryptography and includes a more detailed description of just how the RSA algorithm works.

## Notes

1. See Whitfield Diffie and Martin Hellman, "New Directions in Cryptography," *IEEE Transactions on Information Theory*, volume IT-22, November 1976, pp. 644–654.
2. See Ronald L. Rivest, Adi Shamir, and Leonard Adleman, "A Method for Obtaining Digital Signatures and Public-Key Cryptosystems," *Communications of the ACM*, 21(2), 1978, pp. 120–126.
3. Free versions of PGP were available on the Web in May 2001 at http://www.pgpi.org; information on commercial versions was available at http://www.pgp.com.

CHAPTER 16

# The Impact of the Legislation

THE E-SIGN Act *will* succeed in stimulating increased use of electronic signatures and documents. But the initial increased use will not come in the form of auto purchases, home loans, and other general consumer commerce applications featured in early stories and commentary about the legislation. Instead, the initial use will come in contexts where the issues of trust and authentication are already addressed through existing relationships or mechanisms.

Consider, for example, the relationship between a manufacturer and a supplier in which signatures are required for each order from the supplier, but the overall relationship has been established in an existing purchase agreement. In this case each party can exercise control over the signature authority granted to employees, and concerns about liability and indemnification are already covered in the separate agreement. Dealing with paper or faxed signatures is simply an added cost. If such parties are not already using electronic signatures, the E-SIGN Act should give them the green light to do so now.

Or consider the variety of transactions and the back-and-forth exchange of documents between insurance companies, insurance brokers, and customers. Insurance is a good candidate for early application of electronic signatures and records delivery because the costs of moving everything back and forth in paper are high. Just as important, the insurance company is in a position to create the infrastructure required to make the electronic signatures workable. It can dictate the specific technologies that will be used for signatures, authenticate the signature for each customer, and establish the terms of the agreement between the company and the customer concerning loss or theft of digital keys, forgery, liability, and so on. In short, the insurance company can set up its own authentication infrastructure and liability agreements with its agents and customers and so is free to make immediate use of electronic signatures.

What emerges from these examples is a picture of electronic signature use that is very different from the view that one might begin with when first thinking about the problem. Most people have one handwritten signature. By analogy, one might expect to have one electronic signature and that this signature would be recognized and accepted by your insurance agent, your bank, and by the general business community. But, as we have seen, there are substantial problems associated with authenticating such signatures and with assigning liability for forgery in such a general scheme.

These problems disappear, however, when the parties to a transaction can set up a separate, private agreement, as in the examples presented above. Such case-by-case agreements governing electronic documents and signatures can treat the technology, authentication, and liability issues in ways that are appropriate to the scale and to the nature of the transactions being conducted. So, rather than having one electronic signature, analogous to your one handwritten signature, you will probably have a number of different electronic signatures for use in different business contexts.

## Analysis and Suggestions

Despite news stories that suggest otherwise, the E-SIGN Act is not going to be the catalyst for a sudden revolution in e-commerce. The aims of the bill are more modest than that. The intent is simply to remove legal obstructions that might stand in the way of letting the market do its work in sorting out electronic signature technologies and approaches to authentication. Managers could misread the impact of the legislation if they look for broad, sweeping effects or expect the E-SIGN Act to resolve matters that are still left to the market.

The real impact of the E-SIGN Act is that it removes barriers to the use of electronic signatures in business contexts where such signatures already make business sense. The challenge for the manager is to recognize those contexts. You should look for the following kinds of business situations:

- *A high volume of transactions requiring signatures, so that there are real cost savings or performance improvements from adopting electronic signatures.* Usually, electronic signatures will not make business sense for infrequent transactions between parties. The costs of establishing satisfactory authentication will often outweigh the savings from the use of the electronic signature.

- *Parties that already know each other, or some other already-in-place or easy-to-establish mechanism for authenticating signatures.* If authentication is cheap and easy, then it is easier to make the business case for electronic signature use.
- *The ability to easily create agreements (or use existing ones) covering liability and fraud.* Again, existing infrastructure that can be adapted for use with electronic signatures makes the business case for electronic signatures easier by bringing down the costs.
- *Situations where the cost of fraud is relatively low* (for example, transactions with a low value for each transaction). If your risk of loss is lower, you can accept a greater risk of fraudulent transactions.

As the E-SIGN Act suggests directly, the insurance business is form and paper intensive and deals with a great many transactions that meet at least some of these criteria. Supply-chain relationships are another area in which many transactions meet these criteria. Banking may be yet another.

The E-SIGN Act will also stimulate new areas of business for software vendors and service providers. The problems associated with presenting, tracking, managing, and authenticating electronic signatures and records are opportunities for the companies that can address them. Given the complexity and critical importance of being able to authenticate signatures, there will be interesting opportunities for companies that provide outsourced capabilities for clients or that can provide customer companies with the tools and processes to manage the authentication themselves.

One important point that software vendors and service providers should remember as they address these opportunities is that the early applications will be *industry and situation specific*. For example, insurance companies will need technology and perhaps services in order to set up their own electronic signature management and authentication systems. The same will be true of financial services companies, retailers managing their supply chains, manufacturers sourcing materials from suppliers, and so on. The problems associated with authentication and liability in the general case will ensure that, for a while at least, these applications will be relatively narrow and focused on the needs of individual companies in particular vertical markets. The way for a software vendor or service provider to go wrong here would be to believe the hype about sudden revolution, wish away the authentication issues, and go after an undifferentiated, horizontal market. The technologies will be applied horizontally, but the approach to the markets must be vertical.

If, as Senator Abraham said, the E-SIGN Act supplies the pavement for the e-commerce lane of the information highway, it will be supplying it one stone at a time, at least for awhile. All the same, most businesses will want to begin using the road soon, since early markets are the time to build advantage. But you should also be realistic about how much of the highway is complete and about how rough the ride can be if you drive fast where the pavement is still under construction.

CHAPTER 17

# Learning from the Electronic Signatures Act

THE path to the E-SIGN Act as it was finally signed into law was not direct. Earlier bills that had been introduced to deal with electronic signatures did not always restrain themselves from bias toward particular technologies (they usually focused on digital signatures using a public/private key infrastructure). Some of the proposed bills even skated on the edge of trying to make decisions about authentication and certification authorities.

As an extreme example of replacing market action with government fiat, consider Utah's digital signature legislation, which attempted to prescribe the entire infrastructure required to enable use of digital signatures. For awhile the Utah legislation was considered as model legislation for use by other states.

The thinking behind such ambitious legislation is that government can stimulate business growth by resolving uncertainty. Authentication of electronic signatures, coupled with the associated issue of liability, is a big, complicated problem. So the Utah state legislature rolled up its sleeves to solve it. The E-SIGN Act passed by Congress can seem like a cop-out in comparison. It deals with only a small part of the much larger problem.

But the E-SIGN Act, as finally signed into law, is not at all a cop-out. Instead, it reflects deep understanding of the limits of what we currently know about electronic signatures and of the limits of what Congress can usefully do. The approach that Congress took in the E-SIGN Act reflects the following principles:

- Recognize how little we really understand at present about the problems and opportunities of business on the Internet.

- Restrict government action to the parts of the problem where government is directly involved and is really required—in particular, focus on places where existing policy gets in the way.
- Accept the fact that to find a good solution, markets need time to work—be patient.

## Recognizing How Little We Understand

Humility is, perhaps, easier now that Internet commerce has stumbled. Knowing what will work on the Web seems less certain than it did in late 1999. All the same, it is easy to fall into believing that things are simple and obvious.

Congress was at an advantage when drafting the E-SIGN Act because, with even a little thought, it is clear that the liability and control issues surrounding authentication of electronic signatures are messy and complex. It looks as if the best bet consists of making sure that liability is well aligned with knowledge about the nature of the transaction, which tends to argue for many approaches rather than a centralized approach to authentication. So, it was relatively easy, in the case of electronic signatures, for Congress to recognize how little we currently understand about the problem.

Unfortunately, the same grasp of limits eluded Congress when it came to copyright. Faced with the contradiction between a system of laws that depends on constraining the making of copies, on the one hand, and technology that brings the cost of making large numbers of perfect copies to nearly zero, on the other, Congress reached the surprising conclusion that the solution was easy to grasp and decided to strengthen copyright protections. It is just now becoming clear that there are all kinds of undesirable side effects to this "simple" solution.

In times of enormous, complex, rapid change, business is better served if Congress acts conservatively, recognizing that there is much that can be learned only over time, after we have had more experience with the changes.

## Restricting Government Action to What Is Necessary

This is a subtle, difficult principle, since "necessary" will always look different to different people. The E-SIGN Act provides a good illustration of the principle and so might be useful in making it easier to see how it applies to more complex policy problems.

There are many things that are required—and necessary—in order for electronic signatures to work. The list includes authentication, ways to assign responsibility for loss, and other hard problems. But government is not, strictly speaking, required to work out these issues. Companies can resolve them through contracts and through an appeal to the courts, if it comes to that.

The *one* thing that was needed from government, however, was a clear statement that a contract or other legal document would not be invalidated *solely* because an electronic signature was used to signify a party's agreement. Without that certainty, use of electronic signatures, no matter how secure and well authenticated, involved the risk that a court might decide that the document had not been signed. So, Congress focused its efforts on addressing that one problem and did so as parsimoniously as possible.

The questions of what is necessary, what is properly the government's role, and what should be left to markets are not as straightforward in the areas of copyright and patents. The reason for this is simple: copyright law and patent law are wholly an invention of government. There are no private sector copyright laws and patent laws. Given the central role of government in the areas of copyright and patents, the question of what constitutes minimal and necessary action is cloudier.

The approach in the E-SIGN Act suggests a way to frame an answer: restrict action to areas where the existing law is providing a potential obstruction. Applied to patent law, the obstruction is associated with the difficulty that patent examiners encounter in evaluating business method patents. Congress could address this obstruction by creating mechanisms to bring more public input into the examination process—perhaps using mechanisms similar to those proposed by Representative Berman at the end of 2000. It is instructive to note what such an approach does *not* do. It does not try to decide which kinds of business method patents are good and which are bad; it does not make fundamental changes to the patent law requirements for inventions to be new and not obvious; it does not reverse the direction established by the courts, accepting business methods as patentable content. It restricts itself to addressing the problem of bringing more information to the examination process. In this sense, it would be an example of the kind of conservative change that is restricted to what is necessary.

## Accepting the Fact That Markets Need Time to Work

This principle follows from the others. If Congress is addressing problems where the "right" path is uncertain and is trying to act conservatively, doing only what is necessary, then Congress is implicitly accepting the idea that developing appropriate policy will take time. This is the principle that the Utah state government lost track of when it tried to create a complete electronic signature solution by legislative fiat, putting it in place and telling the markets, "OK, there it is, use it."

In passing the E-SIGN Act, Congress took a small step within a larger process that will take years to work out fully. This may be frustrating to some businesspeople. They might like to see more progress, more quickly. I suppose that we all would like that, in some sense. But it's dangerous for Congress to try to mandate or *create* progress, particularly when we know so little about how things work. So, in passing the E-SIGN Act, Congress decided to simply remove a key impediment and then wait and see what will happen next.

Applying this same measured approach to copyright, Congress should recognize that there, too, it could usefully take a wait-and-see approach, understanding that it will take time for initiatives such as Bertelsmann's agreement with Napster to run their course and produce workable solutions and benefits. Draconian steps to enable new ways to lock up content are not consistent with a view that this matter can be resolved largely in the marketplace and that the solution will evolve over a period of years.

## The E-SIGN Act as Model

The E-SIGN Act that Congress passed in mid-2000 is important as much for what it does not attempt to do as for what it does. The Act leaves the business community responsible for sorting out the different signature technologies and for putting in place workable approaches to use these technologies. The bill does not try to protect business from itself and does not decide what the "right" solution should look like.

On the other hand, the bill does successfully remove uncertainty that existed in key areas—particularly with regard to how electronic signatures would be regarded in courts. In so doing, the bill removes an important impediment to continued development, exploration, and use of electronic signatures by the business community.

The E-SIGN Act's approach to developing new policy provides a model that might usefully be applied in other policy areas, such as patents, copyright, and—as we will see in the next part—privacy. The general principles behind the approach consist of recognizing that there is much that we do not know, restricting government action to what is necessary—particularly to removing legal impediments—and understanding that markets need time to absorb and sort out these changes.

CHAPTER 18

# Electronic Signatures: Further Reading

Biddle, C. Bradford. 1996. "Comment: Misplaced Priorities: The Utah Digital Signature Act and Liability Allocation in a Public Key Infrastructure." 33 *San Diego L. Rev.* 1143. Accessed in January 2001 at http://www.acusd.edu/~biddle/mp.html.

In this useful law review article Biddle takes a very detailed look at the Utah Digital Signature Act and at the broader issues facing digital signatures in general. This article provides an especially thorough examination of liability issues, considering a number of different models for handling liability. If you are interested in thinking through the legal dimensions of liability issues more carefully, this article is a good place to start.

Biddle, C. Bradford. 1997. "Legislating Market Winners: Digital Signature Laws and the Electronic Commerce Marketplace." *World Wide Web Journal* (Summer). Accessed on January 9, 2001, at http://www.w3journal.com/7/s3.biddle.wrap.html.

Another useful article from Brad Biddle. In this article he argues for the kind of legislation that eventually emerged in the E-SIGN Act—in other words, for legislation that does not choose between different approaches for handling the public keys used for digital signatures. He distinguishes between open models, which assume a common key infrastructure used by all, and closed models, where certification is handled in different ways as required for different situations. Once again, the treatment of these issues goes into greater legal detail than I do here.

Singh, Simon. 1999. *The Code Book*. New York: Doubleday.

Singh has written a very entertaining, readable history of codes and ciphers. It contains an excellent history of the development of asymmetric encryption and public/private key approaches to encryption and digital signatures. Singh's history balances the unfolding of the intellectual problems with stories about the people who did the unfolding. It also contains enough detail about the RSA algorithm to enable the reader to work some simple examples by hand.

Stallings, William. 1999. *Cryptography and Network Security: Principles and Practice*, 2nd ed. Upper Saddle River, NJ: Prentice Hall.

This is a more formal, academic presentation of some of the subject matter that Singh approaches through stories. If you are interested in understanding more about how encryption works and about the potential attacks on different encryption methods from an engineering standpoint, this is a good, well-organized text. Encryption is necessarily mathematical, so making use of this book does presume a level of comfort with mathematics.

VeriSign, Inc. 1998. *VeriSign OnSite 4.0 Administrator's Handbook*. Available on the Web in May 2001 at http://www.verisign.com/onsite/doc/adminBook/adminBook/.

VeriSign's *Administrator's Handbook* is a useful resource if you are interested in understanding more about how this major certification authority issues and handles digital certificates.

# PART four

# Privacy

PRIVACY is a big, unruly issue. It affects you in dozens of ways in your dual role as citizen and businessperson. Privacy issues can involve government surveillance, access to encryption technologies, your company's ability to communicate in private internally and externally with customers and partners, and employee monitoring and surveillance.

The aspect of privacy that I focus on in the following chapters concerns what you can do with the information that you collect about your customers. This is the dimension of the privacy debate that is most likely to affect most businesses in the next few years. It is also a part of the debate that is likely to receive attention in the form of congressional policy setting.

Privacy is a substantially different kind of problem than the others that I have examined so far in this book. Patents and copyright exist because of government, and discussions of patents and copyright are, by definition, discussions of government policy. The same is true, to a lesser extent, of electronic signatures, since governments are involved in setting the rules for contracts, notaries, banks, financial transactions, and so on. But in the area of privacy the need for a government role has been much less evident. In fact, the government is usually understood to be one of the primary threats to privacy.

But the business community, too, has emerged as a threat to privacy in the minds of many consumers, and, to some, appears to be a more imminent threat than even the government. The situation today is similar to the one faced by credit bureaus nearly forty years ago in the late 1960s. The public was just becoming aware of the power that computers and databases provided to retrieve individual data from vast stores of information. Vance Packard had just written his best-selling book, *The Naked Society*, and Jerry Rosenberg was writing a book called *The Death of Privacy* that began by recalling Hitler's use of central data archives.

Congress conducted hearings. Privacy advocates argued that credit bureau use of centralized computer databases should be outlawed. Credit bureaus argued that databases provided more control of the use of data and better protection for the public. In 1971 Congress passed the Fair Credit Reporting Act, taking a middle course on the issue, guaranteeing citizens the right to see what is in their files.

Once again, people are turning to the government for help in protecting their privacy against invasion by the business community. This time around, business may have an affirmative as well as a negative interest in potential legislation, since it seems clear that, without assurance that the Web is a safe place, consumer business on the Web will be limited to only a small fraction of overall consumer spending. Perhaps an appropriate set of privacy laws can provide the foundation for consumer confidence that Web business needs.

Consumer privacy is a complicated policy issue. I have placed it last in the sequence of four issues considered in this book in order to have access to the insights and conclusions drawn from the first three. Part of the complexity is that privacy is something of a chameleon: Sometimes it looks like a property issue that can be approached through market mechanisms, sometimes it looks like a right, and sometimes it looks like a political cause. I begin our inquiry with one woman's attempt to make some money from information about herself.

CHAPTER 19

# A Market for Privacy

THE 106th Congress considered more than a half dozen privacy bills during 2000. Even staunch advocates of industry self-regulation, such as the Online Privacy Alliance (OPA), are beginning to take the position that some kind of privacy legislation may be inevitable and is perhaps even necessary.[1] According to research by the Pew Internet and American Life Project, 84 percent of Internet users are concerned that businesses and others will use the Internet to get personal information about Internet users and their families.[2] By a two-to-one margin, Internet users reject the argument that tracking user activity on sites is helpful because it enables better service. The research also shows that 94 percent of the people using the Internet want rules that require that companies be punished for violating privacy policies.

What all of this means is that the days of being able to ignore privacy policy, simply advocating self-governance, are over for businesspeople. It is likely that the 107th Congress will give very close consideration to legislation that regulates how businesses collect and use consumer information. It is therefore critical that you be familiar with the issues and develop a coherent framework for evaluating policy proposals and participating in policy debate.

## Putting a Price on Private Information

In June 2000 Tracy Coyle, a 41-year-old office manager at a Madison, Wisconsin, law firm, reached the limit of her patience with marketers' attempts to extract tidbits of personal information while providing little or nothing in return. Coyle decided that if companies wanted to know what kind of sinus medicine she preferred and whether she bought candy or gum at grocery checkout counters, they could pay for it. So she built a personal profile questionnaire. It contained over 1,300 questions about 378 different activities and identified 262 different product preferences. Someone filling out the questionnaire would reveal what appliances they owned, what medicines they took, what pets they owned, how often they attended church, and much more.

Tracy Coyle's plan was to fill out her questionnaire herself and to then sell the information through an auction.[3] Bidders would be invited to send Coyle e-mail solicitations for products that fit the interests and preferences in the profile. She figured that the information was worth at least $20 and hoped to auction off 250 copies of her profile to the highest bidders. Even if she received bids averaging only a little more than her minimum price, she could make more than $5,000 from the auction. If the auction went well, she planned to set up a registry for other consumers who wanted to sell their own personal profiles. If it all worked, she would be providing a way for consumers to take control of their personal information, enabling individual citizens to actually participate in the marketplace for consumer information, rather than just being the subject matter.

Coyle's auction didn't work out as she hoped; the companies that buy information about consumers did not take her up on her offer to sell her profile. John Keck, a vice president at the marketing firm Foote Cone & Belding who spoke with a reporter for *The Industry Standard* about Coyle's idea, offered an explanation for the lack of interest in Ms. Coyle's auction. "Tracy is definitely in touch with where marketing is headed—her questionnaire has classic direct-marketing written all over it," said Keck. "However, sight unseen, this data is worth, at most, 10 cents to a buck. If she would let us look at the entire profile and then decide if she'd be likely to convert to a customer [for one of our clients], then we might pay between $20 and $100."[4]

The interesting and really useful thing about Keck's response is that it describes a market that values personal information in two very different ways. In the one case the individual information items are not worth much at all—it is the aggregate view that emerges from looking at many individual records all together that has value. At the other extreme the information is essentially a well-qualified sales lead and can be worth a great deal of money to a company with the right product to sell. Note that this is a discontinuous value scheme. The individual records are either part of an aggregate view, in which case they aren't worth much individually, or they are targeted leads. There is no middle ground.

## The Value of Aggregation

Marion Frost is 80 years old. She lives alone; her husband died 18 years ago. She cannot type and has no interest in the Internet, but she owns a WebTV—a box that sits on top of her 30-year-old oak-cabinet television that connects her to the Internet. A company named Knowledge Networks provided Marion Frost with her WebTV. The company even sends someone to switch on the WebTV for her when necessary. Her son usually handles the keyboard.[5]

Knowledge Networks bought a WebTV for Mrs. Frost and for 100,000 other people across the United States because Mrs. Frost and all the others are part of a large random sample of survey respondents that Knowledge Networks has assembled in order to use the Web as a way to do survey research. In return for the free WebTV and free Internet access, the Knowledge Networks survey participants are asked to respond to a 10-minute survey once a week. The surveys reflect the interests and concerns of Knowledge Networks clients, typically focusing on brand strength and product preferences. Mrs. Frost, for example, was asked recently about what other juices she would mix with cranberry juice. Other clients, such as TV networks, use Knowledge Networks for public opinion polling. CBS, for example, used the online Knowledge Networks panel to survey responses to the presidential debates between George W. Bush and Al Gore.

Knowledge Networks promises its survey panelists that it will keep all information about the panelists confidential and will always provide responses to clients in anonymous form, never identifying the panelists. The reason that Knowledge Networks is willing to incur the expense of free WebTVs and free Internet connections for its panelists is that there are a great many companies that want access to such a large random sample of panelists. Knowledge Networks arguably has the largest, most perfectly random sample of consumers available and can track and correlate different interests and changes in preference over time—something that is impossible with telephone surveys.

In terms of John Keck's dichotomous market, divided between valuing one individual's private information at either not very much at all or at $20 or more, the responses that Knowledge Networks is gathering are, when taken individually, of the less valuable kind. Nobody would pay very much to know whether Marion Frost would rather mix her cranberry juice with raspberry juice or apple juice. But when Knowledge Networks can aggregate Mrs. Frost's response with 100,000 others, then it has information that has substantial value. By aggregating Mrs. Frost's answers, again and again, over a period of years, Knowledge Networks can derive enough value to recoup the costs of the WebTVs and other support.

## Developing a Framework for Privacy Policy

What do Tracy Coyle and Marion Frost have to do with privacy and privacy policy? Both of their stories illustrate how personal information—the stuff that most people want to keep private—has come to be treated as a commodity and as property. It is something that has a value and that is bought and sold. If private information can be bought and sold, there is a market. Tracy Coyle's and Marion Frost's stories begin to sketch the unique outlines and character of this market.

Privacy is, of course, much more than something that is bought and sold in a marketplace. Most people would also argue that privacy is a legal right, derived from our unalienable rights to "Life, Liberty and the pursuit of Happiness" claimed in the Declaration of Independence. The belief that privacy is a right, coupled with a belief that this right is being ignored by some businesses, has also turned privacy into a "cause." Consider, for example, that the back jacket copy of a recent book on privacy quotes no one less than Ralph Nader. He describes the book as "a graphic and blistering indictment of the burgeoning technologies used by businesses, government, and others to invade the self."[6] Nader smells a hot issue and is suited up to do battle. As a cause, privacy will also, of course, become a focus of political activity.

Each of these dimensions of privacy, its status as an individual right, as a cause, and as a focus for political and legislative activity, is important to businesspeople. Questions concerning who owns the information that you collect about individual customers, and about the ways in which such information can be used, are coming under intense scrutiny. The answers to these questions are likely to change over the next year or two. Businesspeople need to understand the different sides of the argument. We also need a framework that we can use to make judgments about the different arguments and about the policy proposals that are emerging from them.

Privacy is an exceedingly difficult, complex subject for policy development. It makes patent and copyright policy look comparatively clean and simple. For businesses, a useful, if imperfect, path through this complexity emerges from following Tracy Coyle's lead, framing privacy issues in terms of markets and effects on markets. But before we turn to the task of trying to understand the interaction between privacy concerns and markets, we need to examine the other critically important ways of looking at privacy, as a legal right, as a public cause for concern, and as a focus of political activity.

## Notes

1. *The Industry Standard* published a useful review of the evolution of business's willingness to accept privacy legislation in an article by Keith Perine titled "The Persuader" in the November 13, 2000, issue.
2. From Susannah Fox et al., *Trust and Privacy Online: Why Americans Want to Rewrite the Rules* (Washington, DC: The Pew Internet and American Life Project, August 20, 2000).
3. A number of news sources covered Tracy Coyle's auction as it took place, including the *Financial Times* in an article titled "Observer: Tell Me about Yourself" in its "Avenue of the Americas" column for June 21, 2000. *The Industry Standard* covered the story in a June 14, 2000, article titled "Wisconsin Woman Auctions Personal Info Online" by Diane Anderson. As of May 2001 this article was available on the Web at http://www.thestandard.com/article/display/0,1151,16008,00.html.
4. From Anderson (cited above).
5. Marion Frost's story comes from an article by Michael Lewis, titled "The Two-Bucks-a-Minute Democracy," that appeared in the *New York Times Magazine* on November 4, 2000. The *San Francisco Chronicle* provided a good overview of Knowledge Networks' business in an article by Peter Sinton, titled "Polling Using the Internet Seeks to Improve Accuracy," which appeared on October 28, 2000. More information about Knowledge Networks was available in May 2001 on its Web site at http://www.knowledgenetworks.com.
6. As quoted on the back jacket of the hardback edition of *Database Nation* by Simson Garfinkel (Sebastopol, CA: O'Reilly, 2000).

# CHAPTER 20

# The Right to Privacy

MOST legal principles have been around for a long time. For example, our laws regarding ownership of real property have evolved over centuries. Privacy is different. The legal formulation of a right to privacy is a relatively new idea, and the law is still evolving. There is, for example, no mention of privacy in the U.S. Constitution.

The comparative youth of privacy as a legal and social concern is part of what makes the formulation of privacy policy so difficult. We are not starting from a foundation of broadly shared, generally agreed upon ideas of just what privacy is, much less what is guaranteed by a right to privacy. Our efforts to build a framework for privacy policy must therefore start with two questions: What is the nature of the privacy right, and what is the basis for the right? Until we can articulate at least some broad answers to these questions, attempts to evaluate policy options are as likely to lead us astray as they are to produce useful results.

## The Right to Be Let Alone

Copyright, libel, slander, and other areas of law took shape centuries ago, stimulated by the development of the printing press. Part of the reason that privacy emerged as an issue only within the last hundred years is that it was not until then that new technologies began to create serious threats to privacy. In other words, concerns about privacy are driven in part by technology.

At the time that the Constitution was written, if you were in your home or in a room with a closed door, there was a reasonable expectation that what you said was said in private. Even if you were on the street, only a relatively small number of people could see what you were doing. Like clean air and clean water, it was possible to take the availability of privacy for granted. But by the middle of the nineteenth century the presumption that privacy was freely available had begun to change.

The first significant effort in the United States to assert that there is a right to privacy per se emerged in the form of an article titled "The Right to Privacy" by Samuel Warren and Louis Brandeis that was published in the *Harvard Law Review* in 1890. In the article they explain why it was important, at that time, to begin giving serious consideration to the notion of a right to privacy.

> Instantaneous photographs and newspaper enterprise have invaded the sacred precincts of private and domestic life; and numerous mechanical devices threaten to make good the prediction that "what is whispered in the closet shall be proclaimed from the house-tops." For years there has been a feeling that the law must afford some remedy for the unauthorized circulation of portraits of private persons. . . . The alleged facts of a somewhat notorious case brought before an inferior tribunal in New York a few months ago directly involved the consideration of the right of circulating portraits; and the question whether our law will recognize and protect the right to privacy in this and in other respects must soon come before our courts for consideration.[1]

Warren and Brandeis were responding to the threats to privacy posed by new technologies. Their situation was similar to the one that we find ourselves in a century later; the difference is that today the technologies are even more powerful and invasive.

Warren and Brandeis set out "to consider whether the existing law affords a principle which can properly be invoked to protect the privacy of the individual; and, if it does, what the nature and extent of such protection is."[2] They proceeded by first considering each of the more well-established areas of law, libel, slander, copyright, breach of contract, breach of trust, and so on and by then showing that the application of each of these areas of law does not really match up with what most people would feel is an adequate protection of privacy. The structure of their argument was to show, by elimination, that there really must be something else, a right to privacy, that stands apart from other laws and rights.

They looked particularly closely at the idea that privacy is a kind of property, since, in many ways, protection of property and protection of privacy share similar attributes. Suppose, suggested Warren and Brandeis, that someone accidentally receives a personal letter from a stranger. Under what principle of law, they asked, could one assert that the person receiving the letter does not have a right to publish its contents? There is no contract and no relationship of trust to break, and the letter can reasonably be considered to be the property of the receiver, since he or she would be free to discard it. But publishing the letter's contents seems wrong. Why?

Invoking a now famous phrase, they concluded that the protection provided for the thoughts, feelings, and sentiments expressed in a personal letter or other private writing

> is merely an instance of the enforcement of the more general right of the individual *to be let alone*. It is like the right not to be assaulted or beaten, the right not to be imprisoned, the right not to be maliciously prosecuted, the right not to be defamed. In each of these rights, as indeed in all other rights recognized by the law, there inheres the quality of being owned or possessed—and (as that is the distinguishing attribute of property) there may be some propriety in speaking of those rights as property. But, obviously, they bear little resemblance to what is ordinarily comprehended under that term. The principle which protects personal writings and all other personal productions, not against theft and physical appropriation, but against publication in any form, is in reality not the principle of private property, but that of an inviolate personality.[3]

Warren and Brandeis argued that privacy was, in itself, a right belonging to the individual—apart from property rights, contract rights, and other considerations. Although their essay was recognized as a legal landmark, it took many more years before the courts began to give serious regard to the "right to be let alone." Some would argue that frequent marketing calls during dinner are clear evidence that we still do not recognize and defend that right.

## The Basis for Privacy Rights

Before I continue with the story of the development of privacy law, I need to make a distinction. The distinction is between an individual's right to be let alone by government, on the one hand, and the right to be let alone by other citizens and by businesses, on the other. Given the bad treatment that they suffered at the hands of King George III, the framers of the Constitution were understandably much more concerned about intrusion by government than about intrusion by other private citizens. Consequently, the Constitution, in the Fourth Amendment, guarantees that

> The right of the people to be secure in their persons, houses, papers, and effects, against unreasonable searches and seizures, shall not be violated, and no warrants shall issue,

> but upon probable cause, supported by oath or affirmation, and particularly describing the place to be searched, and the persons or things to be seized.

The Fourth Amendment protects citizens from their government. As we continue in our consideration of privacy law it will be important to bear in mind that protection from government does not necessarily imply protection from other citizens; the government has unique powers that must be constrained in special ways.

This leads to another important distinction: to the extent that there is a right to privacy, it is a right enjoyed by individuals, not by corporations. Corporations have other protections that are similar to an individual's privacy rights, such as trade secrecy protection and trademark protection, but a corporation cannot claim that its privacy has been violated, whether by government, by individuals, or by other companies. Privacy rights are reserved for individual citizens.

What this means is that, as businesspeople, we cannot think in terms of privacy as a protection for our businesses (though, as citizens, we may have personal concerns about privacy and the government). Instead, for us, the interesting business questions are:

- How does privacy law constrain business by providing individuals with protections from business uses of information?
- How does privacy law encourage business growth by providing consumers with the guarantees of safety that are a prerequisite to doing business?

With these distinctions in mind—privacy is for individuals, not businesses, and protection from government is not the same as protection from other people and businesses—we can go ahead and blur them for a bit. The reason for the blurring is that the development of the concept of a right to privacy, of a right to be let alone, has drawn both from cases involving the government and from cases involving private entities. Our quest to understand the nature of and basis for privacy can usefully draw from both government and private examples.

Thirty-eight years after writing "The Right to Privacy" with Samuel Warren, Louis Brandeis got the opportunity to apply the principles articulated in that article as a Supreme Court Justice in a wiretapping case, *Olmstead* v. *U.S.* Roy Olmstead had created a substantial liquor smuggling and distribution business operating in Seattle, Washington, during the time of Prohibition, and federal agents took seriously the task of uncovering such criminal activity and bringing the offenders to justice. To this end, they tapped the wires of the telephones used to receive orders and manage the liquor business and did so without securing a search warrant. The question before the Court was whether the 775 typewritten pages of telephone conversation transcripts were admissible as evidence.

The government asserted that the agents had not violated the Fourth Amendment in compiling these transcripts because they did not actually enter the premises of the business to place the taps and so did not violate Olmstead's security in his person, house, papers, and effects. The majority opinion of the Court, written by Chief Justice and former President William Taft, concurred. If the government had, instead, opened sealed mail messages to and from the business, *that* would have been a violation of the Fourth Amendment, since communications through the mails—a tangible property—are protected by law.

The distinction between information passing over wires and information passing through physical mail is still a relevant one today. When does the government have the right to conduct surveillance of communications passing over the Internet or through wireless channels? In 1928 Justice Taft concluded that "The language of the [Fourth] amendment cannot be extended and expanded to include telephone wires, reaching to the whole world from the defendant's house or office. The intervening wires are not part of his house or office, any more than are the highways along which they are stretched." [4] In short, no one could reasonably expect to have privacy on the phone any more than if they were having a conversation on a public street.

Justice Brandeis wrote a dissent that, forty years later, became more important than the majority's ruling in *Olmstead*. His dissent drew upon two important arguments. The first was that, if the Constitution is to be a living, useful instrument of democracy rather than a historical artifact, it needs to reflect the *intent* of the Founders rather than just the particular details of their time. In short, Brandeis argued that the Constitution talks about "papers" and not "telecommunications" because there were no telecommunications systems in 1791, when the Fourth Amendment was written. Translating the Founders' concern about government intrusion into twentieth-century terms, Brandeis argued that wiretapping was just as much a breach of security in an age when most communications are by telephone as breaking, entering, and seizing papers were when communications were primarily through the mail.[5]

Brandeis's second argument expanded on the themes that he had articulated in "The Right to Privacy" four decades earlier:

> The makers of our Constitution undertook to secure conditions favorable to the pursuit of happiness. They recognized the significance of man's spiritual nature, of his feelings

> and of his intellect. They knew that only a part of the pain, pleasure and satisfactions of life are to be found in material things. They sought to protect Americans in their beliefs, their thoughts, their emotions and their sensations. They conferred, as against the government, the right to be let alone—the most comprehensive of rights and the right most valued by civilized men. To protect that right, every unjustifiable intrusion by the government upon the privacy of the individual, whatever the means employed, must be deemed a violation of the Fourth Amendment.[6]

This is well-constructed, passionate prose; not every generation of justices produces a Louis Brandeis. But his argument was a minority opinion in 1928.

The view set forth in *Olmstead*, that the Fourth Amendment protected only against physical trespass and that wiretapping was legitimate surveillance, persisted all the way up to 1967, when the Supreme Court, in *Katz* v. *United States*, finally reversed the position taken in *Olmstead*. Charles Katz had been convicted in lower courts of running an interstate gambling business over the phone, working from a phone booth. The evidence used to get the conviction had been obtained by attaching an electronic eavesdropping device to the phone booth. In the lower courts the debate had centered around the question of whether a phone booth was a constitutionally protected place, safe from government intrusion, search, and seizure, or whether it was a public place.

The Supreme Court's *Katz* ruling rejected the lower court's focus on trespass and places and brought two important new interpretations to the Fourth Amendment. First, the Court decided that the Amendment governs not only the seizure of tangible items but extends as well to the recording of oral statements. Second, the Court ruled that the Fourth Amendment protects people rather than places, and that, consequently, its reach cannot turn on the presence or absence of a physical intrusion into a particular place. In short, the Court finally came around to agreeing with Brandeis's first argument in his dissent from *Olmstead*: the Court decided that the intent of the Founders should be understood to cover governmental intrusion into private communications, even when the intrusion used means that could not have been imagined in 1791.

But, from the standpoint of privacy law, it is significant that the Court did not subscribe to Brandeis's second, more passionate argument to the effect the Constitution implied a right to be let alone. Justice Potter Stewart, in writing the Court's opinion in *Katz*, said:

> The Fourth Amendment cannot be translated into a general constitutional "right to privacy." That Amendment protects individual privacy against certain kinds of governmental intrusion, but its protections go further, and often have nothing to do with privacy at all. Other provisions of the Constitution protect personal privacy from other forms of

> governmental invasion. But the protection of a person's general right to privacy—his right to be let alone by other people—is, like the protection of his property and of his very life, left largely to the law of the individual States.[7]

So, although there is no explicit mention of privacy in the Constitution, there is general agreement that the Constitution does provide the basis for a right of privacy from government intrusion. But this kind of privacy right does nothing to protect people from the collection and use of data about their Internet shopping preferences, from intrusive marketing calls, or from the use and sale of personal data without their permission. There is no Constitutional basis for such protection. Instead, such privacy rights, to the extent that they exist at all, emerge from a combination of different sources, including federal statutes (for example, it is a violation of federal law to disclose video rental records), state statutes (for example, it is against the law in New York and in some other states to disclose library records), professional ethics (for example, physician–patient and attorney–client confidentiality), and common law that varies from state to state (for example, the legal precedents against voyeurism).

In legal terms these other rights to privacy—the ones apart from protection from government intrusion—are known as *torts*. Torts are causes for civil action that are based on statutes or on legal precedent. Rights based on torts do not have the same quality of feeling chiseled in stone that Constitutional rights have; privacy torts are no exception.

## The Nature of the Privacy Right

After the publication of Warren and Brandeis's article in 1890, privacy, as a legal concept applying to interactions between individuals and between people and businesses, muddled along without the benefit of a consistent notion of just what the right to privacy involved. It was one thing to assert that citizens enjoyed a right to be left alone and another to use that abstraction in a lawsuit. The muddling is partly in the nature of torts: each state is free to pass laws recognizing different torts, and each state interprets torts in terms of the legal precedents established in that state, ignoring conflicting precedents in other states. Consequently, the same privacy complaint could result in very different court decisions in different states. Add to this the fact that the definition of a privacy right is still young and unformed, and therefore likely to be understood in widely different ways, and you have the recipe for a muddle.[8]

This muddle finally got some degree of new clarity in 1960, when an influential legal scholar by the name of Dean William Prosser reviewed the cases that had emerged over the decades, categorized them, and then wrote an article arguing that the privacy tort really consisted of four separate but related torts.[9] Prosser's distinctions and definitions are useful for us as we try to sharpen our own thinking about the nature of the right to privacy. Prosser identified the following four kinds of invasion of privacy:

1. **Intrusion**: the unreasonable, highly offensive intrusion upon someone's solitude. The intrusion can be physical, as when someone enters someone else's house without invitation. It can also be virtual, as when someone obtains someone else's bank balance without permission.
2. **Appropriation**: the unauthorized use of someone's name, likeness, or other information related to identity. Defense against appropriation works differently for public figures than for the general, private citizen because the public figure can more easily make an economic claim on the right to derive value from his or her name or image.
3. **False light**: the highly offensive, false portrayal of an individual. For example, using someone's photo to illustrate a story about rapists when the person is innocent of rape could prompt a lawsuit based on the false light tort.
4. **Disclosure of private facts**: the highly offensive publication or distribution of private information that is not of legitimate public interest. Unlike actions based on libel or slander, an action can be based on the private facts tort even when the facts are true. For example, publication of the fact that someone had a sex change operation, a fact that the person had tried to keep private in assuming her new identity, has been the basis for a successful suit on the basis of the private facts tort.[10]

Since the publication of Prosser's article, these four torts have, in general, been recognized as the only grounds for legal action based on invasion of privacy. Some states have encoded all four torts in statutes, other states have rejected one or more of the torts, and yet others have decided to leave it to the courts to decide which torts to recognize under which circumstances. So, despite Prosser's contribution to clarifying the notion of privacy, it is still currently true that there is no single, clear notion of privacy that applies across the entire United States. Clearly, when we are considering privacy on the Internet, that leads to problems in interpretation and jurisdiction.

### Conflict with Other Laws Adds to the Confusion

An important complication associated with privacy torts, made worse by the state-by-state variations, is that they overlap with other causes of action, such as defamation and infliction of emotional harm. Privacy rights also conflict, sometimes head-on, with other rights that our society regards as important and worth protecting, such as the right to be free from danger or the First Amendment protection of the press. These conflicts have caused some states to outlaw the use of some of the privacy torts as causes for action.[11]

Freedom of the press is an especially well protected right in the United States. Conflicts between the press and assertions of privacy rights are good examples of how claims to privacy are often not easy to evaluate, since they are in conflict with other rights. Consider, for example, Clarence Arrington's privacy conflict with the *New York Times*, described in detail in Ellen Alderman and Caroline Kennedy's book, *The Right to Privacy.*[12] The *New York Times Magazine* used Arrington's picture on its cover to draw attention to a feature story about the black middle class. The *Times* did not get Arrington's name or his permission to use his image. Worse, it turned out that when he discovered his picture on the front of the magazine and read the article, he found that he disagreed vehemently with the point of view and the conclusions drawn in the article. His friends wanted to know why he had agreed to be the principal advertisement for such a disagreeable piece of journalism. Well, he hadn't agreed; he had never been asked. So, he sued the *New York Times* for invasion of his privacy through wrongful appropriation of his image. The courts decided that the right of the press to operate in an unfettered fashion was more important than the man's right to privacy, writing that "An inability to vindicate a personal predilection for greater privacy may be part of the price every person must be prepared to pay for a society in which information and opinion flow freely."[13] In fact, the outcome of this lawsuit was that it stimulated the New York legislature to provide protection for photographers and their agents from such suits in the future.

### Recent Developments: Telemarketing

It is broadly recognized that the right of the press to gather news is highly protected. But how does privacy fare against other assertions of freedom of speech? What about freedom of speech as exercised by telemarketing calls during dinner? What if the freedom is exercised by autodialer, rather than by a human caller?

In the first part of the 1990s, telemarketers, the courts, and Congress got involved in a debate over the use of autodialers to make prerecorded marketing calls to homes. The arguments that pulled this debate back and forth through the courts illustrate just how difficult it is to establish even a narrow kind of privacy claim against claims of free speech, even when the free speech does not involve the press.

The Automated Telephone Consumer Protection Act (TCPA) became law in December 1991. It outlawed many kinds of automated marketing calls.[14] Senator Fritz Hollings, sponsor of the legislation, understood that the privacy concerns addressed in the legislation were in potential conflict with the free speech rights of marketing companies. Citing Brandeis's assertion of the central importance of the right to be let alone, Hollings argued that the individual's privacy concerns, in this case, outweighed free speech claims. After all, as Hollings said on the floor of the Senate: "Computerized calls are the scourge of modern civilization. They wake us up in the morning; they interrupt our dinner at night; they force the sick and elderly out of bed; they hound us until we want to rip the telephone right out of the wall."[15]

Telemarketing companies didn't agree, of course. What was even more interesting was that the American Civil Liberties Union (ACLU) didn't agree either. Working with the National Association of Telecomputer Operators and its president, Kathryn Moser, Charles Hinkle of the Oregon ACLU brought an action in Oregon against that state's anti-autodialing statute, successfully arguing before the Oregon courts that the statute illegally curtailed free speech guarantees.[16] A subsequent attempt to apply this same argument against the federal law failed. At the federal level, the opinion of the Ninth Circuit Court stated that "Congress adequately demonstrated that [automated, prerecorded calls to residences] pose a threat to residential privacy. The ban is narrowly tailored to advance that interest, and leaves open ample alternative channels of communication. Thus, it does not violate the First Amendment."[17]

Despite the direction of the federal verdict, this case illustrates the strength of free speech claims when pitted against privacy claims. It was only because the TCPA states its claims narrowly and because there are alternative avenues of expression that the privacy claim was sustained at the federal level.

### Summarizing the Nature of the Privacy Right

As a relatively new legal concept, privacy rights for individuals, relative to other people and to companies (as opposed to the government), are in a state of flux and confusion. Prosser's separation of privacy actions into four distinct torts helped, but there is still ample cause for confusion and uncertainty over privacy.

- **Inconsistency across jurisdictions**: Clearly, the inconsistency from state to state is a problem for companies trying to come to terms with privacy laws in an Internet business.
- **Limited applicability of Prosser's torts**: Although one could invade privacy in any of Prosser's four ways while using the Internet as the vehicle for the

invasion, it would normally be the case that a number of these torts are not relevant to the concerns of companies as they move to the Web, unless they represent the press. (And, for the press, the problems with publication on the Web are not different from the problems that the press has historically encountered with privacy claims.) In particular, appropriation and false light will not be relevant claims against most businesses. That leaves disclosure of private facts and intrusion as the most important likely causes of action against a business.

- **Potential weakness of privacy as a cause for action**: The disclosure of private facts tort has generally been a very weak cause of action when used against the press. In pitting the standard of what is highly offensive against the standard of what is newsworthy, setting the right to privacy against freedom of the press, the press usually wins. It remains to be seen whether this tort acquires new relevance when "disclosure" can mean selling private data to other marketing companies.
- **Privacy is not ownership**: Nothing in these torts suggests that people "own" private facts about themselves, in the same sense that they can own a car or wristwatch. In fact, as Clarence Arrington discovered, even a claim to ownership of such very personal artifacts as one's image can be set aside in favor of the press's right to gather and distribute news. Tracy Coyle's claims and optimistic business plan notwithstanding, it is clear that the individual does not have a legal right that provides complete ownership and control of personal facts.[18]

## The Law and Privacy

I began this chapter with two questions: What is the nature of the privacy right, and what is the basis for the right?

The review of the short history of privacy law shows that the privacy right actually has two natures. In the first instance, people have a guarantee of privacy against government intrusion. In particular, the Constitution provides a firm basis for protection against unreasonable search and seizure of an individual's person, house, papers, and effects. In the past forty years this protection has been extended to cover wiretapping and has come to be understood as a protection for the individual, not just a protection of property. As with all rights to privacy, this protection from the government applies to people, not to corporations.

The other nature of the privacy right—I call it *private-sector privacy*—concerns protection of one's privacy from intrusion by other individuals or by businesses. It is the kind of privacy right that a person would claim if he or she felt that the *New York Times*, DoubleClick, or an online merchant had violated his or her privacy.

Private-sector privacy is much less firmly formed than the protection against the government. It grows from a generally accepted notion that people have a right to be let alone. Deciding how far that right extends, however, is difficult because it quickly begins to overlap and even conflict with other rights. In particular, the right to keep information private is often in direct conflict with the right of the press to gather and report the news. We also saw that the right to be let alone was potentially in conflict with the right of others to speak freely. In short, the basis for private-sector privacy has not yet developed to the point where such privacy rights are uniformly understood, universally recognized, and regarded as carrying substantial weight when they come into conflict with other rights.

Another important conclusion is that there is an important interaction between technology and privacy rights. Legislation and court activity has tended to define privacy in response to particular technical assaults. In the 1890s Warren and Brandeis were concerned about photography; from the 1920s through the 1960s the courts struggled to come to terms with the central role of the telephone; in the early 1990s Fritz Hollings focused on carving out privacy protection against automatic dialers. This focus on the *means* of privacy invasion is yet more evidence that there is no clear, affirmative notion of what the privacy right is, in itself.

As a point of contrast, consider protection from theft of real property. Most of us share a common understanding of what such theft is. Laws protecting us from theft do not have to take into account the techniques used to accomplish theft in order to define our right to be secure in property. It is possible to write, "Thou shalt not steal" and assume that, in so doing, one has defined protection for a broad class of assaults on real property.

This is not at all the case with the right to be let alone. Lacking a clear, shared notion of just what that right entails, courts and legislatures fall into defining the privacy right piecemeal, by enumerating the different kinds of assaults. This has led numerous commentators to speak of privacy as a *derivative* right rather than an *inherent* right. The right to privacy depends on other things.

The act of defining the privacy right through precedent and in terms of the different means of assault has a number of consequences. First, the definition of the privacy right keeps shifting. This is inevitable since, as I noted at the outset, privacy is a relatively new area of law. But it also adds a substantial degree of uncertainty for businesses trying to base decisions on privacy law.

A second consequence is that our society defines privacy by looking over its shoulder rather than looking forward (for example, waiting until 1967 before acknowledging the central role of the telephone). Understanding privacy in terms of what has happened, rather than in terms of a shared, general principle, has two important impacts on business:

1. Legal frameworks, such as Prosser's categorization of privacy torts, are much more useful for understanding the old threats to privacy than they are as a guide to handling the questions before us now, arising from technologies that were never part of the legal history that Prosser reviewed and cataloged.
2. The courts' attempts to apply precedents based on outdated presuppositions will produce surprising results, as they did in 1928 when the Court distinguished between the protections provided for telecommunications and those provided for paper documents. Looking backwards provides a strange and sometimes distorted perspective on the present when presuppositions keep changing rapidly.

In summary, our survey of privacy and the law shows that the basis for claims of private-sector privacy rights is spotty, inconsistent (particularly across different states), and generally weak, despite a strong, shared sense that there ought to be some kind of right to be let alone. In particular, the idea shared by many people that they somehow "own" the facts and particulars about themselves does not currently have a strong basis in law.

Scott McNealy, CEO of Sun computers, famously remarked, "You have zero privacy anyway. Get over it."[19] When it comes to private-sector privacy, he was not far from the mark. Looking for a strong legal conception of a privacy "right" is the wrong place to start in an effort to inform and shape policy and practice on the Internet.

Although this may appear to be a good situation for business in that it reduces the potential for costs due to successful privacy claims, the appearance is deceiving. Trust is the grease that makes business transactions move quickly and easily. In brick and mortar businesses trust grows from face-to-face contact and from the sense of being able to "size up" a business in a physical visit. Those elements are missing on the Internet, and, worse, customers share a strong sense that their privacy is more at risk on the Internet than elsewhere. The next chapter explores these concerns in an effort to understand just how the weak, confused state of private-sector privacy is creating friction as businesses move onto the Web.

## Notes

1. From the Samuel Warren and Louis Brandeis article "The Right to Privacy," which first appeared in the *Harvard Law Review,* IV(5), December 15, 1890. Accessed in May 2001 at http://www.lawrence.edu/fac/boardmaw/Privacy_brand_warr2.html.
2. Ibid.
3. Ibid.
4. From U.S. Supreme Court, *Olmstead* v. *U.S.,* 277 U.S. 438 (1928). Accessed on the Web at http://caselaw.lp.findlaw.com/scripts/getcase.pl?court=us&vol=277&invol=438 in May 2001.
5. Lawrence Lessig, in his important book *Code* (New York: Basic Books, 1999, pp. 111–121), takes a careful look at the Olmstead case, using Taft's and Brandeis's opinions as examples of two different approaches to retaining fidelity to the Constitution. His analysis is interesting and makes a good read.
6. From *Olmstead* v. *U.S.* (cited above).
7. From U.S. Supreme Court, *Katz* v. *United States*, 389 U.S. 347 (1967).
8. Ellen Alderman and Caroline Kennedy, in *The Right to Privacy* (New York: Vintage, 1997), provide a readable history of the development of privacy law that includes many illustrations of how the right to privacy has been understood in the courts.
9. See William L. Prosser, "Privacy," 48 *Cal. L. Rev.* 383, 389 (1960).
10. The case of the transsexual is described in Alderman and Kennedy (cited above), pp. 167–168.
11. Ibid., pp. 158–170.
12. Ibid., p. 216ff.
13. From *Arrington* v. *New York Times Co.*, 434 N.E.2d 1319, 449 N.Y.S.2d 941 (N.Y. 1982), *cert. denied*, 459 U.S. 1146 (1983).
14. 47 *U.S. Code* § 227.
15. From statements by Sen. Hollings on the Automated Telephone Consumer Protection Act in the *Congressional Record,* November 7, 1999, p. S16205.
16. See *Moser* v. *Frohnmayer,* 315 Or 372, 379-80, 845 P2d 1284 (1993).
17. From *Moser* v. *F.C.C.*, 46 F.3d 970 (9th Cir., 1995).
18. In *Shamans, Software, and Spleens* (Cambridge, MA: Harvard University Press, 1996), James Boyle recounts the somewhat astounding story of John Moore, who underwent treatment for leukemia at the University of California Medical Center. During the course of the treatment the doctors discovered that some of Moore's blood components had significant commercial value because they overproduced

lymphokines. The doctors extracted quantities of Moore's bodily fluids and removed his spleen, arguably as part of his treatment. But they also, without informing Moore, kept these fluids and body parts for use as part of their commercial efforts to create a new, genetically engineered cell line, which they subsequently patented. The courts ruled that Moore had no claim to his body parts and that the ownership rights properly belonged to the doctors.

19. Sun Microsystems CEO Scott McNealy, talking to a group of reporters about his "Jini" Java project, reported in *Wired News*, January 26, 1999. Accessed at http://www.wired.com/news/politics/0,1283,17538,00.html in May 2001.

# Consumer Concerns

EVER since consumers started buying things on the Web, there has been concern about just how much privacy they had on the Internet. As the Pew Internet and American Life Project found in a survey in early 2000, "A strong sense of distrust shades many Internet users' view of the online world, and the uneasiness has grown in the past two years. Eighty-six percent of Internet users say they are concerned about business people they don't know getting personal information about them or their families."[1]

## The DoubleClick Story

In the first months of 2000 a company called DoubleClick gave shape to these consumer fears. Before that time, if an Internet consumer had heard of DoubleClick at all, it was as a company that managed the banner advertising for other companies. What most consumers understood less well was that, in the process of placing ads, DoubleClick is able to assemble a database that profiles the viewing habits and interests of millions of Internet users. DoubleClick does this by sending an identification number, wrapped in something called a "cookie," along with each advertisement that it displays. The ID number is unique to each computer and Web browser. The browser, unless instructed otherwise by the user, stores the cookie containing the ID on the computer's disk. The next time that the user encounters an ad managed by DoubleClick, perhaps when viewing an entirely different Web site, the browser software sends back the cookie information to DoubleClick. Because DoubleClick keeps track of which IDs it sets from which sites, the returning cookies give DoubleClick a way to construct a profile of the different sites that people visit. DoubleClick can tell which pages are viewed, when they are viewed, and how often they are viewed.

Profiling makes a lot of people uncomfortable. It feels strange to know that some company is keeping track of what you do on the Web. The discomfort is made worse by the fact that most users know that they are being watched, but aren't sure just how it is being done. The Pew study found that 8 out of 10 users think their actions are being tracked, but fewer than half the users have any idea that cookies have something to do with the tracking.[2] Having a sense that one is being watched while not being quite sure how makes people uneasy.

For more information about how information collection from Web-site visits works, see the special supplemental section, placed immediately after the current chapter, titled "A Deeper Look: Technical Background on Cookies and Web Bugs."

But DoubleClick had always claimed that the discomfort and caution were unwarranted. After all, the company was just collecting anonymous IDs. As it used to state in its privacy policy:

> DoubleClick does not know the name, email address, phone number, or home address of anybody who visits a site in the DoubleClick Network. All users who receive an ad targeted by DoubleClick's technology remain completely anonymous. Since we do not have any information concerning names or addresses, we do not sell or rent any such information to third parties.[3]

So, the story was that DoubleClick was just collecting anonymous information in order to do a better job of matching advertisements and viewers. Advertisers greatly prefer sending relevant ads. Users, to the extent that they want to see ads at all, would rather see relevant ones. DoubleClick was able to claim that it was creating a win-win situation for shoppers and for companies with things to sell.

But in November 1999 DoubleClick completed its acquisition of Abacus Direct, a company that bills itself as the manager of "the nation's largest proprietary database of consumer, retail, business to business, publishing and online transactions used for target marketing purposes."[4] Abacus's database "contains records from more than 1,100 merchandise catalogs, with more than 2 billion consumer transactions from virtually all U.S. consumer catalog buying households."[5] It contains the names, addresses, and purchasing habits of 9 out of every 10 U.S. households.[6]

After the acquisition, DoubleClick was in a position to combine everything that it knew about a person's Web behavior with all the Abacus direct-marketing information. The promise of anonymity under all circumstances was history. And so DoubleClick changed its privacy policy. The new policy reads:

> However, as described in "Abacus Alliance" and "Information Collected by DoubleClick's Web Sites" below, non-personally identifiable information collected by DoubleClick in the course of ad delivery *can be associated with a user's personally identifiable information* if that user has agreed to receive personally tailored ads.[7]

Some might see this change as breaking the commitment made in DoubleClick's earlier privacy statement, but reading the privacy statement as a "commitment" is naive and unwarranted. As DoubleClick's current statement further warns, "We also recommend that you review this Privacy Statement periodically, as DoubleClick may update it from time to time."[8] It seems that what DoubleClick is really saying is, "Today's privacy statement is worthless as a guide for what we might choose to do tomorrow with the data that we collect from you today. Moreover, if you think that you might not like tomorrow's decision, it is your responsibility to keep checking back to see what it might be. Our collection of data about you today places us under no obligation to continue to honor today's policy about how we respect your privacy or to contact you when we decide to change that policy."

Such a deal. Of course, there is that matter in the new statement about "if the user has agreed. . . . " Doesn't that at least make the change somewhat more acceptable? Perhaps. But a careful reading of the rest of the statement—users need to read these things like they read a legal document if they hope to protect themselves—reveals that DoubleClick assumes that users *do* agree to tie personal information to their Web profiles unless they specifically give instructions to the contrary. Again, from the DoubleClick site:

> Abacus Online is fully committed to offering online consumers ***notice*** about the collection and use of personal information about them, and the ***choice*** not to participate. . . . The notice and opportunity to choose will appear on those Web sites that contribute user information to the Abacus Alliance, usually when the user is given the opportunity to provide personally identifiable information (e.g., on a user registration page, or on an order form).[9]

"Notice" and "choice" sound good when it comes to this "opportunity [!] to provide personally identifiable information," but in privacy policy jargon what DoubleClick is describing is a process known as *opt-out*. Opt-out makes it the *user's* responsibility to pay attention, read the agreements carefully, and find and click all the right boxes on all the different sites that they visit. Have you ever tried to figure out how to send back the Publisher's Clearinghouse entry form in order to be eligible for the $10 Million Sweepstakes award *without* buying a magazine? Check these three boxes, find and affix these two stickers, find and enclose the small pink slip, turn around twice and face south . . . opt-out can be like that.

DoubleClick's $1.7-billion acquisition of Abacus Direct, its movement toward association of Web data with personal identities and mail-order purchasing information, and its decision to rewrite its privacy policy, reneging on what seemed to be commitments to protect anonymity in its earlier policy, all worked together to bring a lot of attention to DoubleClick.

> In short order, lawyers filed 17 class-action lawsuits against DoubleClick, attorneys general in Michigan and New York opened probes to determine if the plan violated their respective unfair consumer practices laws, the FTC launched its own investigation, and the company's stock lost 60 percent of its value between its January high and March.[10]

DoubleClick had stepped over some kind of invisible line, giving a concrete form to people's fears about privacy invasion on the Web. One vendor of an "anonymizer," a service that allows people to visit sites without revealing their identity, experienced a four-fold increase in subscriptions after the DoubleClick announcement moved from business news to nightly news.[11] On March 2, 2000, Kevin O'Connor, DoubleClick's CEO, announced that DoubleClick's plans to merge the DoubleClick and Abacus Direct databases were a mistake and that DoubleClick would seek agreements with the government and with the industry as a whole regarding privacy standards before proceeding.[12]

With regard to the question of whether DoubleClick actually broke any laws, the answer appears to be "No." About a year after the initial blowup, in January 2001, the FTC concluded its investigation of DoubleClick, stating that:

> It appears to staff that DoubleClick never used or disclosed consumers' PII (personal identifying information) for purposes other than those disclosed in its privacy policy. Specifically, it appears that DoubleClick did not combine PII from Abacus Direct with clickstream collected on client Web sites. In addition, it appears that DoubleClick has not used sensitive data for any online preference marketing product, in contravention of its stated privacy policy.[13]

Then, in March 2001, a federal district court judge dismissed all the pending federal claims against DoubleClick, stating that the plaintiffs failed to show that DoubleClick had violated any of the laws under which the plaintiffs were bringing suit.[14]

The fact that DoubleClick pulled back from crossing the line of actually tying click-stream data to personally identifiable information does not make the line or the issue go away. DoubleClick's initial plans and its apparent ability to restate its privacy policy made Web users more conscious that Web sites are collecting profile information and that privacy may be at risk on the Web.

## Consumers and Web Privacy

Nobody wants to do business with a company that breaks implied commitments or that unilaterally changes the terms of an agreement. If you had a supplier that did business that way, you'd sever the relationship as quickly as you could. The dilemma for customers on the Web is that they never wanted a relationship with DoubleClick in the first place and are relatively powerless to terminate it. DoubleClick is more like a nuisance caller than a business partner. The only way to put an end to the relationship is to learn about cookies, invest in software tools to screen cookies, and keep on guard against other attempts, such as Web bugs, to assemble profile information.

This is a fortress mentality rather than a state of mind conducive to doing more business on the Web. Instead of making customers comfortable, such behavior makes them angry. The Pew survey found that 94 percent of Internet users want to see punishment for any company that uses personal information in ways that contradict an earlier privacy statement. And punishment does not mean a slap on the wrist. The majority of the Internet users surveyed advocate punishments in the form of jail terms, fines, or a shutdown of the offending company's Web site.[15] The strength of such feeling is an indication of the degree to which users want business on the Web to be more predictable than it is today. The desire for predictability, enforced by punishment for companies that act in bad faith, motivates the push for legislation to regulate the use of personal, private information on the Web.

With all that said, it is still clear that it is possible to make people comfortable with Web shopping, given the right situation. The Pew study of trust and online privacy found that two-thirds of the people using the Internet are willing to provide companies with names, addresses, and other personal information. But they want to be able to decide when they do that, rather than just have it happen behind the scenes and behind their backs.

Clearly, being willing to provide name, address, and credit card information is a prerequisite to buying things on the Web. According to a Harris survey in the second half of 2000, 59 percent of the people in the United States over the age of 18 have Internet access.[16] The Pew researchers found that 48 percent of their sample of Internet users had bought something online with a credit card. Combining those numbers, we can estimate that the percentage of U.S. adults who have bought something on the Web at least once is perhaps approaching 30 percent. The problem for companies that would like to do more business on the Web, however, is that the overall volume of purchasing is still quite small, accounting for only about 2.5 percent of overall retail spending in the United States.[17] Using Geoffrey Moore's chasm-crossing terminology,[18] retail commerce on the Web is still in the "early adopter" phase. The problem facing businesspeople is how to get across that chasm to start selling to the "early majority."

In Moore's now-classic book he describes how winning the trust and attention of the early majority is what takes businesses and markets from high-flying concept plays to substantial volume and presence. The terms that he uses to characterize the early majority are "pragmatic" and "prudent." Mainstream, early majority buyers are not risk takers. Although there is more than one hurdle standing between Web-based retailing today and selling to the early majority, there can be little doubt that resolving privacy concerns is high on the list. From the standpoint of early majority shoppers, the sense that something sneaky is happening on the Web is enough to make them keep their money in their pockets.

The survey data collected by the Pew Internet and American Life Project, AT&T Labs,[19] and other research organizations is useful in identifying the primary concerns that consumers have surrounding privacy. The list of requirements is short enough to be counted on the fingers of one hand:

- **Let's make a deal**: Providing personal information is like doing a deal.
- **Cede some control**: Consumers want some say-so in the deal.
- **Make it easy**: Exercising say-so needs to be simple and quick.
- **Expand**: These issues are more important as you move beyond early adopters.

### Let's Make a Deal

Consumers think of providing personal information as a trade. They provide information to a company in return for something they value. Tracy Coyle took this idea and made it concrete, offering to auction off private information to the highest bidders. Most consumers don't conceptualize the trade-off as literally as Coyle, but the principle is still present. Typically the trade is for better service, time savings, or something else other than money.

Thinking of the collection and use of private information as a "deal"—as negotiation—is a useful model for businesspeople. It emphasizes the fact that the exchange needs to benefit the consumers in some way they value.[20]

As in any deal, the value depends on what is being traded. The AT&T study found that users had different levels of willingness to divulge different kinds of information. For example, a substantial majority (76 percent) of users are willing to provide their e-mail addresses in order to get access to a site, but only 54 percent are willing to provide their full names without an excellent reason to do so. Users are even less willing to provide their phone numbers and are nearly completely unwilling to provide their social security numbers.

The willingness to provide different kinds of information also depends on context. For example, 58 percent of the respondents in the AT&T study said that they would be willing to provide sensitive information about income, investments, and investment goals in order to receive customized investment advice, but only 35 percent of the respondents would be willing to provide their names in this scenario. On the other hand, almost half (48 percent) of the respondents would be willing to provide their names in order to receive news, weather, and sports information.

Even this one example suggests that consumers are making some pretty complicated decisions about privacy information that are highly dependent on context. Providing financial information is a relatively trusting activity. Yet, in this apparently high-trust context, the users are less willing to provide names than they are in relatively low-trust settings where they are just getting weather information. This seemingly incongruous result makes sense, however, if one thinks in terms of an unwillingness to attach an identity to the financial information. Giving one's name in exchange for weather information seems relatively safe, even if it is (or, perhaps *because* it is) beside the point.

Put another way, Web users are bringing all of the nuance, complexity, and richness of motive to privacy transactions that they bring to doing any other kind of deal, from buying a car to buying shoes. This is a tremendously important insight and one that has not yet found its way into most thinking about privacy. It has two important, immediate consequences for our consideration of privacy policy. The first is that it bodes ill for most efforts to rationalize or automate privacy transactions through simple legislative or technical fixes. No one would ever seriously propose a technical or legislative scheme for handling shoe preferences; the decision is based on too many variables—on preferences—that vary from person to person and time to time. The important insight is that it won't be any easier for privacy.

The second consequence is that it is easy to see why Web users are very uncomfortable with attempts to connect and integrate purchasing and preference information across different contexts and different Web sites. All of the user's nuance and contextual decision making in, say, deciding to provide a name in one context and not in another, is undermined if Web companies aggregate and tie together all of the information pertaining to an individual customer across all the contexts. Integrating and homogenizing the information across contexts interferes with the consumer's ability to do different deals regarding information in different situations with different vendors.

### Cede Some Control

The logic of doing a deal implies that both parties have some say-so. The problem with much of current Web data tracking and collection, from the user's standpoint, is that vendors are making all of the decisions unilaterally. The DoubleClick case is a particularly egregious example, but it is not inconsistent with the general approach that businesses are taking to Web data collection. Starting from the commonly held idea that data collection can and should be relatively surreptitious and continuing through the Web retailer's demands for self-regulation, it seems that Web businesses have been wanting to do deals for private information while holding all the cards, playing both hands if necessary. Notwithstanding the obvious appeal of such an approach, it is short sighted. Curtailing the consumer's say-so in the negotiations over private information will ensure that retail commerce on the Web never gets beyond the early adopters who are persistent enough and sufficiently comfortable with technology to be able to wrest some control back from the retailers. The sizeable early majority of consumers won't bother with such difficult self-protection and will, instead, continue to do most of their business elsewhere.

The push back against too much control in the hands of retailers shows up in the survey data. The Pew survey of trust and privacy online, talking both to people who are on the Web and those who do not use the Internet, found that 63 percent of the sample feels that companies should not be allowed to track user activities. An even larger proportion (79 percent) believes that Internet companies should get permission from people before making use of personal information. When asked who should have the most say-so about how companies track Web-site visitors and use personal information, 62 percent of this mixed sample of users and nonusers felt that it was the people who use the Web sites who should make the decisions; 19 percent of the sample felt that the government should make the decisions, and only 6 percent felt that the Internet companies should have the most say. It seems safe to conclude that the business community has not been persuasive in convincing the American consumer that business is capable of useful self-regulation.

One important policy question concerns the mechanism that a company makes available to Web-site visitors so that they can express preferences about whether personal data should be collected. There are two alternatives, *opt-out* and *opt-in*. DoubleClick's policy, as mentioned earlier, used opt-out. This alternative provides users with a box to check or some other way of asserting that they do not want their personal data collected and used. Opt-out appears to be better for vendors because it allows them to use data from any and all customers unless a customer has provided explicit instructions to the contrary: user inaction equals permission. Opt-out puts the consumer who wants to protect his or her privacy at a disadvantage. Not only do users have to find the privacy statements and privacy options and click on all the right boxes, but they also have to keep doing the looking and clicking on each site visited. Vendors can, if they choose, make it difficult and time consuming to opt out.

The opt-in approach turns the tables. The vendor can collect and use data for a customer only if that customer explicitly gives permission to do so. User inaction equals no permission. This forces a vendor to sell a customer on the idea of sharing information, making the case to users that it is to their advantage to enter into a closer relationship with the vendor, sharing data in return for the benefits of personalized interaction, better targeted information, quicker service, or some other benefit. Not surprisingly, most vendors join DoubleClick in preferring opt-out to opt-in. But the Pew study found that a really overwhelming majority of the Internet users surveyed—86 percent—want opt-in.

These data on user preferences and concerns strongly suggest that the current rules and practices regarding private information, when regarded from the user's point of view, appear to be tilted in favor of the vendors. The result is that users feel that they do not have sufficient control over the use of information about themselves. It appears that they cannot look after their own interests on the Web. This is not an attitude that is conducive to expanding retail Web business beyond its current small niche.

### Make It Easy

When you go into a brick and mortar store for the first time, there is a "feel" to the place. Is the store clean and nicely lit? What do the other shoppers look like? Is it too hot or too cold? Does it have a nice smell? What kind of music is playing? Does the sales staff make you comfortable?

You also pick up on negative signals. In some stores there are two-way mirrors and video cameras everywhere. You know that you are being watched. That tells you something about the store and the clientele.

On the Web most of the cues that shoppers use to make a judgment about a store are missing. Worse, the customer suspects that he or she is being watched.[21] There is even reason to fear that the data collected about the visit and about what the customer buys is being sold to third parties.

If a merchant wants to counteract these negative messages to make the customer feel safe and comfortable, the merchant needs to do this without assuming a lot of technical sophistication or requiring a lot of work on the part of the customer. A customer knows how to go into a brick and mortar store and size things up. Although this is certainly learned behavior, it feels like an intuitive activity, not a technical or legal one. It is much more difficult to get a "good feeling" about a place on the Web from a privacy statement.

The Pew study found that less than half of the Internet users surveyed claimed to know what a cookie is. From my own experience in working with Web users, even with experienced ones, I would bet that a good number of the people who think they know what a cookie is probably don't. Dealing with cookies is just too hard and technical for most people. If customers have difficulty understanding the operation of something as simple as cookies, it seems very unlikely that listing conditions and terms for information reuse, or relying on technical solutions such as anonymizers and pseudonym generators, will make much sense to the typical customer.

If merchants want to build a large base of trusting customers, they need to make it very easy for customers to know that they are safe. It cannot be hard, subtle, or tricky. This ties back to the point about ceding control: if retailers want people to feel safe, then retailers need to take big, unequivocal steps in that direction.

> The World Wide Web Consortium (W3C), the standards-setting organization for the Web, has developed a recommendation for an automated mechanism for publishing and evaluating privacy statements called the P3P or Platform for Privacy Preferences Project. The idea is to make privacy statements easier to use by automating the process. It is a controversial proposal. In a supplemental section titled "A Deeper Look: Technical Background on the Platform for Privacy Preferences Project (P3P)" I provide a description and evaluation of P3P for readers interested in knowing more about it.

### Expand

Remember that today's Internet shoppers are different from your target market. You are now selling to the early adopters, the people who are more technically proficient and more willing to take risks. But the target is the early majority, made up of people who tend to be more pragmatic and cautious. This means that you cannot simply rely on doing more of what works for today's customers; instead, you must look ahead to the concerns of the customers that you are trying to attract.

The Pew study found that 15 percent of the Internet users in the survey had just gotten onto the Internet in the previous six months. The researchers found that this group of newcomers was substantially more concerned about the possibility that businesses and strangers might get access to personal information over the Web.

It is possible that this greater amount of fear and concern among newcomers is just a function of inexperience and that, as they use the Web more, these newcomers will become more comfortable with it. But that runs counter to another observation, which is that concern about privacy among all users has increased, not decreased, with time. It is difficult to argue that more experience translates into more trust.

Another, more sobering explanation is that as Web usage expands, it is extending to new segments of the population who are more concerned about privacy. In other words, the overall increase in concern about privacy reflects a change in the makeup of the population of Web users. This explanation would suggest that we are beginning to bring in some of the first members of the early majority market, which is surely a good thing. But it also means that the expansion is raising the bar for addressing privacy concerns.

## Broader Privacy Concerns

It is important that business people realize that the concern over Web privacy is just one part of a much larger set of concerns. Americans are worried about privacy issues in general. In the consumer's mind, problems with protecting personal information on the Internet are simply one instance of a much broader set of concerns.

Businesspeople should be familiar with this bigger picture because it shapes the consumer's understanding of what is happening on the Web. Providing a complete rendition of this big picture would require a separate book focused just on privacy issues; many such books have already been written. In Chapter 24 I list some of the books and articles that I have found to be most useful in quickly arriving at a picture of broader consumer concerns about privacy. My goal here is simply to highlight some of the most important dimensions of these concerns.

### The Tone of the Concerns

People are afraid of dangers that they don't understand. Much of the writing on privacy is all about showing people just how much they don't know. Consequently, books about privacy speak to people's fears and, in some cases, work to sharpen those fears.

One of the popular books on privacy features a dust jacket with an eye looking through a keyhole. The back of the dust jacket contains this quote from a U.S. Congressman: "a chilling compendium of the myriad methods government and industry have devised to catalog and profile the preferences of American citizens."[22] Another book on privacy has a cover picturing drawn blinds, with one slat in the blinds askew, providing an opening for a Peeping Tom. A third book asks in its opening pages, "If cameras keep getting smaller and more mobile, like wasp-size drones, what kind of defenses might protect us against Peeping Toms, or police spies, flying such devices through the open windows of our homes?"[23]

Businesses will be able to count themselves lucky if they can bring questions about privacy out of the zone of fear of intrusion and into a pragmatic economic framework. Privacy is a topic that is currently charged and polarized, with good guys and bad guys, as DoubleClick discovered.

### Concern about Technology

As the Warren and Brandeis article illustrates, concerns about privacy have always been driven by changes in technology. There are three broad areas of technology that are central to most public concerns about privacy: databases, surveillance, and the Internet. (A fourth area that is important to experts in the area of privacy is encryption, but encryption is too esoteric to be central to public concern at any level of detail.)

The concern over databases grows from the sense that businesses and government are now able to collect enormous quantities of information about people and can now interconnect all of that information. This is not a new concern. The Fair Credit Reporting Act of 1971 focused specifically on ensuring that consumers had rights of access to the data that is maintained in databases by companies that track and sell consumer credit information. But the concern has grown as the amount of information in electronic form has grown and as more powerful computers, coupled with more powerful software, makes it easier to connect the different sources of information.

Surveillance concerns grow from being watched in the most literal sense of the phrase. In the early 1990s towns and cities in Britain began making extensive use of video cameras for the purpose of crime prevention and prosecution. The practice has spread to other countries, including the United States, and there are now well-publicized cases, such as the tapes recorded before the bombing of the Alfred P. Murrah building in Oklahoma City, in which video surveillance cameras have played important roles in solving crimes. The omnipresent cameras also, of course, contribute to a general sense that what one does in public is no longer ephemeral but is recorded.

The Internet provides the network for tying together the databases and surveillance and for making all of this information more broadly available. No longer does someone wanting to find out about you have to travel to your local courthouse to look up the value of your house, ask your neighbors or look up birth records to find the names and ages of your spouse and children, drive by your house to find out what kind of car you drive, or talk to your employer to make a good guess about your income. A trained researcher, using the Internet to access databases, can uncover such information while sitting at a desk. The Internet makes access to private information easier for anyone who is interested in you, whether they work for a company, the government, or a criminal organization. More than just a research tool, the Internet also becomes a powerful way, in itself, to elicit new information. The first paragraphs of Charles Sykes's *The End of Privacy*, one of the many recent books on privacy issues, provides a picture of how this looks to the typical consumer:

> Before breakfast, a businesswoman signs on to the Internet, checks her email, and orders flowers. Even before she has signed off, her on-line movements have left a trail of data that has been added to her profile, including the fact that the recipient of the flowers is a thirty-two-year-old man who lives in the next suburb. Her phone records indicate a number of late-night calls to the man's residence. While she was on-line, every icon she clicked on was tracked and recorded. Someone was learning about her. Several discreet "cookies" are left behind on her hard drive.
>
> Later that week, her purchase of the flowers will be matched and merged with the fact she vacations in Aruba, buys lingerie from Victoria's Secret, uses a high-end hair color, and drives a late model car. Her name will be sold to marketers looking for consumers who fit that profile. The same marketers have a dossier that already runs to more than eighty-five pages about her spending habits. Every time she uses her smart card at her grocery store, her profile expands, including her recent purchase of hemorrhoid medication, contraceptives, and her preference for cabernets. She is unaware that her ex-husband's attorney has just obtained a copy. Others will be interested to learn that she logged onto an Internet message board for patients with breast cancer for the fourth consecutive day. The next week, she will unexpectedly be denied a new home mortgage.[24]

This is a chilling picture. It is not a picture that encourages people to spend more time shopping on the Internet.

## Creating Fertile Soil for Web Business

Concerns about privacy will place constraints on what businesses are able to do with the information they collect about people. That much is certain. What remains to be seen is whether those constraints are imposed by governments, by associations of businesses, or by the individual businesses themselves. We also do not yet know the focus or the severity of the constraints. The shape that privacy policy will take over the next several years will determine the uses that companies can make of customer information and the value of that information.

The business community's current approach to privacy suggests a military metaphor: business is currently approaching this policy debate as if it were a war that business can fight and win on many fronts, all at once, against an inconsequential, divided foe. For example, in late 2000 legislators sympathetic to privacy concerns discovered that despite their best efforts, the credit industry was able to successfully derail legislation that would have required an individual's consent before his or her social security number could be bought or sold. The intent of the legislation was to curtail social security number identity theft. The credit industry evidently felt that even this modest attempt to protect privacy had to be resisted. Such displays of lobbying intransigence suggest that the business community either feels that it can win all battles or that it cannot afford to give ground on any issue without putting all objectives at risk.

DoubleClick's experience, the accumulated messages from consumer surveys, and the tenor and scope of the public's general concerns over privacy all combine to suggest that the strategy of fighting on all fronts, giving no quarter, is mistaken. To the extent that business chooses to approach privacy policy as a battle, it will find that it is a big war against a large and powerfully aroused adversary. This is why military metaphors are not the place to look for suggestions about how to proceed.

Business *is*, in fact, in a position to preserve the ability to manage and use most customer information in innovative ways, to build new markets, and to grow. But to do that the business community will need to decide which information practices are critical to business and where concessions to consumer concerns make business sense. Put another way, just as each business needs to understand that it is involved in "doing a deal" as it interacts with individual customers, so must business in general recognize that the approach to policy will take the form of making a deal.

There are pragmatic reasons to follow such a course that go beyond the satisfaction of putting together a deal in which everybody comes out ahead. The pragmatic reasons center around the fact that until consumers have a basis for greater comfort than they feel today, the scope of Web business will be limited to early adopters, and Web retailing will continue to be a niche play. The solution to this problem requires recognizing consumer concerns, taking them seriously, and constructing policies that provide customers with the comfort and certainty that they need.

Restating all of this in the simplest possible terms, two conclusions emerge from the survey of consumer concerns and attitudes about privacy. The first is that businesses must develop mechanisms to create much greater consumer comfort and trust concerning how private information is used. This is a prerequisite to expanding the amount of Internet retail commerce. The second conclusion grows from the first: businesses must understand that they are negotiating a deal with consumers that involves providing user benefits in return for access to valuable private information. Successful negotiation will require businesses to look carefully at just what kinds of information they most need, identifying and ranking their priorities.

The focus on identifying and understanding priorities is all the more important because it appears increasingly likely that businesses will not be simply dealing directly with customers but will instead be dealing with the public interest as expressed through Congress. The next chapter looks at privacy issues that are emerging as central to the debate in Congress.

## Notes

1. From Susannah Fox et al., *Trust and Privacy Online: Why Americans Want to Rewrite the Rules* (Washington, DC: The Pew Internet and American Life Project, August 20, 2000), p. 12.
2. Ibid., p. 8.
3. Junkbusters (http://www.junkbusters.com) provides a comprehensive history of DoubleClick's activity, including references to other sources of news and analysis. The information about DoubleClick's earlier privacy policy comes from the Junkbusters site. It was accessed at http://www.junkbusters.com/new.html#personally in May 2001.
4. From the home page of the Abacus Direct Web site, http://www.abacus-direct.com, accessed in May 2001.
5. From the Abacus Direct Web site, http://www.abacus-direct.com, accessed in November 2000.
6. From Edward Robinson, "Click and Cover," *Business 2.0*, September 12, 2000, pp. 168–181.

7. From the DoubleClick privacy policy, http://www.doubleclick.com/us/corporate/privacy/, accessed in November 2000.
8. Ibid.
9. Ibid.
10. From Robinson (cited above), p. 176.
11. Ibid., p. 179.
12. "Statement from Kevin O'Connor, CEO of DoubleClick," issued on BusinessWire on March 2, 2000. Accessed on the Web in May 2001 at http://ir.doubleclick.net/ireye/ir_site.zhtml?ticker=DCLK&script=410&layout=-6&item_id=78051.
13. From a letter from Joel Winston, Acting Associate Director, Division of Financial Practices, Federal Trade Commission, to Christine Varney, DoubleClick's attorney, dated January 22, 2001. Accessed in March 2001 at http://www.ftc.gov/os/closings/staff/doubleclick.pdf.
14. *In re DoubleClick Inc. Privacy Litigation*, 00 Civ. 0641 (NRB), U.S. District Court, Southern District of New York, March 30, 2001. Accessed in March 2001 at http://www.nysd.uscourts.gov/courtweb/pdf/D02NYSC/01-03797.PDF. This is an interesting, important ruling. The plaintiffs attempted to argue, among other things, that DoubleClick's placing cookies on a user's machine was an instance of unauthorized access to the user's machine under the Electronic Communications Privacy Act, analogous to the unauthorized access that a hacker might try to get. Clearly, a ruling in favor of the plaintiffs would have had far-reaching consequences.
15. From Fox et al. (cited above), p. 11.
16. Humphrey Taylor, "Internet Access Continues to Grow But at a Slower Pace," *The Harris Poll*, No. 60, October 11, 2000.
17. From a study by the Commerce Department and Boston Consulting Group, quoted by Laura Carr in "100 Numbers You Need to Know," *The Industry Standard*, November 20, 2000, p. 290.
18. See Geoffrey Moore, *Crossing the Chasm* (New York: Harper Business, 1991).
19. Lorrie Faith Crainor, Joseph Reagle, and Mark S. Ackerman, "Beyond Concern: Understanding Net Users' Attitudes about Online Privacy," AT&T Labs—Research Technical Report TR 99.4.3, April 14, 1999. Accessed in November 2000 at http://www.research.att.com/resources/trs/TRs/99/99.4/99.4.3/report.htm.
20. For a much more complete analysis of how data collection and use works as a deal between Web supplier and Web user, see my book *Web Engagement* (Boston: Addison-Wesley, 2000). Chapter 7, titled "Privacy and Customer Engagement,"

looks at the technical issues surrounding the creation of a win-win deal with customers. The subsequent chapters look carefully at alternative approaches to personalization.

**21.** The Pew study found that 79 percent of the Internet users surveyed believed that it was somewhat common or very common for Web sites to track customer visits.

**22.** Rep. Edward J. Markey, quoted on the dust jacket of the hardback edition of Simson Garfinkel's *Database Nation* (Sebastopol, CA: O'Reilly, 2000).

**23.** From David Brin, *The Transparent Society* (Reading, MA: Perseus, 1999), p. 10.

**24.** From Charles Sykes, *The End of Privacy* (New York: St. Martin's Press, 1999), p. 3.

# Technical Background on Cookies and Web Bugs

THIS chapter takes a deeper look at cookies and Web bugs, two common methods used by Web sites and advertisers to keep track of user activity. There is a great deal of misunderstanding about both cookies and Web bugs. Some people greatly overestimate the power of these tools, fearing that they provide surreptitious access to a person's private files on his or her computer. At the other extreme, some people completely disregard the privacy implications of these tools. Neither extreme is healthy. Fortunately, a brief technical explanation of what cookies and Web bugs actually are usually clears up any misperceptions. Readers already familiar with cookies and Web bugs—or those who do not want to know any more about them—can skip to the next chapter.

Cookies and Web bugs are two approaches to providing ad-serving companies like DoubleClick with information about visitor activity on different sites. The two approaches have different strengths and weaknesses for both advertisers and for visitors who wish to control how information about their activities is being collected.

The brief explanation of the differences between the approaches is that cookies provide ad servers with more useful and more accurate information, but they are also relatively easy for users to detect and control. Cookies can also provide truly useful functionality to users—they are not just a tracking tool. As a consequence, understanding the difference between desirable cookies and more intrusive ones is important for users who want to manage cookie activity.

Web bugs, on the other hand, are nearly impossible for users to detect without substantial effort. Further, they provide no useful service to users. Happily, for people who want to protect their privacy, Web bugs also provide ad servers with less in the way of valuable information than cookies do.

To understand cookies and Web bugs in more detail it is necessary to know what they are and how they work.

## Cookies

Cookies were invented to solve a real problem. The HTTP protocol that governs communications between Web browsers and Web servers is intentionally simple. The simplicity is part of what makes the Web work so well. One of the simplifications is that each request from a Web browser for a page from a Web server is independent of every other page request, even when the requests come one right after another between the same browser and server. This means that, in the world of the Web, there is no concept of a "session" or of a related sequence of pages. Normally this is a good thing. It keeps servers from having to track sessions, holding them open. It makes the Web fast. But sometimes connected sequences of pages are really important, such as when you are wanting to put something in a shopping cart, go to checkout, arrange for shipping, and pay for an item. To do even something as basic and familiar as that there needs to be a way to keep track of a transaction over the course of a sequence of page views. Cookies are the solution to that problem.

Cookies work by storing a small amount of "state" information on the computer that is running the browser. Anthropomorphizing the interaction, it is as if the server, knowing that it cannot remember names and faces, much less what happened in the last meeting with a browser, gives the browser a little piece of paper with an identification number and a brief memo regarding just where the browser and server are in the process of their interaction. The next time the browser encounters this server, it gives the piece of paper back. The server looks at the identification number, notes the most recent step in the transaction, and responds appropriately, "recognizing" the browser and proceeding to the next step in the sequence (for example, proceeding to checkout, then to arranging shipping).

This interaction between browsers and servers, setting and sending cookies, proceeds according to some simple but restrictive rules:

- The browser is in charge. When a server wants to set a cookie, it sends a request to the browser to do so, along with the contents that the server would like to write into the cookie. Depending on instructions from the user, the browser will either write the cookie or not.

- Cookies do not allow Web servers to read things from the user's disk, contrary to popular misconception. Again, the browser is in charge. Before it makes a page request from a Web site, the browser examines its collection of cookies to see if there are any that were set by that particular site. If there are, it sends these cookies to the server along with the page request.
- Browsers cannot send one Web site's cookies to a different site. Cookies are returned only to the sites that set them. The information about your shopping cart in the cookie from Eddie Bauer cannot be sent to L.L. Bean.

So, how is it that DoubleClick or some other ad-serving site can collect cookies that show all the different sites you have visited? The answer is that what looks like a single page on a browser is often composed of lots of separate files—particularly if there are images. Advertisements are images. Because links can lead to anywhere on the Web, there is no reason that the images have to come from the same Web site as the main part of the page. For example, if you browse to a page from the *New York Times*, the page structure and news content will typically come from the *New York Times* Web site. But since the *Times* works with DoubleClick to supply advertising for the site, the ads will come from DoubleClick's Web site. So, in loading that one page, your browser will make calls to both the *New York Times* and to DoubleClick.

This means that both the *New York Times* and DoubleClick have the opportunity to set cookies and receive cookies. The DoubleClick cookie contains an identifier so that it will recognize your machine when it "visits" the DoubleClick site again, sending back the cookie as it requests another ad, perhaps on another Web page from another site.

Because DoubleClick gets its cookie back with each ad request, and because it can easily know which customer (the *New York Times,* the *Wall Street Journal*, and so on) owns the Web page that contains the ad, it can build up a profile of the sites that you visit and how often you visit them. What else does it know about you? Not surprisingly, it knows which ads it has sent to your machine and it knows when it sent them. It knows which browser you use. Most important, it knows the IP address—essentially the address on the Internet—that you are using to connect to the Web.

Is the IP address like a street address, providing a unique identifier for you and your family? Usually the answer is no. If you are connecting from your office, knowing your IP address may mean that the ad-serving company can identify the company for which you work but typically means nothing more. (Note, however, that if your company is keeping track of things internally, the *company* can know which sites you are visiting. But this has nothing to do with cookies and IP addresses.) If you are connecting from home, the IP address will usually indicate which company you are using as an Internet service provider but very little more. If you connect through AOL, clearly that information doesn't tell the ad site much since there are millions of AOL customers. If you connect through a smaller, local service provider, the ad service can usually get an idea of the region of the country that you live in. If you connect to the Web through an "anonymizer"—a service that intentionally randomizes IP addresses—the IP address will tell the ad server nothing at all.[1]

The real danger to privacy, as described in the main body of the text, arises when the cookie can be associated with credit card or name and address information that you have provided to a vendor that works cooperatively with DoubleClick, tying the identifiers in the cookies to personal information about you.

Cookies are relatively easy to control once you understand how they work. Newer Web browsers include ways to designate some sites as "trusted"—and to say that you are willing to always accept cookies from such sites. These would typically be sites where you want to use shopping carts or where you want the site to recognize your browser to save you from always having to log into the site. For sites that are not trusted, you can set the browser to ask you whether you want to accept a cookie. There are also relatively inexpensive utility products that can help automate cookie management, building rules about which cookies to accept and which to reject. I use such a tool and routinely reject all cookies from advertisers and from any site other than the one that I am intending to visit. I simply don't see much benefit to me from accepting third-party cookies.

## Web Bugs

A Web bug is a very small graphic, usually one pixel wide and one pixel high. It is often transparent so that there is no way for you to see it on your screen. The sole purpose of a Web bug is to cause your browser to go fetch it. When it does the fetching, your browser identifies itself to the site that is sending the Web bug, providing the IP address you are using to connect to the Web, the make and version of your browser, and so on. The Web bug will also know which page you requested that contained the Web bug. So, if you have a Web site of your own and put a Web bug on your home page that calls out to a graphic on a friend's site, your friend will be able to keep track of how many times your home page is requested and which IP addresses requested the page.

The problem with Web bugs, from the point of view of someone wanting to do surveillance, is that IP addresses don't tell anyone much. If you are connecting through a dial-in service, IP addresses are usually assigned dynamically, which means that you probably have a different IP address each time you connect to the Web. If you are connecting to the Web through a firewall, as would usually be the case at work, you and everyone else behind the firewall share the same IP address and so are indistinguishable from each other.

Unlike cookies, Web bugs have no way to assign a unique identifier to your machine and browser. They are not of much use for tracking individual visitors or even for recognizing when a visitor has returned.

On the other hand, because a Web bug just looks like a small graphic (very small), there is currently no easy way for browsers to detect them and allow you to manage them. When your browser accepts Web bugs you almost certainly don't know it. But you're not revealing much, either, so it's not clear that the lack of detection should be very important. But because most users don't understand how little can be learned from a Web bug, and because of the unfortunate, somewhat sinister-sounding name, many users who have heard of Web bugs view them as a bad, sneaky device. If you use Web bugs on your site, and if people find out about it, you will probably hear about it.

The strong reaction that many people have to Web bugs is somewhat unfortunate, since Web bugs *can* be useful for businesses that simply need to count page views. Content syndication companies, for example, use Web bugs to keep track of how much use is being made of their content. This information is important since it allows them to adjust billing to match usage. Web bugs are a cheap way to do the necessary page counting and are actually less intrusive than cookies.

## More Information

I have written a book that is wholly dedicated to the questions of how to learn more about customers and how to personalize your site for each customer's needs and preferences. It is titled *Web Engagement: Connecting to Customers in e-Business.* Readers interested in learning more about cookies, IP addresses, and the limitations associated with tracking Web visitors will find *Web Engagement* both useful and interesting.

## Note

1. This picture, in which IP addresses typically tell a site very little, is changing some as more users opt for broadband technologies. Some of these technologies do provide users with a fixed, particular IP address that does allow Web sites to consistently associate a particular user with a particular address.

# Technical Background on the Platform for Privacy Preferences Project

THE Platform for Privacy Preferences Project (P3P) is an interesting, important, and, in my opinion, flawed attempt to automate the exchange of information about privacy policies and privacy preferences between Web sites and their visitors. P3P has gained additional momentum and importance due to Microsoft's incorporation of parts of P3P into the company's .NET initiative. Apart from the Microsoft connection, P3P is worth a look because it illustrates the difficulty associated with finding technical solutions to the privacy problem. This chapter provides an overview of P3P, looking at what it attempts to do and how it does it. Readers who are not interested in this side trip into the world of P3P can skip to the next chapter.

The principal tool that Web sites use to tell a visitor what kinds of data the site collects is the privacy statement. There the user can get the answers to important questions such as whether the site tracks user activity, whether names and addresses are shared with others, whether the user has any right to see what has been collected, and so on. Given the substantial concern that Web users have about privacy, one might expect them to read the privacy statement before doing anything else on a site. But, of course, they don't. Reading a privacy statement is a little like reading a contract: it is hard for many people to understand just what the privacy statement means for them. Besides, companies change privacy statements and don't always do what the statement says. It is easy for a visitor to see the privacy statement as just another part of the seduction process.

The Platform for Privacy Preferences Project (P3P) is a technologist's approach to making privacy statements more useful and understandable for consumers. The two ideas behind P3P are that privacy statements should be more uniform and that, given the uniformity, there ought to be a software process to assist users in interpreting the statements. P3P defines a highly structured, machine-readable version of privacy statements. The machine readable form makes it possible to automatically interpret the statements for users. It might even be possible to match the statements against profiles of user privacy preferences. Then, Web browser software could automatically tell people when a site has a privacy policy that is not to their liking.

The P3P initiative is taking shape within the framework of the World Wide Web Consortium (W3C), the same organization that recommends the primary Web standards such as HTML and HTTP. As such, the process of developing the recommendations is open to the public and involves participation from interested companies and from nonprofit organizations such as the Center for Democracy and Technology. In the case of P3P the recommendation process has encountered more debate and disagreement than is usual for a technical recommendation. As always, privacy is a volatile topic.

The debate centers around how useable P3P is, whether it is biased against consumer interests, and whether the business community is using it as a smokescreen to avoid providing real protection through legislation. The debate raises some complicated questions. Privacy statements *are* too hard for people to use effectively, but it is not clear that P3P really solves this. But if P3P is not the answer, what is?

P3P is also important to consumers and to other businesses because it is an integral part of Microsoft's approach to privacy. Microsoft's Internet Explorer 6.0 browser incorporates a simplified form of P3P as the mechanism for expressing a user's privacy preferences and then checking them against the policies of different Web sites. It is also a key part of Microsoft's .NET initiative, through which Microsoft hopes to move from licensing software for personal computers to building a new business around distributed Web services. In the context of Microsoft .NET, P3P is central to the way that the Microsoft services will handle personal information about users.

The summary of P3P in the preceding paragraphs may be all that you need to know about P3P. On the other hand, it will be worthwhile for some readers to really understand how P3P is attempting to devise a technical solution to privacy problems. If nothing else, P3P is an important, visible attempt to address a tough problem. Even if it turns out not to be successful, there are things to learn from the attempt. Achieving that learning requires understanding a little more about just what P3P is.

## What Is in a P3P Privacy Policy Statement?

The first version of the P3P recommendation includes the basic elements that are required in order for Web browsers to find and interpret privacy policies on Web sites. It provides standard ways to locate and access policies, some simple communications protocols to request and send them, and a vocabulary and syntax for expressing just what the policy is. One useful feature of the recommendation is that it is possible to set up different policies for different parts of the site. For example, a company might have a policy of collecting little or no identifying information on the site's home page but of collecting and saving name, address, and billing information deeper within the site when a customer places an order. P3P would be able to keep a browser apprised of the applicable policy as a customer moves around on the site.

P3P policy statements answer questions about the general privacy policy and about the specific kinds of data that the site would like to collect and use. The full specification is intricate and detailed,[1] but it is possible to get a quick overview of the scope of P3P by looking at the kinds of policy information that it can express.

With regard to a policy (remember that a single site might have several policies) P3P formalizes and automates the transfer of the following information regarding the policy as a whole:

- **Who is doing the collecting?** The policy provides identification and optional contact information for the entity collecting the data. The only thing that is absolutely required in P3P is the legal name of the entity. State laws or certification requirements imposed by industry oversight or certification groups might require more specific contact information.
- **Can the user get access to personal information that is collected?** If the site doesn't collect anything that is identifiably associated with the user, this question is moot. But if identifiable information is being collected, P3P requires the entity to state whether the user can review contact information (for example, physical address, e-mail address) and other information (for example, billing history).
- **How are disputes resolved?** This is an optional part of the privacy policy. It provides the Web site with the ability to list the mechanisms that are available in case a user has problems with the information that is being collected. For example, a Web site might want to indicate that disputes should be resolved by calling the company's customer service department. In describing a dispute resolution mechanism, the Web

site can also describe the remedies that it provides. For example, the policy can guarantee that any incorrect information will be corrected.

- **Where is the human-readable version of the policy?** Every P3P policy specification must be accompanied by a version that can be read by people, not machines. The machine-readable version must have a link to the human-readable version.

In addition to the general policy statements about access and dispute resolution, a P3P specification must answer the following question:

- **What is being collected?** The policy must describe the information that is being collected. This information can be described both by naming individual data elements (for example, "User's Name," "User's Birth Date," "Pages Requested") and by referencing entire categories of information (for example, "Physical Contact Information," "Demographic Information," and "Navigation and Clickstream Information"). The categories are quite broad and each contains many individual data elements. As we will see later, this breadth is a cause for concern for some critics of P3P.

For every data element that is collected, the policy must answer the following questions (the policy creator can make this simpler by grouping the data elements—in many cases the answers to these questions will be the same for all the data elements collected on a site):

- **What is the purpose of collecting the data?** If a Web site is collecting information, it must tell the user how it will use the data. Possible uses include completion of the current activity (for example, a purchase), research and development to improve the site in general, customization to reflect individual user interests, telemarketing, and so on. The Web site can also tell the user whether he or she has any choices with regard to permitting each particular use. For example, a site might explain it will sell name and address information to telemarketers unless the user opts out of such use of data. Alternatively, a site can assert that the user *must* permit a particular use of data if he or she wants access to the site.
- **Who has access to the data?** The company that collects the data might share it with a variety of other entities, including delivery services, marketing analysis companies, telemarketers, and so on. A P3P policy description must specify which other kinds of entities, if any, will receive the data and whether these entities have privacy policies that differ from those of the site that is doing the collection.

- **What is the retention policy for managing the data?** If a Web site collects data it must tell the user how it manages it over time. Options range from "No Retention" (the data are not logged and are discarded immediately) to "Indefinitely" (there is no policy and the data could sit in a database or on tapes forever). One important intermediate option is "Retention to Meet Legal Requirements," which would apply, for example, to transaction data that must, by law, be retained for some period of time for auditing purposes and so that users can dispute claims or review invoices.

## User Agents and Services

Even this brief review of the breadth and depth of the P3P recommendation should give you a sense of its ambitious goals. Only the most privacy-aware Web sites currently articulate privacy policies that have the kind of detail and specificity that P3P would establish as standard practice. If nothing else, the P3P recommendation could raise the bar for normative industry practices. From the "service" side of the interaction, which is the P3P term for describing and communicating a privacy policy on a Web site, it is difficult to find much fault with the P3P recommendation beyond its hopeful, ambitious assumptions about what might be possible.

The problems with P3P, to the extent that they exist, turn up on the other side of the interaction, in the design of the "user agents" that interpret and respond to the policies described by P3P services. If sites are sending out these detailed, well-structured privacy policy statements, what is the user's computer supposed to do with them? Clearly, just generating something for the user to read isn't the answer—we already know that people don't read privacy statements, despite their substantial concerns about the use of private information. Something more automatic is required.

In order to enable automated processing on the user end of the exchange, P3P is paired with a sister recommendation called A P3P Preference Exchange Language (APPEL).[2] APPEL gives users a way to express privacy preferences. The general idea behind the combination of P3P and APPEL is to take a site's privacy policy, expressed according to P3P, and compare it with the user's preferences, expressed in APPEL. If the site's policy is consistent with the user's preferences, then the user gets access to the site and the user should have no objection to the site's getting access to the specified user data. On the other hand, if the policy involves kinds of data or uses of data that are inconsistent with user preferences, the user and the site either need to reach some new agreement or need to part ways. That's the theory.

The problem with APPEL is that it is really very complex. This isn't surprising. It has to include all of the detail of P3P, by reference, since the user preferences and rules necessarily relate to the information found in privacy policy statements. Then, in addition to all the things in P3P, APPEL needs to provide a way to create rules that say what the user agent should do in response to different privacy policies and combinations of data requests, uses of data, third-party uses of data, retention policies, and so on.

Things get even more complicated. Recognizing that one's privacy preferences at home might be different from one's preferences at work or in some other context, APPEL allows users to create different "personas" and to create separate policies for each persona. Presumably, this allows users to begin to express some of the contextual dependencies that the survey data, described in the main body of the text, suggest are routine in a user's interaction with different sites in different contexts. The reality, however, may be simply that layering personas on top of APPEL's already complex structure may take a difficult situation and turn it into an impossible one. The APPEL working group itself, in its April 20, 2000, draft of the APPEL language draft, said, "When the first draft of this document was released, the working group felt that, although it had met the requirements it had set, the resulting language was complex and difficult to grasp fully."[3]

In short, if APPEL is a fair representation of the intellectual effort involved in setting up a user agent (and it is, after all, the W3C's best shot at that task at the moment), then most people will not be able to express their privacy preferences to a user agent unless they happen to be computer scientists or mathematicians. This difficulty in describing user preferences is a real problem for the whole P3P concept. After all, if there is no easy way to express user preferences, what is the purpose of having machine-readable descriptions of privacy policies? Are we back to asking people to read policies and make their best guesses as to what they mean?

It is too soon to write the problem off as hopelessly complicated. Perhaps user-friendly software tools will emerge that allow users to express their preferences graphically and that can then, behind the scenes, create an APPEL specification. Or perhaps software can learn about user preferences as the user responds to different policies on different sites. The approach that Microsoft is taking in Internet Explorer 6.0 is to greatly simplify the options and scope of P3P. According to a preview of the privacy features in the emerging product (still in development at the time) that Microsoft provided in April 2001, the approach will focus mostly just on controlling cookies and will allow the user to choose between five preset levels of privacy protection.[4] It remains to be seen whether this simplification will result in something that is both useable and useful.

It is worth noting that most users have difficulty simply managing cookies. Whatever emerges surrounding P3P will have to be pretty simple and intuitive before it sees enough use, with enough consumers, to have much impact on people's sense of trust and comfort while shopping on the Web.

## What Bothers Privacy Activists

It is not the complexity in using APPEL and P3P, limiting the potential use of P3P, that causes concern among privacy activists. Instead, they are concerned that P3P will actually do too much or will do the wrong things. The objections to P3P revolve around three issues in addition to its complexity:

1. The belief that P3P is biased in favor of industry and against the individual. Critics assert that it encodes the marketing industry's view of the value and use of private information.
2. The fear that P3P might make it much easier to collect private information, effectively reducing privacy on the Web.
3. The sense that P3P, in appearing to offer a solution, is a distraction from the really important issue, which is that we need laws to protect privacy.

Any businessperson interested in P3P, for whatever reason, should be familiar with these concerns. To the extent that the concerns have substance, P3P could actually hinder rather than help the effort to increase consumer trust in e-commerce.

### Encoding the Industry View of Privacy

P3P specifies scores of data variables about users. Some of them are quite detailed. For example, one of the elements of the P3P demographic profile is the user's age. But rather than specifying the age as a range (for example, 35 to 44), or even just as an age in years, P3P is set up to record an actual birth date. This is information that many might view as related more to personal identity than to demographic profiling.

Contrasted with this level of detail and precision in collecting user data, P3P provides the user with very little information about the entity that is collecting the information. Users might want to know how to contact the entity, whether it is owned or affiliated with some other company, the size of the entity, and many other things. The only information that P3P guarantees that it will provide to the user is the entity's name. Some critics look at this imbalance in the quantity and quality of information exchanged between Web sites and users and see it as part of an overall pattern of imbalance in the fundamental structure of P3P.[5]

The greatest tilting toward the interest of data collectors, rather than individuals, lies in one of the fundamental assumptions behind P3P and therefore at the heart of how P3P works. P3P is built around the assumption that if a site is asking for data that a user does not wish to provide, then the user should be warned about the site. That's it: check to see if the site wants something that a user wishes to keep private; if so, warn the user. The basic idea—and this is what bothers critics—is that if the user chooses not to provide personal information, then he or she should not make use of the site.

Critics contend that this set of assumptions means that users who are concerned about privacy incur the cost of being fenced off from part of the Web. Mark Rothenberg, Director of the Electronic Privacy Information Center (EPIC), argues that the effect of P3P is akin to "redlining"—people concerned about protecting their privacy are zoned out of Web neighborhoods.[6]

P3P critics argue that, instead of penalizing the user, the tables should be turned so that the costs and consequences fall upon the data collectors. If a site wants access to data against a user's wishes, then that site should have to do without the data, rather than telling the privacy-aware user to do without the information on the site. The difference, in the minds of the critics, is between *access* and *consent.* They argue that P3P starts out by focusing on access and assuming that its job is to facilitate a trade: you get access to my site if I get access to your personal information. Instead, they say, the focus should be on finding a way to ensure that no data is ever collected from users without their consent.

### Making Data Collection Easier

Earlier drafts of the P3P recommendation included mechanisms to automatically transfer user data if the user agreed to the site's policies. Not surprisingly, this alarmed a number of people and added fuel to the argument that what P3P is really all about is automating data collection rather than protecting privacy. This part of the recommendation has been set aside in order to get a basic recommendation completed more quickly. Of course, the fact that the W3C committee has set this mechanism aside for the moment does nothing to prevent a company that is implementing P3P mechanisms from also implementing automatic transfer on its own.

Apart from automating transfer of private data, critics are concerned about the sheer level of detail and amount of data that users might be unwittingly assenting to provide through P3P.

### Distracting from Creation of Meaningful Privacy Regulations

Perhaps the greatest concern that critics have with P3P is that they think it misses the point. P3P critics contend that people need legal guarantees that their privacy information cannot and will not be collected and sold at will. They argue that creating a complicated technical mechanism for securing access to information overlooks the fact that what people want is really very simple: they want to know that if they provide information—name and address, phone number, credit card number—it will be used only for the immediate purpose that they had in mind when they provided it. The fact that vendors would like to use this information for other purposes is irrelevant. Cooking up a complicated way to describe those other uses doesn't help. People don't want to enable buying and selling of their data, period. So, say the critics, business should just stop asking.

Most P3P critics take this argument one step further: They argue that P3P is being used as an excuse to stall legislation that will provide effective privacy protection. Even though the P3P working group acknowledges that P3P requires laws or other enforcement mechanisms to be effective, there are other groups that do, in fact, hold up P3P as evidence that the direct marketing industry can police itself and that privacy legislation is not necessary. As Jason Catlett describes it, P3P should stand for "Pretext for Privacy Procrastination."[7]

## P3P in the Business Context

Even if one does not agree with Jason Catlett's political analysis of the uses of P3P, it is clear that P3P cannot be viewed as anything more than a technical contribution to a much larger business and legal problem. There is nothing in P3P that would ensure that policies are followed, either in terms of what is actually collected or how the data are used. Business organizations opposed to privacy legislation assert that if P3P is complemented by independent privacy seal organizations such as TRUSTe or the Better Business Bureau Online (BBBOnline), then it can provide an effective guarantee of privacy protection. But, as Forrester Research has noted, "because independent privacy groups like TRUSTe and BBBOnline earn their money from e-commerce organizations, they become more of a privacy advocate for the industry—rather than for consumers."[8]

## Is P3P a Good Thing?

P3P is a complicated proposal, technically and politically. There are privacy advocacy groups, such as the Center for Democracy and Technology, that feel that P3P has the potential for contributing to real progress in the effort to protect user information and to create a more favorable environment for business growth. The key assertion behind this argument is that P3P has the potential to bring useful transparency to the problem of deciding what a company's privacy policy is and how it will use and safeguard user data.[9] There are also organizations that believe, just as sincerely, that P3P will interfere with progress. There is a third segment of people who believe that P3P is irrelevant because it is too complicated to ever achieve broad adoption and does not really serve the needs of any constituency.

My intent has been to provide you with enough technical information and a broad enough survey of the arguments on all sides of the question so that you can formulate your own opinion.

My opinion, for what it is worth, is that concerns about P3P getting in the way of meaningful legislation are overblown. It seems likely that the 107th Congress will pass at least basic legislation guaranteeing that users receive notice when information is being collected and choice about whether to provide data. P3P won't stop that.

The greater likelihood, I believe, is that P3P will turn out to be too difficult to use. As I have already noted, most Web users cannot figure out how to manage cookies, where there are only a few alternative choices about preferences. It is difficult for me to believe that very many users will have confidence in their ability to deal with the bewildering array of choices in P3P. Even more discouraging, we know that a user's willingness to provide information is dependent on context; expressing the relationship between context and changes in preferences will be very difficult. One potential unfortunate result of the use of P3P in popular products like Microsoft Internet Explorer 6.0, then, might be that users never learn to use the P3P functionality and end up thinking that they are enjoying a level of privacy protection that is largely illusory.

Having said all that, the idea of having a more standard, transparent way to express privacy policies is very appealing. Perhaps the legislation that emerges over the next two years will actually help simplify the problem by constraining the number of possible policy choices to a more workable set of options. Legislation might provide customers with assurance that, whatever choice they make, they are guaranteed to have at least basic protection. Then perhaps P3P could be much simpler, dealing with a smaller range of choices. A subset of P3P—or a set of specific P3P applications—could then focus simply on adding clarity to an interaction that already has a basis for trust firmly in place. That would be a much more manageable role for P3P, rather than having to take on the entire burden of creating trust by itself, through a technical fix.

## Notes

1. The W3C Web site has a section devoted to specifying, describing, and discussing P3P. It is located at http://www.w3.org/P3P/. The site includes a brochure that provides a general description of P3P but with less detail than the description I provide here. More useful, and available from this site, are the working drafts of the P3P recommendation,

list of articles describing and critiquing P3P, and access to tools, such as IBM's P3P Policy Editor, which automates the task of creating P3P policy descriptions.

2. APPEL is described in a W3C working draft document available at http://www.w3.org/TR/P3P-preferences.
3. From Lorrie Cranor, Marc Langheinrich, and Massimo Marchiori, "A P3P Preference Exchange Language (APPEL), W3C Working Draft 20 April 2000," Appendix A. Available on the Web at http://www.w3.org/TR/2000/WD-P3P-preferences-20000420.
4. Aaron Goldfeder, "Privacy in Internet Explorer 6 Public Preview," Microsoft Corporation (April 2001). Accessed in April 2001 on the Web at http://msdn.microsoft.com/workshop/security/privacy/IE6PrivacyFeature.asp.
5. See, for example, Karen Coyle's paper titled "P3P: Pretty Poor Privacy?—A Social Analysis of the Platform for Privacy Preferences (P3P)," June 1999. Accessed on the Web at http://www.kcoyle.net/p3p.html in December 2000.
6. The Rothenberg quote is from a paper by Christopher D. Hunter titled "Recoding the Architecture of Cyberspace Privacy: Why Self-Regulation and Technology Are Not Enough." His paper provides an excellent overview of the concerns about industry self-regulation and about P3P. It also includes an extensive list of articles dealing with this subject. Accessed at http://www.asc.upenn.edu/usr/chunter/net_privacy_architecture. html in December 2000.
7. From Jason Catlett, "Open Letter of September 13, 1999, to P3P Developers." Accessed on the Junkbusters site at http://www.junkbusters.com/standards.html in December 2000.
8. As quoted in Junkbusters' public comment by Jason Catlett for the FTC Public Workshop on Online Profiling. Accessed at http://www.ftc.gov/bcp/profiling/comments/catlett.htm in December 2000.
9. See the Center for Democracy and Technology's paper titled "P3P and Privacy: An Update for the Privacy Community," available in May 2001 on the Web at http://www.cdt.org/privacy/pet/p3pprivacy.shtml.

CHAPTER 22

# The Privacy Debate in Congress

WE are at the leading edge of what may become a period of intense Congressional activity regarding privacy. The 106th Congress, which adjourned at the end of 2000, introduced scores of privacy bills. Few of them made it to the President's desk for signature; no bills passed that dealt in any broad way with consumer privacy issues. That is likely to change. Christine Varney, former Federal Trade Commissioner and now a lobbyist and advisor to the business community for privacy legislation, looked ahead toward the 107th Congress and said: "We have a two-year Congress that is very committed to getting itself re-elected. . . . Privacy legislation will happen."[1]

Privacy legislation covers a lot of territory, of course. Speaking very generally, legislative activity will focus on four different areas of concern.

1. **Access to technology**: In the past the U.S. government has restricted use and export of encryption technologies, treating encryption as a weapon. It has also sponsored the development of technologies that provide the government with a "back door" into encrypted information (for example, the Clipper chip) but has refused access to underlying algorithms. The degree to which encryption is available to entities other than the government is an important policy question.
2. **Government surveillance**: The Internet, coupled with high-speed computers and databases, provides the government with surveillance tools that increase its ability to monitor its citizens' activities as well as communications from foreign governments. Policy and legislation to limit the reach and use of government surveillance of citizens is obviously an important concern for democratic societies. An important, closely related issue concerns the government's right to

demand or guarantee access to encryption keys (an area of concern generally referred to as *key escrow.*)

3. **Employee privacy rights**: The courts have consistently ruled that employers have a right to monitor what their employees write while at work, where they go on the Internet while using company computers, and what they do while on the job. There is, however, debate over what responsibilities employers have to inform employees of their practices and over what regulations, if any, should control use of such monitoring data.
4. **Consumer privacy protection**: The Internet has increased any business's ability to collect information about customers, prospects, and consumers in general. It enables detailed monitoring of shopping activities and makes it easier for businesses to build and use customer profiles. There is substantial debate over what uses businesses can make of such information, particularly with regard to selling it to others. *Protection of children* from online data collection is a special instance of the broader consumer protection focus and one that has already received legislative attention in the Children's Online Privacy Protection Act (COPPA).

Each of these policy areas is important. Businesspeople are citizens. Many people involved in information technology or senior management are in a better position than most other citizens to understand privacy issues and technologies. They can play a leading role in shaping the debate over critical concerns such as government surveillance. But, judged in terms of immediate impact on business performance, the most important of these four areas is the last one: what kinds of policies and legislation will we put in place to protect the privacy of individuals as they use the Web? How can this legislation expand the Web marketplace by guaranteeing that shopping online is not at the expense of privacy?

Consumer privacy policy will take shape through debate over competing philosophies, objectives, and legislative vehicles. It will be messy and, on the surface, hard to follow. However, there is a relatively small set of key issues at the core of this debate. Any businessperson wishing to follow the discussion or contribute to it will want to identify these issues and know how they impact his or her business. Fortunately, the list of issues is short enough to be counted on your fingers:

- **Coverage**: What kinds of information will the laws protect and regulate?
- **Consent**: What will constitute consent to use the information?
- **Access**: Will people have access to the information collected about them?
- **State laws**: How will federal legislation fit with state laws?

- **Enforcement**: What mechanisms will be used to ensure that companies are complying with the laws? What remedies will be available when companies don't comply?
- **Safe harbor**: Will there be provisions for using industry organizations or other voluntary programs to certify compliance?
- **Notice of change**: What will happen when a company changes its privacy policy?

Readers who have been following privacy policy might observe that this list does not include one of the most frequently mentioned elements of proposed privacy legislation, which is "notice." The reason is that there is no longer much disagreement about the idea that companies should provide notice of their privacy policies and of what they do with information they collect. All legislative proposals start with that assumption. Where they differ is with regard to what kinds of activities require notice, what rights users have in addition to notice, and so on.

I begin with a brief look at each of these issues to identify the different points of view. This will provide the foundation needed to sort through policy options and to begin to think about a more comprehensive framework for evaluating national privacy policy.

## Coverage

The first question to ask about any privacy legislation is what it considers to be private: what kinds of information is the legislation proposing to regulate and control? There are three dimensions that different legislative approaches use to define the scope of what is protected:

1. **Identity**: Most proposed legislation distinguishes in some way between personally identifiable information and anonymous information that is not related to an identifiable person. Personally identifiable information is, of course, given more protection. Some bills provide very little protection with regard to anonymous information.
2. **Purpose**: Gathering information to complete an immediate task (for example, responding to an e-mail, shipping a product) is generally viewed as nonintrusive if the information is just used and deleted. If information is used for secondary purposes, such as analysis of customer preferences, it is more likely to be viewed as information that should be regulated. Transferring information to a third party is typically viewed as an even more intrusive use that calls for even closer regulation.

3. **Definition of *personally identifying***: A third dimension on which proposals can differ concerns just what is considered to be personally identifying information. Most proposed bills regard a name or social security number as personally identifying information. There is, however, a range of other information, such as birth dates and places of birth, that might be regarded as personally identifying information in some legislative proposals.

There is very little debate over the notion that basic, personally identifying information such as name, address, and phone number should fall within the scope of whatever protections a privacy bill provides. There is, on the other hand, substantial debate over whether legislation should regulate the collection of information that is not tied to individual identities. As an example, Senator Ernest Hollings proposed a bill in May 2000 that would regulate collection of anonymous information such as the general usage information that is collected in Web server log files (for example, how many pages are requested from the site, which pages are requested most, and so on). Businesspeople might reasonably ask why such information should be regulated in any way and how it impinges on anyone's privacy.

The "purpose" dimension is just as important as the "identity" dimension in defining the scope of a proposed regulatory policy. Some legislation would regulate use of personally identifying information for any purpose other than responding directly to a customer transaction. In other words, a Web site would not be able to retain names and addresses of customers without their permission. Other legislation sees no harm in any use of personal information so long as it stays within the company; these bills attempt to regulate only the exchange or sale of personal information. In other words, a company could collect whatever it wants about you without your consent, so long as it keeps the information in house.

## Consent

How does the consumer or Web-site visitor signal his or her willingness to allow information to be collected and used? The principal choices are:

- **Opt-out**: The user has to actively forbid use of the data. The absence of an expression of preference from a user is understood to be tacit permission.
- **Opt-in**: The user has to actively affirm permission to use the data. No expression of preference is understood to mean that consent has been withheld.

Industry marketing associations are adamant in their claims that opt-out is the only workable approach, arguing that too many people will fail to bother with checking privacy preferences.

A reasonable response to this argument is that it begs the question of *why* the data are collected and what benefit this collection is providing to users. If the data are being collected for the user's benefit, and if that benefit is attractive to the user, it should be easy to get permission through opt-in, right? And if it is not for the user's benefit, what's going on?

The argument for opt-in is not based only on concern for user benefits; there are also advantages to businesses in an opt-in policy. The most obvious advantage is that opt-in is what customers want: the Pew Internet and American Life study of privacy preferences found that an astounding 86 percent of Internet users want access to personal information based on an opt-in approach.[2] If the primary focus of privacy legislation is to build a foundation of trust and comfort with Web shopping, opt-in might be the smart choice.

There is yet another argument for opt-in, one that goes back to the question of why a business wants personal contact information in the first place: if the purpose of the information is to generate a sales lead, that lead is clearly much more valuable if the person has said that he or she wants to receive e-mail and other ads that are of interest. Knowing that someone has said "Yes" is much more valuable than only knowing that they didn't say "No." As David Moore, CEO of 24/7 Media said,

> We don't do any spam—it's all opt-in, and we're very conscious about not sending people too much e-mail. If you opt in, and I'm sending you a new advertisement every single day, you're going to say, "Get me out of here!" and we'll lose you. But if we send you an e-mail once a week, every 7 to 10 days—and it's on target, I'm going to have you as a customer for a long time.[3]

The question of opt-in versus opt-out needs to be combined with the question of coverage before it really makes sense. Just what kind of information collection and use is the customer opting into or out of? The Hollings bill (S. 2606, 106th Congress), for example, uses an opt-in approach to guarantee that people really have provided consent for any collection and use of personally identifying information beyond what is immediately required for a transaction, but the bill settles for opt-out when the information is not tied to personal identities.

Contrast this approach with the one adopted by Senators Conrad Burns and Ron Wyden. Their bill (S. 809, 106th Congress) requires only an opt-out procedure. But what is even more important is that it requires only opt-out even when the information would be disclosed to third parties. In S. 809 a company's desire to collect personally identifiable information for internal use is subject to neither opt-in nor opt-out. S. 2606 and S. 809 present very different views of what is private and very different policy choices.

The point is simple: it is not enough to look simply at whether an approach requires full consent through opt-in or merely allows an opt-out process. One also has to look at what kinds of information are covered by the consent mechanism.

## Access

It is one thing to give someone permission to collect information about you; it is another to actually be able to review the information yourself. The question of whether or not people should have access to the personally identifiable information that a Web site collects about them is another important, and debated, issue in the construction of privacy legislation.

The primary argument that business advances against providing people with access to the information collected about them is that providing access is expensive and cumbersome. If you provide access, inevitably you will need to provide mechanisms for correcting information. This involves customer support expenses, more complicated user interfaces, and so on.

One sharp response to these complaints is that if the information is not valuable enough to a business to warrant the expense of providing access, then the business wouldn't lose much by discarding the information. The idea that a company can collect information from you and about you, and then forbid you from seeing it simply because it is not convenient for the company, is consistent with the impression that the Web is not a safe place for consumers to do business. This is the problem we are trying to correct.

There are, however, also important, affirmative reasons for businesses to give customers access to their records. The most important is that it is almost certainly the cheapest way to make sure that customer records are accurate. For example, I recently learned that my Internet service provider will stop offering e-mail services. So, I have a new e-mail address. I went to the primary e-commerce sites and publications where I do business, logged into my accounts, and changed my own e-mail address, keeping records for these vendors up-to-date for them, investing my time, not theirs. Customers who have opted into a Web service that they value are motivated to keep records accurate. Business wins, the customer wins.

Access also provides a very inexpensive regulatory check to ensure that businesses are not overreaching their stated privacy policies in collecting information, misrepresenting the customer, or using information in ways that are inconsistent with their privacy policies. No industry oversight group or government regulatory body can provide a more cost-effective auditing mechanism than the self-interested consumer. Providing customers with access is an important component of making regulatory schemes lightweight and manageable. It provides a way to have oversight without requiring burdensome record keeping and auditing requirements that would make it difficult for smaller businesses to use the Web.

Not all legislative proposals mandate access to personally identifiable information. Some do provide for access but do not provide Web users with the right to amend or delete information. Finally, as was the case with consent, it is important to consider just *what* users have access to. For example, S. 809 provides consumers with access only to information that is disclosed to third parties and not to information that the company keeps and uses internally. This kind of approach will fail to achieve the benefits of accuracy and self-regulation that come from providing consumers with access to all their personally identifiable data.

## State Laws

Normally, the laws that pertain to contracts, fraud, consumer protection, and other business issues are state laws, not federal ones. Protection from intrusion, from disclosure of private facts, and from other invasions of privacy has also been handled as a matter of state law. The National Association of Attorneys General, which represents the attorneys general of the 50 states, is actively engaged in monitoring and supporting privacy legislation. It is very likely that, absent federal action on privacy, there will be a great deal of state activity. There may be state activity in any case.

The business community needs to seek a federal law that brings a measure of consistency across the different state activities, preempting state laws that conflict with federal law. A patchwork of different state regulations will not address the key requirement to increase consumer trust in Internet commerce by making it more predictable; conflicting state laws could, in fact, make the situation more uncertain and confusing. In addition, since many businesses use the Internet to do business within a number of states, a federal baseline for privacy protection reduces the compliance burden for businesses.

Most federal legislative proposals regarding privacy include language that preempts state legislation that is in conflict with the federal legislation. Proposals differ with regard to how common law in the different states intersects with federal legislation. They also differ with regard to the states' roles in enforcement.

## Enforcement

What happens when a business violates its own privacy policy or acts in ways that violate whatever guidelines Congress establishes? There are a number of approaches to answering this question:

- Place enforcement in the hands of the Federal Trade Commission (FTC) or some other regulatory agency
- Rely on an industry association to handle first-level enforcement
- Allow the states to handle enforcement
- Allow individual parties whose privacy has been violated to initiate legal action

Different privacy proposals introduced in the 106th Congress approach enforcement in different ways. There is general agreement that states and the FTC should be involved in enforcement. There is disagreement over the question of whether there should be a private right of action to enjoin companies from violating privacy policies or to recover damages for accidental or intentional misuse of private information.

This is a complicated question for businesses, and it's not one for which the answer is simply that less enforcement is better. The goal for businesses as well as for consumers is to create a predictable, uniform environment for commerce. Companies that work toward the creation of such an environment should not have to compete unfairly against other companies that do not play by the rules, nor should they have their efforts to create trust on the Web undercut by such companies.

Enforcement is also often connected to record-keeping requirements. The goal should be that businesses that play by the rules will bear the lightest regulatory burden possible. This ties back to the discussion of access: guaranteeing individual consumers the right to inspect their records may turn out to be the least expensive way to ensure accuracy of the records and to provide an oversight mechanism.

This is almost certainly an area where policies will need to evolve as we get more experience with what works and what doesn't. Businesses should ensure that legislation provides for regular review of enforcement mechanisms. The focus of the review should be on questions of fairness, predictability, and minimization of the regulatory burden.

One of the more popular approaches to enforcement is to turn the task over to the industry itself. Such self-regulation is usually coupled with a "safe harbor" mechanism.

## Safe Harbor

A "safe harbor" provides for self-regulation by marketing and online industry organizations. An organization that wants to offer a safe harbor applies to the designated regulatory body (usually the FTC in most legislation) with a description of a certification program that meets or exceeds the requirements imposed by legislation. After a public review and comment period, the FTC approves or rejects the safe harbor program. If it is approved, companies can achieve compliance with the legislation by acquiring certification through the program.

The Children's Online Privacy Protection Act (COPPA) includes a safe harbor provision that can serve as an example of how safe harbor might work in a more general privacy protection program. Once regulations governing COPPA were established, the FTC received applications to create safe harbor programs from TRUSTe, the Entertainment Software Rating Board, the Council of Better Business Bureaus, and others. Typically these programs provide companies that have been certified as members of the programs with a "seal" that can be displayed on Web sites and in marketing materials. The programs describe requirements that certified companies must meet, compliance-monitoring programs, processes for handling consumer complaints about violations, and so on. Typically the penalty for violating safe harbor program requirements is revocation of the seal.

Safe harbor is also the mechanism that has been proposed for meeting requirements imposed by the European Union on companies that want to collect information from European citizens. An agreement reached with the European Commission in early 2000 specified that U.S. companies could enter the safe harbor if they met requirements to provide notices of what information is collected and how it is used, the choice for users to opt out of data collection, user access to records, and guarantees that data would be handled securely.[4]

The advantages of safe harbor arrangements are that they can reduce the regulatory burden for all parties and allow industry to continue to regulate itself. The disadvantage of safe harbor arrangements is that the consumer can reasonably ask whether an organization that is dependent on its members for funding, rather than on the general public, can ever be adversarial with those paying members. As *Wired* reported in writing about TRUSTe's investigation of RealNetworks' surreptitious data collection (after which TRUSTe eventually decided not to revoke its seal from the RealNetworks site):

> Since its inception in 1996, TRUSTe has investigated hundreds of privacy violations—some minor, some egregious—by some of the largest online companies, including Microsoft and Deja.com, that have signed a contract to abide by certain data-collection standards. In return, companies may post a bright green "TRUSTe" logo on their Web site.
>
> But so far, TRUSTe investigators have never revoked a company's ability to display that logo, which is designed to tell consumers that they can trust that firm.[5]

## Notice of Change

The Pew Internet and American Life Project found that 94 percent of Internet users felt that a company should be punished for violating its own privacy policy.[6] Since privacy policies do change, and since doing something contrary to an older policy can look like a violation, keeping consumers updated about changes in privacy policies seems both smart and fair. Some proposed privacy legislation requires notifying people when the use of the data that has been collected from them changes; others permit changes without notice. Given the outrage that DoubleClick encountered when it unilaterally changed its policy, business's interest in creating a safe, predictable commercial environment is consistent with a requirement for notification. The advantage for conscientious businesses in having such a requirement spelled out in legislation is that it levels the playing field.

## Assembling the Pieces

There are other key elements that are critical to creating a legislative foundation for consumer privacy on the Web. For example, Web sites must institute security procedures so that private information stays private. But the issues in this list are the ones over which there is debate; they are the issues on which you need to focus as you evaluate legislative proposals.

But a list of issues is not an outline for a privacy policy. Assembling these different issues into a coherent whole requires a return to considering the overall objectives behind the drive for a national privacy policy. What does business need out of all this? Here is a list of objectives and guiding principles that could usefully shape the decisions about individual issues and policy details.

- **Assurance of safety**: The principal motivation for privacy legislation is to create an environment that is conducive to fluid business activity. Just as well-established contract laws, laws protecting property, and broadly accepted processes for dispute resolution are requirements for vibrant, free business activity in the offline world, so are they essential in the online world.

It is clear that consumers do not currently have assurance that they have control over personal information once they divulge it, for whatever reason, on the Web. Privacy policy can provide that assurance. It is from this perspective that the business community's resistance to opt-in consent and user access to data seems to be an instance of losing sight of the primary objective. Legislation that does not give consumers what they need in order to feel safe in using the Web is just an irritation and a burden for everybody.

- **Predictability and consistency**: Whatever policy we adopt needs to be consistent across geographic entities, kinds of businesses, and different companies. This is part of making the Web a safe place for commerce: Knowing that the rules are the same from place to place contributes to confidence and safety.

  In practice this means that we do need federal law rather than 50 state laws and that the federal law should apply in a consistent, predictable way across different areas of business and business models. We should not, for example, have one set of privacy regulations for financial services companies and another set for retail trade. We need a comprehensive approach to privacy.

  This concern about creating a consistent, predictable environment should also be reflected in decisions about matters such as safe harbor arrangements. We lose our primary objective if the desire for self-regulation leads to dozens of different regulatory micro-environments, each with a slightly different way of handling compliance, consumer complaints, and so on. This is not to say that safe harbor is a bad thing but instead that safe harbor must be handled in a way that reflects the focus on providing predictability and consistency.
- **Minimal regulatory burden**: The strength of the Internet and its potential to create something that is really new is due, in part, to the way that it opens new opportunities for small businesses as well as large ones. A foolish regulatory policy could make it difficult for small businesses to collect information about customers, personalize their sites, and innovate on the Web. Requiring a company to build the infrastructure necessary to provide each individual customer with secure access to his or her information is one thing; having to build an administrative structure to keep up with record keeping and auditing requirements is another. As I have noted, the need to minimize the burden of conformance for companies that want to play by the rules argues for sharing responsibility for data accuracy and compliance monitoring with consumers.

- **Neutrality regarding technology**: It would be easy, and a great mistake, to write legislation that deals with particular technologies. If you think back to the discussion of copyright legislation, you see that there is strong precedent for such narrowly focused legislation that attempts to patch particular problems without taking a broader view. For example, it would be easy to fall into the trap of trying to deal specifically with cookies or deciding to mandate particular security practices. If there is any lesson to be learned from Internet development over the last five years it is that technology moves forward quickly. Privacy policy should focus on broad principles and objectives, not on trying to solve particular, current problems.
- **Preservation of Internet character**: Even allowing for the hard times that Internet businesses have been through during the past year, the Web has been an astounding agent of change and growth. There are a handful of architectural and functional characteristics of the Web that have contributed significantly to this power. Control of the Web is distributed, the architecture is open, barriers to fundamental use are low. A successful privacy policy will be consistent with these core characteristics. I have already written of the importance of keeping regulatory burdens light, which ties into ensuring that barriers to use remain low. Open architecture is consistent with providing a transparent view into how private information is collected and used. Distributed architecture is consistent with providing users with full access to personal data and with employing users in the oversight process. It is conceivably also consistent with well-designed safe harbor policies.

Creating good legislation to address concerns about privacy and trust will be difficult and, at times, confusing. One of the closing paragraphs from testimony by Jerry Berman, Executive Director of the Center for Democracy and Technology, delivered before the Senate Commerce Committee summarizes the challenge:

> The privacy issue must not be left to meander through Congress for the next two years, to be resolved in end-of-the-session horse-trading. Nor should it be left to the states to sort out 50 different sets of rules. As information becomes the backbone of our economy, concerns about the privacy of personal information will continue to intensify. The time to build privacy into the infrastructure through laws, code, and self-regulatory activities is now. In doing so, Congress should stick to fair information practice principles, seek technology and business model neutrality, minimize regulatory burdens and maximize predictability. Industry should use technology to aid transparency, educate

> users, and enable individuals to exercise more nuanced control over data flow. Only through a balanced mix of baseline legislation, self-regulation and privacy enhancing technologies will privacy be protected on the Internet.[7]

Berman is primarily concerned with privacy protection. Businesspeople are primarily concerned about expanding the amount of business done on the Web. These are two sides of the same coin. Berman's advice is as good for business growth as it is for privacy protection.

## Notes

1. As quoted by Carolyn Duffy Marsan in "Online Privacy Law Anticipated," *Network World*, November 30, 2000. Accessed in December 2000 at http://www.infoworld.com/articles/hn/xml/00/11/30/001130hnprivacylaw.xml?p=br&s=9.
2. From Susannah Fox et al., *Trust and Privacy Online: Why Americans Want to Rewrite the Rules* (Washington, DC: The Pew Internet and American Life Project, August 20, 2000), p. 6.
3. As quoted by Lydia Lee in "Opt-in rules!," *Salon Magazine*, March 6, 2000. Accessed in December 2000 at http://www.salonmag.com/tech/view/2000/03/06/moore/.
4. For more information about the safe harbor privacy agreement that the Department of Commerce negotiated with the European Commission, see the International Trade Administration site at http://www.ita.doc.gov/td/ecom/menu.html (document was accessed in May 2001).
5. From Declan McCullagh, "Is TRUSTe Trustworthy?," *Wired News*, November 5, 1999. Accessed in December 2000 at http://www.wired.com/news/politics/0,1283,32329,00.html.
6. Fox et al. (cited above), p. 11.
7. From testimony by Jerry Berman before the Senate Commerce Committee on October 3, 2000. Accessed in May 2001 at http://www.cdt.org/testimony/001003berman.shtml.

CHAPTER 23

# A Privacy Framework

THE pragmatic, nuts-and-bolts analysis of policy issues in the preceding chapter presents an important view of privacy policy options. But there is also something unsatisfying about it. It is so thoroughly grounded in the detailed realities of the current debate that it provides very little in the way of a broader perspective. How did we get into this situation? Where is all of this headed? Why is it that consumers and their concerns about privacy rights are suddenly able to cause the business community to give up on self-regulation and think seriously about privacy legislation?

Summarized succinctly if a bit unfairly, the pragmatic, narrow view boils down as follows: "Consumers are spooked about privacy. So, business needs to do something to make them feel better."

OK. That is accurate as far as it goes. We need to provide methods for notice, consent, access, and so on. But where are the boundaries of the consumer demands? What is "enough" privacy? Without knowing what problem we are trying to solve, it will be difficult to know when we have solved it.

These kinds of questions would be easier to answer if we had a broader theory of privacy. Then we might be able to elevate our view of policy from this year's legislative options to an understanding of business mechanisms and consequences. The preceding chapters, which have examined the idea of privacy as a right, as a consumer concern, and as a political debate, set the stage for considering such a broader view.

## Privacy as a Right

Most people regard privacy as a right, in the same sense that freedom of speech is a right. There is strong appeal in Warren and Brandeis's notion of a "right to be let alone." When the popular press writes about privacy, the underlying assumption is generally that it is dealing with some kind of legal or universal right. So, the idea of starting with this notion of a right as the basis for policy has intuitive appeal.

Unfortunately, upon closer inspection, trying to construct a policy framework around a right to privacy is as likely to confuse as to clarify the problem. Drawing a sharp boundary around the right to privacy is very difficult, as the discussion in Chapter 20, "The Right to Privacy," illustrated. Part of the difficulty is due to the differing privacy laws in different states, a problem that could presumably be solved with a federal law. But part of the difficulty is also centered in the privacy right itself. The boundaries of what is private and protected by law blur as privacy runs up against other rights. Even automated telephone dialers can be tied to free speech rights that are weighed against privacy rights. It is as if, notwithstanding the general agreement that there should be a right to be let alone, we have no consensus as to what that right is.

In order to place the difficulties associated with a rights-based approach into sharper focus, let's move away from the Internet for a minute and consider some friends of mine who run an art gallery and frame shop in a coastal village in Maine. People come in and pick out matting and frames for the pictures they like, then fly home when their vacations are over. My friends ship the framed pictures to the people at their homes in Massachusetts, New York, and so on. Of course, my friends keep a file of these names and addresses, along with a list of what pictures each customer has bought. When an artist comes out with a new painting or a new print, my friends send letters to the people who have bought other work by the artist, often enclosing a picture of the new piece, offering the prints and the original for sale. In the very unusual event that someone does not want to receive these mailings, my friends remove them from the list (opt-out). But they don't ask permission to compile this list. It is just a part of doing business. More important, that list of customers represents years of work and experience. My friends have made a big investment in compiling it. I am sure they would say that they own that list. They view it as a business asset. If they ever sell their gallery, I am sure that the list will go to the new owner and that the new owner will continue sending out the occasional mailing as artists produce new work.

The point of this story is not that my friends clearly have a *right* to run their business this way. Just the opposite. The point is that the question of rights is unclear. It is enough to note that since they have been running this business this way for a long time, serving an increasingly large list of customers who are happy to receive the mailings, it is not at all apparent that they do not, in fact, *own the list* of customer interactions as a business asset that can be sold. Many would argue that the list of customers is often the primary asset when someone sells a small business, particularly a service-based business. But do they have a *right* to the information? If so, why wouldn't a Web business have a right to sell its customer list?

Let's push the rights question a little further. You have dozens of friends and hundreds of acquaintances. In your dealings with these people, you have been gathering information—things that happened between you and them and impressions that you have formed. Do you have a *right* to talk about these people to others, or do you have to get consent first? If someone in your acquaintance treats you badly, do you have a right to tell your friends? Or do you have to first get consent from the person who hurt you before you can share information about them?

My point is simply that it is very difficult to make the case that people "own" all of the facts about themselves as they interact with the world and that they have the right to exercise complete control over this information. Interactions are two-way, and both parties come away with new information as a result. Should we decide, on the basis of some concept of rights, that one party owns the information and that the other party must forgo use of it? Is all information jointly owned, requiring sign-off from all parties? Do we want a government agency that regulates the creation of individual reputation?

This is not to say that privacy should not be regarded as a right. On the contrary, surveys and public comment consistently indicate that it is important to accept the idea that some kind of privacy right exists and should be respected. And this is not to say that there should not be some kind of regulation of uses of information collected on the Web. The point is simply that making the case for legislation in terms of "rights" and expecting those rights to be clearly defined, black and white, leads to some real difficulties. If we are going to place privacy policy in a broader framework that makes objectives and choices clearer, we need to start from some foundation other than our conception of privacy rights.

## Monetizing Privacy

Another approach to framing and understanding privacy policy is to think of privacy as a kind of property, as something you can put a value on and buy and sell. This is an attractive idea. After all, my friends expect to sell their customer list. If we could figure out how much private information is worth, then companies wanting to collect information would know what kind of compensation they need to provide to people in return for the use of the information. Or we could put the shoe on the other foot and assume that the information actually belongs to the companies once they collect it. Monetizing privacy would then determine the going rate for people who wanted to buy their information back.

Thinking about privacy as property suggests a famous—many would say "infamous"—economic theory known as the Coase Theorem, named after the man who thought it up, Ronald Coase, winner of the 1991 Nobel Prize in Economics. The Coase Theorem goes as follows:

> Given well-defined property rights, low bargaining costs, perfect competition, perfect information and the absence of wealth and income effects, resources will be used efficiently and identically regardless of who owns them.[1]

The Coase Theorem is used primarily as a way to analyze the effects of "externalities," which are costs—such as the cost of air pollution—that stand outside the normal operation of the market. The theorem has acquired notoriety, and a bad name, from use by conservative thinkers who look at the first phrase and the last phrase and leave out the middle, asserting that if you fully distribute property rights you will get the most efficient outcome. This sometimes degenerates into an argument to let companies buy the right to pollute and then keep on polluting. Liberal thinkers focus on the requirements in the middle—perfect competition and perfect information—and argue that since these can never be met, the theory has no practical value.

My goals here are more modest than a search for theoretical truth: I am looking for insight into a hard problem. The interesting and useful thing about the Coase Theorem is actually the middle conditions that conservative thinkers overlook and liberal thinkers write off as impossible. These conditions—low bargaining costs, perfect competition, and perfect information—can be lumped together as "transaction costs." Applying the Coase Theorem to the question of how to assign and regulate privacy rights focuses attention on these transaction costs. Rather than writing off the situation as imperfect (we knew that to begin with—we are trying to figure out how to make better decisions in the midst of imperfection), we might usefully ask if there are ways that we can work to minimize these costs. Our course in pursuing a regulatory strategy might focus on minimizing transaction costs so that we can make as much use of market forces as possible.[2]

Tracy Coyle, whom I introduced in Chapter 19, was trying to put Coase's Theorem into practice when she answered her own 1,300 questions about preferences, interests, and other personal information and then offered the package of information to the highest bidders. She copyrighted the questionnaire and her answers, thus establishing a clear property right, and set up an online auction to minimize bargaining costs. Then she waited for the bids to roll in so that she would enjoy profits from making the most efficient use of her resources.

Nothing happened; there were no bidders.

Coase's Theorem helps explain what went wrong. First, there is the matter of requiring "perfect information" in order to facilitate a frictionless transaction. Unfortunately for Tracy Coyle, information was actually what she was trying to sell. As John Keck, Vice President at the marketing firm Foote Cone & Belding, said in evaluating her proposal, "Sight unseen, this data is worth, at most, 10 cents to a buck."[3] He suggested that it might be worth a lot more if he could evaluate it and see that it really contained something of interest to his clients. But there is substantial irony and perhaps difficulty—an economist might call it "moral hazard"—in the notion of having to give the information away in order to have it be worth more.

Tracy Coyle ran up against the fact that information about individual consumers acquires value in one of two very different ways. First, it can be aggregated with information from many other consumers to provide an understanding of the market and of market segments. The overall picture is very valuable, but each datum within the picture is worth very little—as Keck suggested, maybe a dime. Only the vendor or some other data aggregator can pull together the pieces to create the valuable composite view; the individual consumer has very little leverage in this scenario.

The second way that information acquires value is when someone turns personally identifiable information about preferences and needs into a sales lead. Well-qualified sales leads can be very valuable: for expensive items a well-qualified lead can be worth $100 or more. But, by definition, you cannot provide your own name as a sales lead. You can go into a car dealer and say that you want to buy a car, but you cannot get a car dealer to pay you $100 for that information.

In Coasian terms, this market not only has imperfect information but also suffers from a very unbalanced competitive structure. The people who collect and aggregate the information are solely capable of making the information valuable. The individual consumer is in a position akin to that of someone with a handful of sand trying to bargain with a factory that makes silicon wafers for semiconductors. The buyer appears to hold all the cards.

This predicament has stimulated some creative thinking about new business models. Most notably, John Hagel III and Marc Singer published a book titled *Net Worth* in early 1999 that argued that a new kind of business will emerge that will aggregate customer information for the customer and represent the customer in interactions with sellers. They called these new businesses "infomediaries."[4]

It is an interesting idea: buyers counter the apparent ability of vendors to create small information monopolies by creating a massive monopsony. Hagel and Singer describe the possibilities:

> No consumer has the power (or the time) to challenge vendors alone. . . . As a result, vendors make the rules about products, price, services, and company policy on any variety of topics, from employment practices, to customer service, even to environmental impact. Customers can basically take it or leave it. . . .
>
> As infomediaries aggregate millions of consumers into one voice, they will broadly increase consumer influence in both commercial practices and public policy. Think of trade unions. . . . What if, in other words, infomediaries were to aggregate the individual voice of the consumer into a "collective will" wielded against vendors on such important consumer issues as product safety, the environment, privacy and information capture, prices, warranties, and customer service, just to name a few? In this kind of scenario, one could imagine consumer advocate Ralph Nader in the role that Jimmy Hoffa used to play for unions.[5]

Apart from how one might feel about this new role for Ralph Nader, it is fair to say that Hagel and Singer's proposal would replace one kind of regulatory problem with another. Aware of this, they spend some time talking about how it would be necessary to protect the massive aggregation of personal information, entrusted to the infomediary, from being seized by governments anywhere in the infomediary's worldwide operations. Following this reasoning, suddenly Ralph Nader as Jimmy Hoffa looks like the least of our problems. Hagel and Singer, without intending to, make a very strong argument for one of the controlling principles identified in the last chapter: approaches to dealing with personal information should concentrate on retaining the current character of the Internet, a key component of which is its distributed architecture.

The reason for thinking about the Hagel and Singer proposal at all is that it brings the apparent competitive imbalance in the information "market" between customers and vendors into sharp focus. We are a very long ways from meeting Coasian conditions for a market that could make use of distribution of information property rights as the means to optimal allocation and use of personal information. There is a strong, understandable impulse in the business community to look for some way to treat privacy as an economic good that can be managed through market mechanisms. Unfortunately, the fundamental requirements for market activity, even when understood in Coasian terms, are simply not present in the interactions between consumers and businesses with regard to private information.

## The Fallacy of the Powerless Customer

Consideration of private information as an economic good makes it appear that, in this particular exchange, the consumer is relatively powerless. But it sounds contradictory to talk about the powerless consumer. The usual story about the Internet is that it gives the customer more power than ever. After all, according to the usual assumptions about consumer e-business, the Internet puts competitors only a couple clicks away from each other. The Web provides customers with more access to product information, pricing information, and alternative sources of supply than ever before. How is it that now, with regard to privacy, customers are all of a sudden at the mercy of the vendor?

They're not. Keep in mind that the percentage of overall retail trade that is accounted for by the Internet is just pushing 1 percent.[6] Faced with the fact that the economics of private information on the Web currently favors vendors, customers are pushing back in the way that is most readily available to them: they are taking their business elsewhere. This is, in fact, precisely the problem that businesses need to solve if they want to succeed in building consumer transaction volume on the Web.

Individual stories don't prove an argument, but they sure can help illustrate it. My dental hygienist was late in starting her holiday shopping this past year. What was her solution? She told me that she planned to curl up on the couch with a big stack of catalogs. What about doing shopping on the Internet? She said that she didn't trust it.

## My View

Our society's shared understanding of privacy rights is still too loosely formed to permit an approach to policy based solely and cleanly on an expression of rights. Lacking a nice, straightforward solution based on rights, the next best thing would be a good, self-regulating approach based on markets. But trying to simply let the market determine a value for private information turns out to be just as messy as a rights-based approach. When it comes to bargaining over personal information, vendors hold most of the cards. The result is that consumers find another game.

Many of them, like my dental hygienist, choose mail order over the Web, supporting a volume of transactions through mail order that is nearly an order of magnitude larger than retail e-commerce.[7] The interesting thing is that mail order companies are just as aggressive in using personal consumer information as are Web business operations. More, they literally know where people live. Looking at the information available to catalog sales operations and to companies that sell over the Internet, it is difficult to understand why one kind of operation should be an inherently safer place for the consumer and his or her personal information than the other.

One possible explanation for the greater comfort with mail order, and the consequent greater volume of business, is that it is much more familiar to most people. The idea of looking through a catalog, calling an 800 number, and giving a credit card number over the phone is decades old. The idea of doing the same thing through a Web browser is only a few years old. Add to that the fact that new technologies stimulate privacy concerns, and you very possibly have all the explanation that you need for why people feel more at risk on the Web than in shopping over the phone.

This line of reasoning suggests that maybe all that Web business really needs to do is wait and be patient. Rather than trying to shepherd in a new era of trust through ambitious new regulatory schemes to guarantee and monitor protection of consumer information, business might be just as well served by providing good service, treating the customer right, and giving this new idea another five years to become more familiar to more shoppers.

Accepting this view does not necessarily imply that legislation is a bad idea, but it does suggest one particular focus for the objective of legislation: legislation should assist business in regulating itself and in guaranteeing a uniformly good experience for Web shoppers as they share personal data with companies. Legislation should put the structure in place so that the parties to business on the Web can approach transactions with confidence that each knows what is really involved in the transaction.

Framed this way, some of the ideas appearing in current legislative proposals, such as the idea that consumers should have access to personal information on sites so that they can guarantee its accuracy and help monitor its use, make a great deal of practical sense. Other ideas, such as the assertion that customers should be able to exercise control over how companies use that information internally, make much less sense in this pragmatic framework.

In short, it looks to me like the best course for business is to take reasonable steps to make customers aware of what information is being collected and, in a general way, how it is being used. Certainly, customers should be able to review what a company has collected, correct it, and ask the companies to keep it in house. Beyond that, business should simply give customers some time to adjust to this new commerce medium and should argue for a legislative approach that adopts such a measured, patient strategy.

## Notes

1. This statement of the Coase Theorem is taken from a useful critique of the theorem by Steve Kangas titled "Ronald Coase and the Coase Theorem," accessed in May 2001 on the Web at http://www.huppi.com/kangaroo/L-chicoase.htm.
2. *Reason* magazine published an interview with Ronald Coase in its January 1997 issue (Thomas W. Hazlett, "Looking for Results: An Interview with Ronald Coase"). This interview provides a richer view of Coase than is generally admitted by either conservative or liberal theorists, suggesting that his theorem is more important as a way to see things from a different point of view and to raise questions than as an attempt to express a formal truth. The interview was available on the Web in May 2001 at http://www.reason.com/9701/int.coase.html.
3. As quoted by Diane Anderson in an article for *The Industry Standard,* cited in Chapter 19.
4. John Hagel III and Marc Singer, *Net Worth* (Boston: Harvard Business School Press, 1999).
5. Ibid., pp. 258, 259.
6. The United States Department of Commerce tracks changes in retail e-commerce sales on a quarterly basis. This figure was taken from a report accessed in May 2001 at http://www.census.gov/mrts/www/current.html.
7. The National Mail Order Association estimated that in 1998 the U.S. mail order market reached $357 billion. U.S. consumer e-commerce for 2000 is estimated to be $45 billion (Jupiter Research, as quoted in "100 Numbers You Need to Know," *The Industry Standard*, November 20, 2000, p. 290).

# Privacy: Further Reading

## Printed Resources

Agre, Philip E., and Marc Rotenberg. 1998. *Technology and Privacy: The New Landscape.* Cambridge, MA: MIT Press.

This is a collection of academic articles looking at technical, legal, and policy dimensions of privacy. It includes useful articles on cryptographic issues, evaluating the success of efforts to create laws to protect privacy, data protection, and other important matters. This is not the place to start one's readings about privacy (I would recommend a combination of Alderman/Kennedy and either Garfinkel or Sykes), but it makes a good second-round resource when you want to dig more deeply.

Alderman, Ellen, and Caroline Kennedy. 1997. *The Right to Privacy.* New York: Vintage.

This is an excellent introduction to how privacy law works in practice. Using scores of stories about actual violations of privacy in different contexts, Alderman and Kennedy illustrate just how complex and inconsistent our society's response is to claims of rights to privacy. This is perhaps the best single overview of privacy issues for nonattorneys. It does not deal in any serious way with the intersection of privacy and Web technology.

Boyle, James. 1996. *Shamans, Software, and Spleens.* Cambridge, MA: Harvard University Press.

I provide a strong recommendation of this book, along with a more complete explanation of what it is all about, in Chapter 5. Boyle's examination of complicated issues associated with public and private ownership of information is important background for thinking about privacy: is the information in your spleen yours?

Brin, David. 1999. *The Transparent Society.* Reading, MA: Perseus.

Brin sets out the thesis for this book in his opening tale of two cities. Both cities have surveillance cameras on every lamppost and in all public spaces, providing a complete view of what people do in any public space in the city. In one city the cameras are all connected to a central viewing facility at police headquarters. In the other the images are placed on a network and available for all citizens to see. His argument is that democracy and freedom are better served in the second scenario than in the first. His assumption is that surveillance will happen in any case, whether we want to acknowledge that fact or not. Given that, we should share the information rather than trusting to an elite police group. This is an important argument; the book is worth a quick read.

Garfinkel, Simson. 2000. *Database Nation: The Death of Privacy in the 21st Century.* Sebastopol, CA: O'Reilly.

This book provides a very complete overview of the different ways that technology is affecting privacy, including discussions of satellite surveillance, the Web, databases, surveillance cameras, and many more intrusive technologies. A well-written catalog of things to be worried about, it serves as a useful reference to different dimensions of the privacy debate. It is also a good example of the tone of the public expression of privacy concerns.

Lessig, Lawrence. 1999. *Code.* New York: Basic Books.

I provide a more complete description of *Code* in Chapter 5. In short, it is an important book that informed my thinking in writing this book. Lessig provides a good though brief overview of the legal aspects of privacy and relates them to his primary concern about the way that the computer code that makes up the Web becomes, with laws, a constraint on what one can do on the Web.

Perine, Keith. 2000. "The Persuader." *The Industry Standard,* November 13, pp. 155–170.

An excellent, well-organized overview of the struggles, debate, players, issues, and changes of course as the business community has moved from a strident self-regulation position to one that is better able to come to terms in constructive ways with privacy legislation.

Sykes, Charles. 1999. *The End of Privacy.* New York: St. Martin's Press.

Like Garfinkel's *Database Nation,* this is an overview of privacy issues written for the general reader. It provides a survey of the concerns and issues regarding privacy and a picture of what the threats are. It focuses less on technology than does Garfinkel's book and more on the role of government.

Zoellick, Bill. 2000. *Web Engagement: Connecting to Customers in e-Business.* Boston: Addison-Wesley.

I wrote *Web Engagement* because I found that many businesspeople needed a basic introduction to how Web sites can collect and use information gathered about Web-site visitors. The book starts out by looking at what can be learned about visitors and goes on to discuss techniques for strengthening a Web site by tailoring it to customer needs and preferences. It looks carefully at clickstream data, cookies, and recommendation and preference engines, placing these technical considerations in the context of business objectives.

## Web Sites

There are a great many sites dealing with privacy issues and tools—this is far from a complete list. It is, instead, a list of resources that I have found to be useful in assembling the information in the preceding chapters. (Site addresses are those used on the Web in May 2001.)

Center for Democracy and Technology, http://www.cdt.org/.

This site contains papers, positions, and legislative summaries regarding privacy, encryption, and other issues. Interesting arguments supporting P3P.

Electronic Privacy Information Center (EPIC), http://www.epic.org.

EPIC is a public interest research group that takes strong positions against commercial practices that threaten privacy. It is an excellent source for news, lists of resources, position papers, and access to privacy protection tools. The group opposes P3P—see http://www.epic.org/reports/prettypoorprivacy.html.

Junkbusters, http://www.junkbusters.com.

The Junkbusters site is primarily focused on a fight against spam and other intrusions into your e-mail, phone, and Web browser. It contains information about technical resources to help Web users protect anonymity. Its position is stridently in favor of privacy. The site also contains numerous articles arguing against various privacy intrusions, as well as links to other resources.

Karen Coyle, http://www.kcoyle.net/p3p.html.

Coyle has written an important paper arguing against P3P, titled "P3P: Pretty Poor Privacy? A Social Analysis of the Platform for Privacy Preferences (P3P)," which is available on her Web site.

Kidz Privacy, http://www.ftc.gov/bcp/conline/edcams/kidzprivacy/index.html.

The FTC sponsors this site, which provides resources, news, notices of official actions, tips for parents, and other useful information regarding the Children's Online Privacy Protection Act.

Online Privacy Alliance (OPA), http://www.privacyalliance.org.

The OPA is an industry-sponsored privacy organization that historically has argued that business should police itself and has argued against government regulation. The site contains good resources for businesses that want to do a better job of dealing with privacy issues.

# Epilogue

THE idea behind this book is that the Web will be what we make it.

The Web does not have an immutable nature of its own. Instead it reflects constraints and requirements imposed by the technology that makes it work, by governments, and by the business community. My belief is that the business community is central to this interaction.

I have had two objectives throughout this book. The first is to encourage and enable a much broader segment of the business community to become actively involved in shaping the Web. This requires that more businesspeople have a solid understanding of the background and implications of some of the key issues that we face. Much of this book is an effort to provide that understanding.

The second objective is to develop a handful of principles—an approach to making decisions about the Web—that businesspeople can use as they address new issues.

Developing a workable, reliable approach to dealing with new issues is urgently important. A good example gained prominence during the final weeks of working on this book. A French judge ordered Yahoo, Inc. to block French Web surfers from access to pro-Nazi sites. In short, the judge asserted that French law should govern what will be available on the Web in France. German courts have expressed similar intent. Saudi Arabia would like to place religious constraints on what is available to its citizens. The United States would like to restrict access to offshore gambling sites.

The question of sovereignty is not one that I have considered in this book, but many of the technologies and concerns treated in the preceding chapters apply. The same abilities to track Web behavior and to identify Web-site visitors that stimulate concern about privacy would enable the control over sovereignty that the French court wants. Electronic signature technologies could be applied to provide even more perfect control over authentication of identity and therefore of citizenship. The kinds of control over content required to perfect copyright protection schemes could be used as part of a censorship program.

My point is that, as you confront different proposals to change the Web in some way, as the French court would do, the fundamental technologies and applications treated in the preceding chapters will be useful in understanding what is involved in implementing the change. But there is much more than that. The detailed discussion of the four problems considered in the preceding chapters provides a set of general principles that you can use in structuring your approach to such proposals for change. So far, my expression of these principles has been largely implicit within the analysis of the four problems. It is worthwhile, now that the discussion of the four problems is complete, to state the principles explicitly as well. What follows is both a quick summary of the conflicts and problems described in the preceding chapters and a statement of the principles that seem, to me, to emerge from these conflicts.

## Respect the Conflict

None of the problems examined in this book is simple. The changes that happen when new technical capabilities disrupt existing assumptions about value run deep. Respect for the complexity of the conflict and the dimensions of its reach needs to be the starting point for developing a response.

Electronic signatures is perhaps the simplest of the problems considered in the preceding chapters. The technical solution is readily at hand and, on the surface, the goal seems apparent. But in looking more closely at the issue it is clear that questions of weighing certainty against risk and questions of liability make even the electronic signature problem very complex—much too complex to be addressed by a solution imposed from above as Utah attempted to create.

There are many people who would assert that the extension of copyright protection to the Web is a simple problem. Former Attorney General Janet Reno even tried to reduce the conflict to "theft, pure and simple." But copyright conflict is, instead, incredibly complex. It reflects the struggle between existing, physical distribution systems and new ones that would transport bits of information rather than atoms with mass and volume. The conflict is made even more difficult by the fact that the existing scheme for protecting content works better for atoms than for bits: counting copies is almost certainly not the way to protect information on the Web. Copyright also provides an instructive example of the outcome of quick Congressional action in the form of the DMCA, which is based on the hope that the problem really is simple. The result is unintended and almost certainly undesirable side effects.

Similarly, the question of what to do about the increased use of business method patents eludes simple answers, despite the assertions on one side that such patents are simply the way things work and, on the other, that they carve up the "glorious open playing field" of the Web "into a proprietary wasteland." There is a real need to shelter and encourage attempts to build something new on the Web, rather than just rushing to copy what the other guy did and then get to market faster. At the same time, the people critical of recent patent activity are pointing at a real problem—it does appear that some apparently patentable inventions are not much more than the application of established ideas in a new context.

There are perhaps fewer people who believe that the issues surrounding consumer privacy are simple. But, even here, there is an impulse to reduce the issues to a question of simply protecting a "right" that is being violated. Coming from another direction, there are impulses to simply treat privacy as a commodity that can be bought and sold. Closer examination of the issues strongly suggests that neither of these simple formulations really addresses the problem.

In considering each of these conflicts it is apparent that their complexity and reach create uncertainty about what a successful resolution will look like. Respecting the conflict means finding ways to incorporate this uncertainty into decisions about how to proceed.

## Let the Conflict Show the Way

The conflicts I have examined in this book are not accidents, like a train wreck, to be cleaned up and avoided. They reflect serious efforts by different parties to create something new amidst the existing way of doing business. Certainly, there are individuals who use the uncertainty and commotion surrounding a conflict as a cover for fraud and other illegal activity. But that is not what is happening in the conflicts surrounding Napster, Amazon, or DoubleClick. Such conflicts unmask important problems and opportunities.

The great value of a conflict is that it can illuminate the bad fit between existing practice and the opportunity to create something new. In the case of electronic signatures the conflict leads in the direction of focusing on a workable alignment of risk and the information required to assess it. In the case of copyright the conflict directs attention to the need to develop a transition strategy from one distribution mechanism to another. For patents the conflict points at finding better ways to determine what is "obvious to one having ordinary skill in the art at the time the invention was made," when technology and applications are changing so quickly that nothing seems obvious and yet nothing is surprising. With regard to privacy the conflict points to the questions of what is behind the substantial consumer distrust of Internet business and why consumers are so anxious to punish businesses that betray trust.

## Use the Force of the Conflict

Just as a conflict can show the locus of the resolution, so can it contribute to the means of resolution. The most striking example of this may be Bertelsmann's realization that Napster provides what is perhaps the most efficient means to explore subscription and license-based distribution models and to develop the technology required to support them.

It is important to note, in contrast, that the course adopted by Congress in passing the DMCA is an attempt to resist the force of the conflict in the case of copyright, rather than to work with it and use it to advantage.

To the extent that government is involved at all in finding ways to move forward in conflicts between Internet technologies and existing ways of doing business, the involvement should focus on removing barriers that keep the conflict from working productively, and certainly not on creating them. The Electronic Signatures Act is a good example of productive government action: the E-SIGN Act restricts itself to guaranteeing that electronic documents are not thrown out simply for lack of a physical signature. Having removed that key barrier to signature use, Congress stepped aside to let the power of the conflict between different approaches to signatures uncover more workable solutions than are available today.

Congress could take a similar approach to patents, where the force of the conflict leads to unprecedented levels of attention to questions of novelty and obviousness—to the point where there are even private ventures attempting to come to terms with the need for better ways to identify prior art. Congress has the opportunity to make constructive use of this energy by taking steps that make it possible for the public to participate at an earlier point, and to greater effect, in the patent examination process. This will not resolve the conflict, but it will help ensure that the conflict moves in productive directions, leading toward a shared understanding of the proper use and scope of business method patents.

Privacy, too, provides an opportunity to make productive use of the strength and momentum of a conflict. Rather than trying to prescribe rules for information collection and trying to set up expensive auditing and monitoring mechanisms, government could, more simply and more usefully, require that consumers be able to review the personally identifiable information that is being collected, leveraging existing consumer focus on this issue. This won't "solve" anything in itself, but it would succeed in engaging the consumer as auditor. This might be a step in the direction of increased consumer confidence and would almost certainly move the conflict forward, closer to resolution, by leading to a clearer articulation of which kinds of information use are really objectionable and which kinds of use are understood to bring useful benefits to the consumer.

## Give the Conflict Time to Work

The problems underlying the conflicts examined in the preceding chapters are complex and sometimes reach deeply into questions of physical and market infrastructure. The conflicts bring real issues to light and provide energy that can be used to move toward resolution. Given all of this, it is critical to recognize that exploring the issues by letting a conflict lead the way will take time.

It is possible, for example, that time is mostly what is required to establish increased consumer confidence in the Web. Real consumer access to the private information that companies collect will help too but will not, of itself, bring about a quick shift in consumer attitudes. Only time and continued experience can do that.

The conflict between copyright protection and VCR technology, starting back in the 1970s, took a decade to find resolution in the form of new markets that were favorable to both VCR manufacturers and the owners of copyrights. There is no reason to believe that the development of mature markets for new approaches to music distribution and digital information distribution in general will take any less time.

Buying the time for a conflict to work its way to resolution sometimes requires political savvy and creative deal making. As the conflict surrounding Napster illustrates, it is necessary to find a way to acknowledge the claims of existing ways of doing business while not cutting off the needs of the new businesses. It can sometimes be hard to sustain such forward motion under tension for months, let alone years. Cross-investment, so that each party shares in the other's potential upside, helps make it easier.

In the area of privacy legislation, buying time takes the form of reasonable, useful steps—such as providing consumers with access to data—while giving the larger process time to work. For electronic signatures, buying time consists of focusing initially on vertical applications where the use of electronic signatures is least risky and most useful. For patents, buying time very probably means proceeding slowly and stepwise, first providing full funding to the PTO and then enabling opposition proceedings just for business method patents, however defined. After learning from that experience and letting the conflict continue to identify problems, it might then be possible to move on to more substantial changes.

The DMCA, once again, provides a useful point of contrast. It attempts to resolve the conflict quickly by criminalizing copyright circumvention. Rather than giving the copyright conflict time to work and to develop new approaches to protecting property, it tries to freeze old approaches in place.

## Favor Decentralized, Heterogeneous Responses

One of the key qualities of the Internet that has made it so useful in different business applications and such a fertile ground for innovation is its decentralized architecture. As anyone familiar with the history of the Internet knows, this design reflects the initial system's genesis as a military tool and the desire to make it capable of functioning even in times of military emergency, when parts of the system could be inoperable due to enemy attack. But the decentralization has also been an important component of the system's success as a commercial environment. It has enabled innovation at many levels of scale and deployment in an exceedingly broad variety of settings.

The Internet has also been, from the outset, a mixture of many kinds of hardware and operating systems, rather than a homogeneous collection of devices and software that reflects a single approach to doing things. Like decentralization, heterogeneity has made an important contribution to the ability to use the system for so many different things, in so many different ways.

These characteristics of the Internet are well established at the foundation level and have, over the years, propagated up to the level of applications and the users' experience on the Internet and the Web. Users experience the Web not as one thing but as many things, used and encountered in many ways. One of the consequences has been the ability to deal with the Web anonymously and privately, using multiple personas if desired. Another consequence has been the general sense that the Web is not easily controlled. The peer-to-peer file sharing that underlies Napster is a good example of a higher-level application that brings the fundamental design characteristics of decentralization and heterogeneity up to the surface of the Web, available to the end user.

There is no reason that decentralization and heterogeneity *must* be available to businesses and consumers operating at the surface of the Web. In fact, from the standpoint of asserting control over the use of the Web, keeping these fundamental architectural characteristics hidden below the surface of the Web might look like a good thing. If you wanted to move in the direction of a system such as that demanded by the French court that wants to ensure that sites with Nazi memorabilia and pro-Nazi literature are not available to French citizens, you would want a system where there is more uniform control over access to the system. The same thing is true for people who would advocate more control over use of copyrighted content.

It is not difficult to imagine the creation of an application environment over a period of, say, the next five years, in which users would need to present a digital certificate identifying themselves in order to get access to much of the Web. The means to such a system could consist of laws assigning significant legal and financial responsibility to companies for the actions taken by customers and Web-site visitors—essentially an expansion of the contributory infringement argument that is being used against Napster. The motivation for such laws would be the desire, on the part of different nations, to exercise more control over what their citizens can do and see on the Web, preventing misappropriation of content, gambling, access to pornography, and so on.

I am not numbered among those who believe that such control would be the end of civilization as we know it, a fatal abridgement of freedom, and so on. It seems that such control is no different than what one would encounter in trying to use, say, a corporate EDI system. Life would go on. But I think we would have lost something that is valuable—valuable for citizens and valuable for businesses. We would have lost an environment that has, to date, been able to support generous growth and many kinds of commercial development coming from unexpected directions in unexpected ways. The ability of the Web to surprise us and to enable companies to create new things grows from allowing decentralization and heterogeneity to flow up to the surface of the Web. I think we will derive the greatest overall benefit by continuing in that direction, rather than locking things down and controlling them. It is a choice. We cannot have it both ways.

If you accept this viewpoint, then you will want approaches to policy that encourage decentralization and heterogeneity, rather than imposing uniformity. The Electronic Signatures Act is a strong example of how that works. The E-SIGN Act, as written, places no constraints on what an electronic signature can be. An electronic signature, under the Act, can be impossible to authenticate and worthless as an assertion of identity or assent. The nature of the signatures is uncontrolled and broadly heterogeneous. The working assumption is that the marketplace will sort things out. Similarly, the E-SIGN Act makes no attempt to create central controls for certification authorities (CAs). CAs can be within companies, can offer themselves to the marketplace as VeriSign does, could be offered through banks and other systems, and are otherwise broadly decentralized. The legislation recognizes that we do not yet know what is best and consciously encourages competition between many approaches so that we can discover what works best. Such legislation is not consistent with creating the kinds of controls required to satisfy the needs of the court in France, but I believe that it will turn out to be consistent with stimulating continued growth and innovation.

Applying this preference for heterogeneity and decentralization to copyright leads to tolerance for what Napster and its emerging, record company–sponsored competitors are trying to accomplish and a desire to work in ways that will enable us to see where peer-to-peer sharing and other new distribution mechanisms will lead. Applied to patents, it leads to tolerance for the idea of patenting new ways of doing business while, at the same time, wanting to constrain the ability to create overly broad monopolies with such patents. Bringing broader public engagement into the patent examination process and into discovery of prior art is consistent with heterogeneity and decentralization. With regard to privacy, maintaining heterogeneity and decentralization tends to argue against broad government control and regulation of information collection and use, moving more in the direction of ensuring that consumers have access to the information they need to protect themselves.

## Going Forward

Good decisions and good policy will always be based on a broad understanding of the particular and unique considerations surrounding an issue. For example, policies and decisions for protecting content need to consider the limits associated with protecting copies, the changes in distribution mechanisms, established control over the distribution of physical media, the consolidation of control over media into a handful of powerful companies, and so on. There are other sets of particulars that apply to business method patents, electronic signatures, and privacy. They are different for each different conflict, but they share the common properties of complexity, deep roots, broad reach, and critical importance to useful action in response to the conflict.

In focusing on four conflicts, each in detail, I have tried to provide you with a useful view of the particulars for each conflict. Just as important, I have tried to provide a picture of how history, technology, existing laws, and industry structures interact to shape such conflicts. If I were to write a longer book, going on to consider conflicts over taxation, sovereignty, censorship, and other "hot spots" in the collision of the Internet and the world as we know it, the same pattern of complex constraints, broad reach, big implications, and difficulty in seeing what is ahead would emerge, again and again, in each case.

This is why arriving at some general principles to guide decision making is so important: in each case, respect the conflict, let it show you new things, use the force of the conflict to move forward, create laws and business arrangements that give the conflict time to work, and bias decisions toward heterogeneity and decentralization.

The time for believing that the Web, by the force of its own innate nature, can radically change business, open enormous new opportunities, and create a sustainable, more productive economic order is over. We know better now. We need to take responsibility for shaping the nature of the Web. Protecting the Web's ability to create new opportunities will require vision, patience, and creativity. The Web will be what we make it.

# Index

*Note:* Page numbers followed by the letters *f* and *n* indicate figures and notes, respectively (*n* followed by note number)

**Y**



**Z**

www.**informit**.com

OPERATING SYSTEMS

WEB DEVELOPMENT

PROGRAMMING

NETWORKING

CERTIFICATION

AND MORE...

**Expert Access. Free Content.**

**Solutions from experts you know and trust.**

- Free, indepth articles and supplements
- Master the skills you need, when you need them
- Choose from industry leading books, ebooks, and training products
- Achieve industry certification and advance your career
- Get answers when you need them from live experts or InformIT's comprehensive library

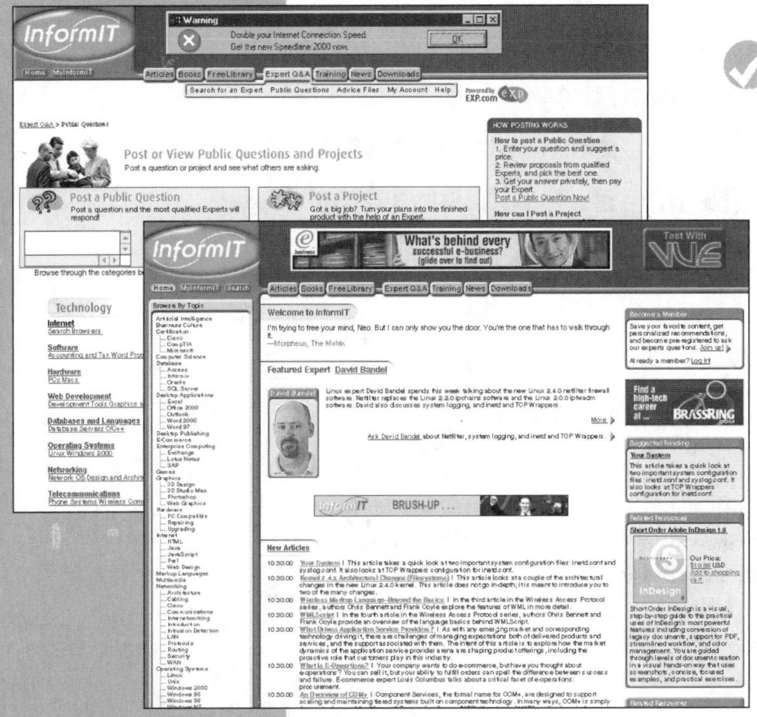

Addison-Wesley and InformIT are trademarks of Pearson plc / Copyright©2000 pearson

www.**informit**.com

# Register Your Book

## at www.aw.com/cseng/register

You may be eligible to receive:

- Advance notice of forthcoming editions of the book
- Related book recommendations
- Chapter excerpts and supplements of forthcoming titles
- Information about special contests and promotions throughout the year
- Notices and reminders about author appearances, tradeshows, and online chats with special guests

## Contact us

If you are interested in writing a book or reviewing manuscripts prior to publication, please write to us at:

Editorial Department
Addison-Wesley Professional
75 Arlington Street, Suite 300
Boston, MA 02116 USA
Email: AWPro@aw.com

Addison-Wesley

Visit us on the Web: http://www.aw.com/cseng